LUTHER'S THEOLOGY OF THE CROSS

LUTHER'S THEOLOGY OF THE CROSS

WALTHER von LOEWENICH

translated by Herbert J. A. Bouman

Augsburg Publishing House
Minneapolis, Minnesota

LUTHER'S THEOLOGY OF THE CROSS

Contents

Foreword 7

Preface to the Fifth Edition 9

Introduction 10

Part One
THE THEOLOGY OF THE CROSS IN THE HEIDELBERG DISPUTATION

The Formulation of a Concept 17

Part Two
DEVELOPMENT OF THE CONCEPT OF THE THEOLOGY OF THE CROSS

I. Luther's Doctrine of the Hidden God 27
   A. The Heidelberg Disputation 28
   B. The Bondage of the Will 31
   C. Lectures on Isaiah 38

II. Luther's Doctrine of Faith 50
   A. Critical Delimitation of the Concept of Faith 52
      1. *Faith and Synteresis* 52
      2. *Faith and Understanding* 58
      3. *Faith and Reason* 65
      4. *Faith in Opposition to Experience* 77
      5. *Faith and Hope* 89
   B. Positive Realization of the Concept of Faith 91
      1. *Faith as Experience* 93
      2. *The Substantive Definition of Faith* 101
   C. The Unity of the Two Definitions of Faith 107

III. Life under the Cross 112
   A. The Hiddenness of the Christian Life 114
   B. The Christian Life as Discipleship in Suffering 117
   C. The Cross and the Christian Life 123
   D. Humility, Trial, Prayer 128
      1. *Humility* 129
      *Excursus on the Concept of Humilitas in
      St. Bernard* 132
      2. *Trial* 134
      3. *Prayer* 139

Part Three

THE THEOLOGY OF THE CROSS AND MYSTICISM

Introduction 147

I. Preliminary Systematic Considerations 149

II. Historical Investigation 152
    A. Tauler 152
    B. German Theology (*Theologia Deutsch*) 159
    C. The New Piety (*Devotio moderna*) 163

CONCLUSION 167

Notes 169

Bibliography 209

Addendum to the Fourth Edition 217

Abbreviations

W. = Weimar Edition of Luther's Works (cited by vol., page, and line)

W. Br. = Weimar Edition, Letters

LW = Luther's Works, American Edition (cited by vol. and page)

RE³ = Realencyclopädie (Hauck), 3rd ed.

RGG¹ ² ³ = Die Religion in Geschichte und Gegenwart, 1st, 2nd, and 3rd ed.

Foreword

The Luther Renaissance which began with the publication of the great Weimar Edition of Luther's works and which began in 1883 has now in the course of almost a century become a concentration of international scholarship almost without parallel in the learned world. It is a feature of it that almost every ten years there has appeared some seminal study after which scholarship has never been quite the same again. Such were the essays of Vogelsang on Luther's Christology in his early lectures; Regin Prenter's *Spiritus Creator;* the *Fides ex auditu* of Ernst Bizer and most recently Lienhardt's *Luther, Témoin de Jesus Christ.*

One of the most important of such influential studies has been Walther von Loewenich's *Luthers Theologia Crucis.* It is a work which should long ago have been turned into English, for it is almost indispensable for anybody studying Luther's doctrine of salvation in the context of modern critical scholarship. This theology of the cross which von Loewenich rooted in the famous Heidelberg Theses of 1518 represents constant stresses in Luther's thought, discernible in his first lectures on the Psalms but no less in his last sermons and in his final great course of lectures on the Book of Genesis.

In important prefaces to later editions of his work, von Loewenich has related his study to more recent editions of Luther, notably the edition of the Psalms by Professor Ebeling published since World War II and also to more recent theological discussion, not least in learned articles by himself. These few pages are to be care-

7

fully noted and the references followed up. In relation to mysticism, Walther von Loewenich has softened an attitude which suffered from a too rigid German approach to the problems of mysticism, and he now writes more sympathetically of Luther's debt to Tauler and the *Theologia Germanica.* But here is a deeply learned study in depth which is still a "must" for the modern student, and even more for the research worker and scholar. It is still a work to which one turns again and again and I am very glad that its publication in English will enable a wider audience of English readers not only to deepen their understanding of Luther himself but to come into contact with one of the most illuminating theological writers of our age, a man of deep understanding and of ecumenical sympathies as well as a distinguished representative of a great historic Lutheran theological school.

Gordon Rupp
Cambridge
All Saints' Day 1975

Preface to the Fifth Edition

The fourth edition of my first book, *Luthers Theologia Crucis* (1929), appeared in 1954, published by Chr. Kaiser. An addendum to the fourth edition provides information on the doubts about such a new edition and on the reasons why author and publisher decided in favor of it after all. For more than five years that edition has been out of print. This edition in a new format is being published in response to urgent requests from circles of younger theologians.

Again I was unable to undertake a complete revision; the reasons have already been stated in the addendum to the fourth edition. They are still valid for me today. I must call the reader's attention to the retractions and critical considerations voiced there. By way of supplement I call attention especially to my report on "Luther Research in Germany" in *Lutherforschung heute* (published by Vilmos Vajta, Lutherisches Verlagshaus, Berlin, 1958, pp. 150ff.), and to my book, *Luther und der Neuprotestantismus* (Luther-Verlag, Witten, 1963). The interpretation of Luther that I presented there in the third chapter, does not do away with my commitment to the abiding concern of Luther's theology of the cross (cf. especially paragraphs 29-32). It appears that in our day there must again be a parting of the spirits in their attitude toward the theology of the cross—both within Protestant theology itself and in the inter-confessional dialog. What took place at the end of World War I as a new departure of Reformation Christianity should remain alive also in the current generation.

If this new edition of *Luther's Theology of the Cross* can contribute to that end its purpose will have been served.

WALTHER V. LOEWENICH
Erlangen

Introduction

There may be widely divergent opinions concerning the so-called dialectical theology. Some may think that it needs to be supplemented and improved; others may take definite positions against it. This much must be conceded in any case, that it largely dictates the questions for contemporary theology. Some problems have agitated certain circles of Christian theology perhaps longer than some proponents of dialectical theology may want to admit, but these problems were not clearly heard above the din of the theology of that day. The same problems have now suddenly moved into the center and become the focus of universal interest. Some think that we are now witnessing the collapse of the theology that has prevailed to our day, the theology determined by Schleiermacher in the 19th and early 20th centuries. Our present situation is in fact characterized by a greater uncertainty regarding the traditional positions than the previous generation experienced. The question so often discussed today, "What is theology?" is a symptom of this uncertainty.

One result of the present situation is that we have become aware of the uniqueness of theology in comparison with other areas of thought. No leading theologian would seriously think of substituting the science of religions for theology, for today we see the differences between Christianity and the world of religions too clearly. For this negative result we are indebted to the work of the history-of-religions school. Not only does the particularity of the material to be treated by theology confront us more clearly today than before;

we have also learned again that this special material requires a special method. To the outsider theology may appear as an untenable compromise between history, philology, and philosophy, but today's theologian has again become aware that his discipline has a very decided character of its own. Today we are again speaking more emphatically of theological thought.

What, then, is the nature of this special theological method? It is that in none of its statements does theology lose sight of the fact that it speaks only on the basis of the revelation in Jesus Christ. Christian theology is theology of revelation. And this is not merely a formal criterion. Not only the "that" of revelation, but also the "what" and the "how" have essential significance. This means that the Word *(logos)* to which all theology must be related is the word of the cross.

Someone may perhaps object that this is an arbitrary limitation; that by one-sidedly accenting the cross Protestant theology has unfortunately blocked its way to the fullness of the New Testament message. But the question remains, "Can one penetrate to the decisive content of the New Testament message and yet bypass this word of the cross?" Once the fact of the cross is taken into account, it soon becomes evident that this fact moves into the center quite unawares. For the uniqueness of the New Testament message is nowhere seen so clearly as at this point. Hence the word of the cross was the characteristic that dramatically separated primitive Christianity from the syncretism of its surrounding religious world.[1]

It was therefore no accident, but profoundly based in the situation, when the first Christian theologian labeled the message entrusted to him the word of the cross (1 Cor. 1:18). To Paul the Jew, the cross was the great offense, but to Paul the Christian, the cross opened up a completely new understanding of God. For Paul the knowledge of God and the word of the cross move into the closest relationship. The word of the cross is indeed "foolishness," but this is Paul's great new insight, that God can manifest his wisdom only in foolishness. The fact that the Crucified One is the Messiah—something unheard of for Jewish ears—opened his eyes to the rule that governs God's revelation. God reveals himself in concealment, God's wisdom appears to men as foolishness, God's power is perfected in weakness, God's glory parades in lowliness, God's life becomes effective in the death of his Son. But this means, furthermore, that a direct knowledge of God is impossible for man.

The world in its wisdom did not know God, and his eternal power and godhead remained hidden to it. Hence there is revelation and knowledge of God only in the folly of what we preach.

For that reason the "foolishness of God" is wiser than the wisdom of men, the "weakness of God" is stronger than the strength of men. Thus a re-evaluation of all values results from the cross. Precisely what is lowly in the world, what is nothing, God has chosen. Only he who shares in Christ's dying can attain to fellowship with him. The life of the Christian is hidden with Christ in God. Thus in the cross Paul sees both the rule that governs God's revelation as well as the rule that governs the knowledge of God and the life of the Christian. The entire thought of Paul is controlled by the thought of the cross; his is a theology of the cross.

In no theologian of the Christian church have these thoughts of Paul experienced such a revival as in Luther. At Heidelberg in the spring of 1518 Luther placed his theological paradoxes—the theology of the cross—in explicit opposition to the theology of glory, the prevailing theology of the church. He openly employed this formula because in it he found the distinctiveness of the gospel characterized most crisply and pertinently over against the official theology. It is the heritage of Paul (note the citations in Luther's Works [LW], Vol. 31, pp. 42-43) that Luther holds aloft with his theology of the cross against a church that has become secure and smug.

What does Luther mean by this formula? The purpose of the following investigation is to clarify this question. But first we must make some prefatory remarks. In current research it is generally regarded as settled that Luther's theology of the cross must be understood as his pre-Reformation theology. It is true, one rarely finds any clear definitions of just what the theology of the cross really entails.[2] Usually the formula appears as something that needs no further discussion. But this seems to be basic to most of the incidental references as a tacit assumption that in the theology of the cross we are dealing with an early pre-Reformation stage of Luther's theology. Otto Ritschl gave the clearest expression to this view by devoting a separate chapter in his *Dogmengeschichte des Protestantismus*, Vol. II, 1, to this pre-Reformation theology of Luther. Ritschl claims that the theology of the cross bears a typically monkish stamp and thereby proves to be only a preliminary stage of the real Luther.

In opposition to this view we defend the thesis that the theology of the cross <u>is a principle of Luther's entire theology</u>, and it may not be confined to a special period in his theological development. On the contrary, as in the case of Paul, this formula offers a characteristic of Luther's entire theological thinking. <u>Hence our investigation has to do not with a specific stage of development, but with the demonstration of a principle of theological thinking in Luther.</u>

What observations have led us to the thesis just enunciated? In the Heidelberg Disputation Luther has lucidly stated how he wants the theology of the cross to be understood (see also the definition on the *Explanations* of 1518, W. I, 522ff.; LW 31, 83). What are the implications for us?

1. First of all, I do not see how the Heidelberg Disputation (1518!) can be attributed to the pre-Reformation Luther. This disputation belongs to the clearest and most basic statements of Luther in our possession.

2. It must surely be our first task to pursue carefully those statements of Luther if we want to get a reasonably correct picture of the concept of the theology of the cross. It is surprising that this task has been so often neglected. For that reason we begin our work with a presentation of the theology of the cross, by which the Heidelberg Disputation may in fact be distinguished.

3. It follows then that in Luther's theology of the cross we are not dealing with paraphrases of the monkish ideal of humility, but with a distinctive principle of theological knowledge that corresponds exactly to the apostle Paul's theology of the cross. Once one has recognized this and then reads a later writing of Luther's (e.g. *The Bondage of the Will*), one notices that the same principle of knowledge is applied there, too, consciously or unconsciously, hiddenly or openly.

It is the aim of our investigation to trace the significance of this principle of knowledge in Luther's thought. It is hoped that this will help, first of all, to fill a gap in past Luther research. The presentation itself will have to demonstrate whether our approach is a fruitful heuristic principle. We do believe it will shed new light on a number of contexts and that much that has hitherto received little attention will gain significance in this framework.

Furthermore, we must not fail to note that this undertaking is based on the assumption that Luther still has something to contribute to theological discussions today. And this precisely by way of his theology of the cross. Are we not today experiencing a return from a theology of glory to a theology of the cross similar to the one we observe in Luther? Hence our work is motivated by a living concern.

We are not here pleading our case with anyone to whom this approach already appears to be a deficiency in scholarly attitude. We do indeed question whether such a person knows anything about true scholarship. Scholarly objectivity is never a matter of neutrality, least of all where theological knowledge is concerned. But with this last statement we have already taken our position on the ground of the theology of the cross.[4]

PART ONE

THE

THEOLOGY OF THE CROSS

IN THE

HEIDELBERG DISPUTATION

The Formulation of a Concept

The church of Luther has always gloried in the cross. Her special concern has always been the question concerning the certainty
of salvation. If her perception of the corruption of human nature
stands out more prominently than that in the Catholic church, then
the question concerning a means of salvation must also be more
urgent for her. In the cross of Christ we have redemption, here and
nowhere else. This is the truth that the Evangelical church has
emblazoned on her banner. This attitude toward Christ's sacrificial
death is still regarded as the shibboleth of all genuine Lutherans.
It is beyond doubt that the Lutheran church in her estimation of
Christ's death can appeal to Luther himself. For him Christ is
the mediator between God and man, the only mediator (cf. W. II,
521, 28ff.; LW 27, 268; W. XL, 1, 451, 15; 503, 5ff.; LW 26, 289f.
325). He is the mediator by his blood. Through his death he effects
reconciliation between God and man.[5] God's wrath is, for Luther,
a reality that is removed only in Christ. As we shall show later,
propter Christum, "for the sake of Christ," has basic significance
for him. The doctrine concerning the work of Christ is also the
innermost sanctuary of theology for him.

Yet this is not what Luther had in mind in his early years when
he chose to label his theology the theology of the cross. For Luther
the cross is not only the subject of theology; it is the distinctive mark
of all theology. It has its place not only in the doctrine of the vi-
carious atonement, but it constitutes an integrating element for all

17

Christian knowledge. The theology of the cross is not a chapter in theology but a specific kind of theology. The cross of Christ is significant here not only for the question concerning redemption and the certainty of salvation, but it is the center that provides perspective for all theological statements. Hence it belongs to the doctrine of God in the same way as it belongs to the doctrine of the work of Christ.

There is no dogmatic topic conceivable for which the cross is not the point of reference. In this sense Luther's theology desires to be a theology of the cross. And now it must be said: While the Lutheran church has clung faithfully to the "for the sake of Christ" (propter Christum) it surrendered Luther's theology of the cross all too quickly. The theology of glory that Luther opposed has made a triumphal entry also into his church. One occasionally wonders whether the doctrine concerning the cross has not even been forced to pay tribute to this theology of glory.

What is the meaning of Luther's concept of the theology of the cross in the Heidelberg Disputation of April, 1518? [6]

The decisive statements are in Theses 19 and 20. Luther, commenting on who may rightly be called a theologian, says:

> That person does not deserve to be called a theologian who looks upon the invisible things of God as though they were clearly perceptible in those things which have actually happened. He deserves to be called a theologian, however, who comprehends the visible and manifest things of God seen through suffering and the cross (LW 31, 40; W. I, 354, 17ff.).

What is involved here is the question about the knowledge of God. The nearest path to it is simply to trace the footprints of God in creation, for creation speaks a powerful language. The invisible things of God, his power, wisdom, justice, and goodness, and so forth (LW 31, 52; W. I, 361, 35), shine forth from creation. We will not move far from the sense of this thesis, but see its implications more clearly if we substitute our modern concepts of nature, history, and personality for "through the things that are made." By one of these three ways modern man wants to attain to the knowledge of God. Whether one becomes aware of God's glory by contemplating the eternal laws of nature or by quiet prayer and adoration in view of the inexhaustible riches of creaturely life; whether one sees history as the Eternal's unconcealed revelation, or whether because of the mystery of personality one is convinced

of the certainty of the Uncaused, in every case the attempt is made
to reach the knowledge of God by way of creation.

Luther does not reject this way altogether (Thesis 24, W. I, 354,
27; LW 31, 41). There really should be a knowledge of God on
the basis of his works; but there isn't. Without reservation Luther
agrees with the apostle's verdict in Romans 1:22. The knowledge
of God's invisible nature on the basis of the works of creation does
not make one wise. "The recognition of all these things does not
make one worthy or wise (W. I, 361, 36; LW 31, 52). Proof: "This
is apparent in the example of those who were 'theologians' and
still were called fools by the apostle in Rom. 1:22" (*ibid.*). The
failure of this way of knowledge was strongly emphasized by Luther
when he pointed out that the theology of glory followed this way
of knowledge. Thus it has passed judgment on itself. It is no "proper" theology. A true theologian "comprehends the visible and
manifest things of God seen through suffering and cross." This is
said in sharp antithesis to Thesis 19. The "visible and manifest
things of God" are substituted for the "invisible things," the
"through suffering and cross" is substituted for "through the things
that were made," and the "comprehends" at this place corresponds
to the "looks upon." What does this mean?

1. For the theologian of the cross it cannot be a question of
brooding over God's being in itself. For example, he is not interested
in a doctrine concerning God's attributes that substitutes quiescent
abstractions for living acts. In fact he considers that extremely
dangerous. God does not want to be known in his invisible things
but in his visible things. True theology must understand clearly
that it has to be a theology of revelation. God has spoken, and
therefore we are able to speak about God. God has shown himself
and therefore we know where we must look.

2. This revelation is, of course, an indirect revelation. Like Moses,
the man of God, we too see God only from the rear (see also the
chapter on the hidden God). A direct knowledge, a viewing of
God's face is denied us.

3. This really means that we know God not on the basis of works,
but through suffering and the cross. What is the meaning of works?
In connection with Theses 19 and 20 they can only refer to God's
created works. For Stange's view that Luther interpreted Romans
1:20 tropologically is incorrect.[7] It is true that in the "Proofs" the

word "works" is otherwise always used to designate the ethical achievements of man. Hence the expression at this place suffers from a certain ambiguity. But this ambiguity may give us a clue to an important insight.

Ethical works and the works of creation, insofar as they are considered to be ways to God, are on the same level for Luther. He rejected not only the way of works but also the way of knowledge. By fighting against the theology of glory he laid bare the common root of moralism and rationalism. Althaus is right in saying that this discovery belongs "to what is most profound in Luther's theology." [8] Religious speculations and holiness by works [9] are two consequences of a single human desire—the desire for an unbroken and direct communion with God. (Ethics and epistemology are not unrelated, but rather condition each other reciprocally.) But for Luther this desire for unbroken communion with God constitutes the theology of glory. The theologian of the cross has knowledge only through suffering and the cross. "God can be found only in suffering and the cross" (LW 31, 53; W. I, 362, 28f.).

Here we may observe the same ambiguity as above in the term "works." "Cross" and "suffering" refer, in the first place, to Christ's suffering and cross. But Luther is thinking at the same time about the cross of the Christian. (For Luther the cross of Christ and the cross of the Christian belong together.) For him the cross of Christ is not an isolated historical fact to which the life of the Christian stands only in a causal relationship (cf. W. I, 219, 30), but in the cross of Christ the relationship between God and man has become evident. The essence of the ultimate character of reality has become clear at this point. There is no honest communion with God that tries to go behind this evidence (cf. Thesis 21; LW 31, 40; W. I, 354 21f.). This evidence, however, cannot be grasped by pure contemplation. Precisely because the total character of reality has become evident here, a decision concerning my existence has been made. Thus if I want to acknowledge this evidence seriously, I must affirm it with my whole existence. That is to say, the cross of the Christian corresponds to the cross of Christ. To know God "through suffering and cross" means that the knowledge of God comes into being at the cross of Christ, the significance of which becomes evident only to one who himself stands in cross and suffering.

The theologian of glory sees God everywhere present. The theologian of the cross knows that "true theology and recognition of God are in the crucified Christ." To seek God elsewhere would be "flighty thought." When Philip (John 14:6), "according to the theology of glory," asked Christ, "'Lord, show us the Father,' Christ forthwith pointed him to his own person and said, 'Philip, he who has seen me has seen the Father'" (LW 31, 53; W. I, 362, 18f.). The "wisdom which sees the invisible things," which only "puffs up, blinds, and hardens" (LW 31, 40f.; W. I, 354 24), God has rejected in favor of "the wisdom of visible things."

4. But what are the visible things of God? Luther mentions human nature, weakness, and foolishness. Precisely in the things we regard as the counterpart of the divine, God has become visible.[10] That leads us back to point 2 above. There it was said that there can be only indirect knowledge of God. Here we are told why that is so. It is because God can reveal himself only in concealment, "in the humility and shame of the cross" (LW 31, 53; W. I, 362, 12f.). There is no such thing as a direct knowledge of God because God's revelation is itself an indirect revelation. "Now it is not sufficient for anyone, and it does him no good to recognize God in his glory and majesty, unless he recognizes him in the humanity and shame of the cross" (*ibid.*). For it is precisely as the God of revelation that God is the hidden God. "Truly, thou art a God who hidest thyself" (Isa. 45:15). In order to reveal himself he has hidden himself beneath suffering and cross, "so that those who did not honor God as manifested in his works should honor him as he is hidden in his suffering" (LW 31, 52; W. I, 362, 9f.).

Thus the formulation in Thesis 20, which "comprehends the manifest things," (in distinction from that of Thesis 19), appears well thought out. "Manifest things" means God has revealed himself; he has permitted us to see his visible things (acts). We need only look toward the Christ crucified. And the "comprehends" adds to it the dialectical supplement. Revelation is there, of course, but only in concealment. Revelation addresses itself to faith. In his early years Luther uses the word "understanding" to designate the perceiving organ of faith (more later!). The theology of the cross is theology of faith.[11] "Our life is hidden in God (that is, in the simple confidence in his mercy)" (LW 31, 44; W. I, 357, 3).

5. Suffering, therefore, gains a special significance for the theology of the cross. We recall again the ambiguity of the words "works" and "cross." The knowledge of God derived from the works of creation was opposed to that which arises at the cross of Christ, and

holiness by works is now opposed to the thought of suffering. "Through the cross works are dethroned and [the old] Adam, who is especially edified by works, is crucified" (LW 31, 53; W. I, 362, 30f.). For that reason he does not, like the theologian of glory, flee sufferings but regards them as the most precious treasure. To all that is humble and lowly he turns in love; that is "the love of the cross, born of the cross, which turns in the direction where it does not find good which it may enjoy, but where it may confer good upon the bad and needy person" (LW 31, 57; W. I, 365, 13). For as one "reduced to nothing through the cross and suffering" (LW 31, 55; W. I, 363, 29), he knows that "sinners are attractive because they are loved; they are not loved because they are attractive" (p. 57; W. I, 365, 11f.).

Thus we have sketched with broad strokes Luther's concept of a theology of the cross. Five aspects emerged as essential.

1. The theology of the cross as a theology of revelation, stands in sharp antithesis to speculation.

2. God's revelation is an indirect, concealed revelation.

3. Hence God's revelation is recognized not in works but in suffering, and the double meaning of these terms is to be noted.

4. This knowledge of God who is hidden in his revelation is a matter of faith.

5. The manner in which God is known is reflected in the practical thought of suffering.

It is clear that with these thoughts Luther proves himself a faithful pupil of Paul. Together with him he rejects the way to the knowledge of God described in Romans 1 and sides with the "foolish preaching" of 1 Corinthians 1. Paul is the father of Luther's theology of the cross. But Luther's discipleship is not one that is externally conditioned, as something that arose only from loyalty to the authority of Scripture. No, in these thoughts Luther sees the expression of his own personal concern. He is able to reduce the entire antithesis over against the traditional theology to the formula that the wisdom of he cross was no longer being heard in it (W. V, 42, 8ff.; LW 14, 305: "Truly, this wisdom of the cross and this new meaning of things is not merely unheard of, but is by far the most fearful thing even for the rulers of the church. Yet it is no wonder, since they have abandoned the Holy Scriptures and have begun to read unholy writings of men and the dissertations on finances instead").

To this can also be traced the whole deplorable condition that afflicted the church within and without, and that evoked the demand for a reformation in head and members (cf. also W. 5, 300, 1ff.). As long as we live in security we have no ear for the "foolish preaching," since it does, in fact, signify the upsetting of all values and relationships, a reversal that must be offensive to natural man.[12] No wonder, then, that the wisdom of the cross is practically unknown. "The wisdom of the cross is today very much hidden in a deep mystery" (W. V, 84, 10). Where it is no longer understood, the Bible, too, remains a closed book, for the cross of Christ is the only key to it. (W. I, 52, 15ff. The cross of Christ is the fountain from which the understanding of Scripture is drawn). Therefore Luther equates wisdom of the cross with true doctrine (W. V, 372, 30f.).

To avoid unnecessary repetition, we shall for the present content ourselves with this brief outline of the basic concept. It will be our task to demonstrate how this concept is carried through in Luther's view of the hidden God, of faith, and of the life under the cross. Only then will we be in a position to judge the extent to which Luther himself remained faithful to his theology of the cross.

We close this section with a summary comparison of the theology of the cross and the theology of glory, which Luther himself furnished in the clearest possible way in his *Explanations of the Disputation Concerning the Value of Indulgences,* 1518:

> From this you can see how, ever since the scholastic theology—the deceiving theology (for that is the meaning of the word in Greek)—began, the theology of the cross has been abrogated, and everything has been completely turned upside down. A theologian of the cross (that is, one who speaks of the crucified and hidden God) teaches that punishments, crosses, and death are the most precious treasury of all and the most sacred relics which the Lord of this theology himself has consecrated and blessed, not alone by the touch of his most holy flesh but also by the embrace of his exceedingly holy and divine will, and he has left these relics here to be kissed, sought after, and embraced. Indeed fortunate and blessed is he who is considered by God to be so worthy that these treasures of Christ should be given to him (LW 31, 225f., W. I, 613, 21ff.).
>
> A theologian of glory does not recognize, along with the Apostle, the crucified and hidden God alone. He sees and

speaks of God's glorious manifestation among the heathen, how his invisible nature can be known from the things which are visible and how he is present and powerful in all things everywhere. This theologian of glory, however, learns from Aristotle that the object of the will is the good and the good is worthy to be loved, while the evil, on the other hand, is worthy of hate. He learns that God is the highest good and exceedingly lovable. Disagreeing with the theologian of the cross, he defines the treasury of Christ as the removing and remitting of punishments, things which are most evil and worthy of hate. In opposition to this the theologian of the cross defines the treasury of Christ as impositions and obligations of punishments, things which are best and most worthy of love (LW 31, 227; W. I, 614, 17ff.).

PART TWO

DEVELOPMENT

OF THE

CONCEPT

OF THE

THEOLOGY OF THE CROSS

I.

Luther's Doctrine of the Hidden God

The theology of the cross rejects speculation as a way to knowledge. Metaphysics does not lead to a knowledge of the true God.[13] For Luther all religious speculation is a theology of glory. He condemns this theology of glory because in it the basic significance of the cross of Christ for all theological thinking is not given its due. The cross of Christ makes plain that there is no direct knowledge of God for man. Christian thinking must come to a halt before the fact of the cross. The cross makes demands on Christian thought—demands which must either be acted on or ignored. If Christian thought ignores the demands of the cross it becomes a theology of glory. If the cross becomes the foundation of Christian thought, a theology of the cross results. For the cross cannot be disposed of in an upper story of the structure of thought.

What is the meaning of the cross for the idea of God? We have said that it forbids every attempt at a direct knowledge of God. God's essence cannot simply be derived from the works of creation. The knowledge of God must disclose itself to us in the cross of Christ. But even there we at first see nothing of God. For the moment, the riddle of the cross makes only one thing perfectly clear to us: Our God is a hidden God. "Truly, thou art a God who hidest thyself" (Isa. 45:15).

The doctrine of the hidden God is a disputed chapter in Luther's thought. What does it mean? Is the hidden God one and the same as the revealed God, or is he to be associated with the absolute God of scholasticism? Is faith concerned with the thought of the hidden

God, or is it a product of speculation? Is it a creation of the dilemma into which Luther fell because of his extreme and daring polemics, or is it intimately entwined with Luther's central thoughts? Above all, does the thought remain substantively the same in the course of Luther's theological development? How can his later polemics against this idea be reconciled with his constant evaluation of the writing against Erasmus? We can arrive at a systematic resolution of these questions only by a detour through a historical investigation. For me it seems by no means settled that Luther uses the concept in the Heidelberg Disputation, for example, exactly in the same way as in *The Bondage of the Will* or in his great lectures on Genesis. Here we shall investigate first the early theology of Luther, then *The Bondage of the Will*, and finally the period after 1525, in order to arrive at a comprehensive result.

A. The Heidelberg Disputation

The idea of the hidden God appears here in a strict inner connection with the program of the theology of the cross. The theology of the cross is a theology of revelation. The "wisdom of invisible things" is expressly rejected. The "invisible things of God" should really become clear from the works of creation. In these works God has manifested himself. There should be something like a natural knowledge of God. For this the pagan world provides the best demonstration. A knowledge of God that does not understand itself properly is the root of all idolatry.[14] But, in fact, there is no such thing as a natural knowledge of God. Men have abused the "knowledge of God on the basis of his works." Through man's fault the direct way has proved itself unable to lead to the goal. The visible God was not recognized. The revelation of God in creation failed its purpose. For man it became not a revelation but rather a concealment of God's essence and will. Yet God wants to be known, his being seeks revelation. How, then, shall God reveal himself so that his revelation might really become a revelation for man? Men have failed to honor the God who was manifest in his works. And so God now chooses a different way to reveal himself to man. The cross now becomes the revelation of God.[15]

But what do we see when we see the cross? There is "nothing else to be seen than disgrace, poverty, death, and everything that is shown us in the suffering Christ" (W. V, 108, 1ff.). These are all things that in our opinion have nothing divine in them but rather point to man's trouble, misery, and weakness. (There especially no one would of himself look for God's revelation. Into such a concealment God enters in order to reveal himself. If there is to be revelation of God, the visible God must become the hidden God. God becomes "hidden in sufferings."[16] As God hides himself, the "visible things of God" become manifest: "His human nature, weakness, foolishness" (Explanation of Thesis 20, Heidelberg Disputation, W. I, 362; LW 31, 52).

Thus God becomes visible as he conceals himself, and only in this concealment does he become visible. "Now it is not sufficient for anyone, and it does him no good to recognize God in his glory and majesty, unless he recognizes him in the humility and shame of the cross" (*ibid.*). Hence, even if the theology of glory should arrive at a knowledge of God, it is of no value. God wants to be recognized only in the humility and shame of the cross.[17]

If God himself is hidden in sufferings, it is clear that also the works of God, in which his activity confronts us, bear the same character. The "works of God are always unattractive" (LW 31, 39; W. I, 353, 21), deformed. They are so deeply hidden that they only appear "under the opposite form" (W. LVI, 376, 31ff.; LW 25, 366). God's power reveals itself in weakness (LW 10, 250; W. III, 301, 35ff.). God's help remains invisible to man who considers himself most forsaken by God when God's help is nearest (LW 10, 251; W. III, 302, 20ff.). God's wisdom is indeed wisdom, but it seems like foolishness to us. It is "God's wisdom in concealment, a wisdom which is in secret things" (W. LVI, 237, 20ff.; LW 25, 223). As such we must seek to know it, we must receive an eye for the hidden character of the divine properties and works, for God will never disclose himself to direct, metaphysical contemplation.[18] If man is not to go astray here, the wisdom of the cross must be granted him. This wisdom, however, is considered foolishness by the world. Therefore, "he who wishes to become wise does not seek wisdom by progressing toward it but becomes a fool by retrogressing into seeking folly. . . . This is the wisdom which is folly to the world" (LW 31, 54; W. I, 363, 10ff.).

What follows from all of this concerning the meaning of the hidden God in Luther's theology before his writing against Erasmus?

1. The idea of the hidden God is most intimately connected with Luther's theology of the cross. It has its central significance there. It is no accident that the concept, even though citing Scripture,

appears especially in the Heidelberg Disputation, the basic document of the theology of the cross.[1] This means indirect knowledge
of God; the hidden God is the God whose nature and work can
only be recognized "under the opposite form."

2. The hidden God is none other than the revealed God. God is
hidden for the sake of revelation. Revelation is possible only in
concealment, the revealed God must as such be hidden.[20] A few
more references will substantiate what has already been said. In a
sermon of 24 February 1517, the following explanation for the
necessity of God's concealment is offered: "Man hides his own
things in order to deny them, God hides his own things in order
to reveal them. . . . By his concealment he does nothing else than
remove that which obstructs revelation, namely, pride" (W. I, 138,
13ff.). Accordingly, the concealment would have to be regarded
as an "alien work" performed only for the sake of the "proper
work."[21] The proper place for this concealment of God—which
takes place for the sake of the revelation, indeed is revelation in
precisely that way—is the cross of Christ. This leads us back to
point 1. The hidden God is none other than the crucified God.
Who is a theologian of the cross? A theologian of the cross is one
who speaks of the crucified and hidden God (W. I, 614, 17ff.; LW
31, 225). A theologian of glory is one who does not recognize, along
with the Apostle, the crucified and hidden God alone (ibid.). "Crucified and hidden alone" makes thoroughly clear that the hidden
God cannot be a hypostasis in or behind God, but is the one living
God who is manifest as he is concealed in the cross of Christ.

3. It follows that the hidden God is no product of speculation.
On this point the antispeculative tendency of Luther's early theol-
ogy reaches its climax. If we may put it thus, the concept of the
hidden God must be construed in a strict Christological sense ("he
who does not know Christ does not know God hidden in suffering"
[LW 31, 53; W. I, 362, 23], a reference to the theology of glory).
Affirming omnipresence and omnipotence of God is very pointedly
described as characteristic of the theology of glory (LW 31, 227;
W. I, 614, 17ff.). On the contrary, the hidden God is the crucified
God. There on the cross, at this one place and cloaked in deepest
weakness, God becomes visible. For that reason Luther cannot
warn enough against the "flighty thought" of seeking God anywhere
else than in the crucified Christ. Speculation that endeavors to
plumb the depths of God in reality places itself above God; it is

obvious that it must be rejected from the perspective of the revelation idea of the theology of the cross.[22]

B. The Bondage of the Will

Luther dealt in greatest detail with the significance of the hidden God in his tract against Erasmus, *The Bondage of the Will* (LW 33, 15-295; W. XVIII, 600-687).[23] We will first investigate the contexts in which the term appears there. The tract against Erasmus does not deal primarily with the problem of the hidden God, but, as the title also indicates, with the problem of the free and/or the enslaved will. In fact the term "the hidden God" appears directly only twice. In support of his theses on the free will Erasmus had cited certain Bible passages. Among others he advanced the famous passage from Ezekiel, "Have I any pleasure in the death of the wicked, says the Lord God, and not rather that he should turn from his way and live?" (Ezek. 18:23). Erasmus interprets the passage as follows: If God grieves over the sinner's death, then he cannot be the one who causes the sinner's death. Rather, the one and only cause of the sinner's death is his own free will.

What is Luther's response?

1. Luther says that the *Diatribe* of Erasmus misunderstands the difference between law and gospel. For the passage from Ezekiel is "an evangelical word and the sweetest comfort in every way for miserable sinners" (LW 33, 136; W. XVIII, 683, 11). If these divine promises were lacking, what sinner would not despair? But the free will can in no way be proved from such promises. The *Diatribe* is turning this evangelical word into a word of law and thus spoiling the whole matter. It does not say, "I do not wish the sin of man," as the *Diatribe* interpreted, but "I do not wish the death of the sinner." The evangelical word addresses itself in a consoling and invigorating way to the sinner who feels his sin and suffers because of it, not to the person who indeed has sin but is not concerned about it. Hence this Ezekiel passage, according to Luther, furnishes a strong argument against free will. "For here we are shown what free choice is like, and what it can do about sin when sin is recognized, or about its own conversion to God; that is to say, nothing but fall into a worse state and add despair and impenitence to its sins, if God did not quickly come to its aid and call it back and raise it up by a word of promise" (LW 33, 138; W. XVIII, 684, 15f.). Gospel and free will are related like fire and water.

2. However, Erasmus' line of thought has not yet been invalidated by charging him with confusion of law and gospel. The real difficulty lies elsewhere altogether. The chief weight of Erasmus' argumentation lay on the question: Is it conceivable that the God who weeps over the death of his people causes this very death? Yet one is forced to this conclusion, which is impossible for Erasmus, if one denies man his free decision. If man has no freedom of choice, then, according to Erasmus, he cannot be made accountable for his sins either. Then not he but God himself is the originator of man's sin. Consequently God causes the sinner's death since he is the true author of sin. But how can this be harmonized with the statement, "I have no pleasure in the death of the sinner"? One of the two must be wrong. This is how Erasmus poses the problem and solves it by having recourse to his view of man's free will.

This leads to the second argument which Luther advances against the interpretation of Erasmus. In this connection we find the term "the hidden God." Luther distinguishes a preached, revealed, worshiped God from one who is not any of these. We must speak about both in a different way. Luther did not invent this distinction, but appeals for it to Paul, 2 Thessalonians 2:4.

> We have to argue in one way about God or the will of God as preached, revealed, offered, and worshiped, and in another way about God as he is not preached, not revealed, not offered, not worshiped. To the extent, therefore, that God hides himself and wills to be unknown to us, it is no business of ours. For here the saying truly applies, "Things above us are no business of ours." And lest anyone should think this is a distinction of my own, I am following Paul, who writes to the Thessalonians concerning Antichrist that he will exalt himself above every God that is preached and worshiped (2 Thess. 2:4). This plainly shows that someone can be exalted above God as he is preached and worshiped, that is, above the word and rite through which God is known to us and his dealings with us; but above God as he is not worshiped and not preached, but as he is in his own nature and majesty, nothing can be exalted, but all things are under his mighty hand (LW 33, 139; W. XVIII, 685, 3ff.).

Then a few lines farther on this God who is not preached is called the hidden God. This is the context in which the term "hidden God" appears in *The Bondage of the Will*. Two things must be noted.

1. Luther has recourse to the doctrine of the hidden God in an exegetical predicament. From a purely exegetical point of view Erasmus is obviously in a more favorable position. How can Luther uphold his religious intuition over against the letter of Scripture? He finds a way out in the doctrine of the hidden God. But is the significance of this doctrine only to provide Luther a means of escape in his polemics, or does it also stand firm and independent of all polemical intent?

2. Luther introduces the doctrine of the hidden God as something familiar. This already speaks against a purely polemical conception of this teaching. On the other hand, it raises the question of how the view of the hidden God harmonizes with Luther's other views of God and how these relate to his concept of faith in *The Bondage of the Will*.

What is the relationship of the hidden God to the revealed God? What strikes us first of all is the difference. "We have to argue differently" about the hidden and the revealed God. The *Diatribe* of Erasmus must be charged with ignorance for not observing this basic distinction (p. 140; W. XVIII, 685, 25). God confronts us first of all in his word. In his word he is "known to us" and "has dealings with us." In it he has offered himself to us. We are directed to God's revelation in the word. God himself could not be grasped by us but would crush and annihilate us in his majesty, for he is a consuming fire. For that reason God wraps himself in his word. He becomes the "clothed" God. With him alone can we have any dealings. God must conceal himself in the word in order to be able to reveal himself. The revealed God is the clothed God.

Indeed, the revealed God is nothing else than the word of God (p. 140; W. XVIII, 685, 26). That word, however, is clear, "I do not wish the sinner's death." The revealed God is unconditional salvific will. The preached God will have all men to be saved and come to the knowledge of the truth. His word is in earnest (Matt. 23:37). This God cannot be the author of sins. Rightly we say, "The good God does not deplore the death of his people which he works in them, but he deplores the death which he finds in his people and desires to remove from them" (p. 139f.; W. XVIII, 685, 18f.). The death of the people may not be traced back to the preached God. His work is not to kill but to create life. He is the physician who heals the people's wounds *(ibid.)*. The gospel is the glad news of the healing and saving God.

Is that all that must be said about God? No, says Luther. While we are dealing with the revealed God we dare not forget about the hidden God. God has indeed revealed himself in his word, but God is greater than his word. God has not confined himself within the limits of the word. God's supreme attribute is his freedom. We may not approach too closely to that freedom, even when we appeal to the word. "For there he has not bound himself by his word, but has kept himself free over all things." God is not exhausted in his word. Therefore we must distinguish between "the word of God and God himself" (ibid.). For "God does many things that he does not disclose to us in his word; he also wills many things which he does not disclose himself as willing in his word." In so far as God does not reveal himself in his word he remains hidden for us. His will is inscrutable. His activity is placed in sharp antithesis over against the activity of the revealed God. He is enthroned "in his own nature and majesty," and in this regard we have no dealings with him, nor can we have any. Yet even though his activity remains hidden from us, he is still the one who does everything, he "works life, death, and all in all" (ibid.).[24] Hence the word, "I do not wish the sinner's death," does not apply to him, as surely as it does to the revealed God. "Thus he does not will the death of a sinner, according to his word; but he wills it according to that inscrutable will of his." "God hidden in his majesty neither deplores nor takes away death." This hidden God is the God of double predestination. He hardens Pharaoh, he has rejected Esau before the boy came into being. "Inscrutable will," indeed, "completely inscrutable and unknowable"! Hence, if Erasmus thinks he can prove the necessity of free will from the Ezekiel passage, he is mistaken; he has failed to take the hidden God into account.

Thus the hidden God and the revealed God are sharply differentiated. One cannot affirm of the former what applies to the latter, and vice versa. The two concepts really appear to stand in a diametrically opposite relationship. But can the unity of the godhead still be maintained under such conditions? Has it not hopelessly fallen prey to a fatal dualism? Can it still be asserted that Luther's picture of God is "not only the most living and definite, but also the most thoroughly pondered and the clearest that Christian theology has ever produced"?[25] Has this not made revelation illusory?

But all of theology is based on revelation. Is it to pine away and limit itself to a few scanty references to "the unknowable"? Furthermore, what happens to any kind of certainty for man, if he must constantly take into account a hidden will of God that is put in opposition to the revealed will? To answer these questions we must once again examine the concept of the hidden God in *The Bondage of the Will*. For we can attempt to solve the decisive question about the relationship between the hidden God and the revealed God only if we uncover the relationships of the concept of the hidden God to Luther's concept of faith, which he has formulated in definitive statements particularly in *The Bondage of the Will*.

"To the extent, therefore, that God hides himself and wills to be unknown to us, it is no business of ours. For here the saying truly applies, 'Things above us are no business of ours'" (p. 139; W. XVIII, 685, 5ff.). The hidden God does not want to be known by us. He is not only a hidden God, but a God who has concealed himself.[26] "It is no business of ours" does not mean that as such he is no concern of ours, but we have no dealings with him. God does not will it. Above all, we must not meddle with God's inscrutable will with our human questions. All our inquiring will not lead to the goal anyway.

Is the hidden God, then, a God who cannot be considered for fellowship with man at all, a God by himself? It almost seems so when we hear Luther saying, "God must therefore be left to himself in his own majesty, for in this regard we have nothing to do with him, nor has he willed that we should have anything to do with him" (p. 139; W. XVIII, 685, 14f.). Luther advises us to pay attention to the word, that is, the revealed God, and leave the secrets of the hidden God alone. But does not Luther by this request arrive at the same result as Erasmus? He, too, conceded that Scripture contains dark teachings, but their very obscurity indicates that they are not necessary. Hence one should not, like Luther, disseminate them among the people where they might only cause confusion.

Luther had already vigorously rejected this attitude of Erasmus (pp. 61ff.; W. XVIII, 632, 21ff.). The "we have nothing to do with him" cannot be meant in the sense of Erasmus. On the contrary, we must *know* about the hidden God. Erasmus, alas, knows nothing about this. But even if man cannot understand the inscrutable will of God, he should nevertheless "fear and adore" him (p. 140; W. XVIII, 686, 3). There must be more involved in the hidden God for Luther than a polemical concern. "Adoration" is due the hidden God; thus the term cannot be taken in a speculative or polemical sense. If we look more closely we will notice that in spite of seemingly contradictory statements of Luther, the concept of the hidden God is not a marginal item in Luther's theology, but is intimately related to his view of faith, and thus reaches into the very core of his theology.

What is faith? Throughout his life Luther regarded Hebrews 11:1 as having the force of a definition, namely, that "faith has to do with things not seen" (W. XVIII, 633, 7; LW 33, 62). This states the indispensable prerequisite for every possible object of faith. "Hence in order that there may be room for faith, it is necessary that everything which is believed should be hidden. It cannot, however, be more deeply hidden than under an object, perception, or experience which is contrary to it" (ibid.). Faith can only look to what is hidden. If anything is to become an object of faith it must be concealed to the point of unrecognizability, yes, be hidden under the opposite.

Just as, according to Luther's Heidelberg Theses, revelation is possible only in concealment, we are now confronted by the other side of the matter, namely that faith can be directed only to what is concealed, hidden, and invisible. In The Bondage of the Will Luther guides this thesis to its logical conclusion. As surely as we confess, "I believe in a holy catholic church," the church, too, insofar as it is an object of faith, is not visible to the physical eye. "The church is hidden, the saints are unknown" (W. XVIII, 652, 23; LW, 33, 89).

What is commonly called church may not have anything to do with the true church by a long shot. It is even extremely probable that the church of God is not to be sought where the official church exists. "Who knows but that the state of the church of God throughout the whole course of the world from the beginning has always been such that some have been called the people and the saints of God who were not so, while others, a remnant in their midst, really were the people or the saints, but were never called so, as witness the stories of Cain and Abel, Ishmael and Isaac, Esau and Jacob?" (W. XVIII, 650, 27ff.; LW 33, 86).

Concealment is an essential characteristic of the objects of faith. This, however, demands the conclusion that God, too, must be hidden if faith is to be directed toward him. Thus Luther does in fact demand that the divine righteousness has to be incomprehensible, if it is to be called divine. "For if his righteousness were such that it could be judged to be righteous by human standards, it would clearly not be divine and would in no way differ from human righteousness. But since he is the one true God, and is wholly incomprehensible and inaccessible to human reason, it is proper and indeed necessary that his righteousness also should be incomprehensible" (W. XVIII, 784, 9ff.; LW 33, 290). Now we can conclude that if the revealed God is really to be present for faith, he must also be the hidden God. Consequently the revealed God would be none other than the hidden God.

Only now, however, we have entangled ourselves in the real difficulties. We have arrived at the insight that in *The Bondage of the Will* the concept of faith demands a hidden God. The idea that faith therefore rests on a fiction must be excluded. How else but in faith could we deal with the one true God? For "it is in the nature of faith not to be deceived" (W. XVIII, 652, 7; LW 33, 88). Hence the hidden God must be identical to the revealed God. But this fact is opposed by the clear distinction Luther made between the hidden God and the revealed God on the basis of the Ezekiel passage. We simply cannot erase the fact (as Kattenbusch does in *Deus absconditus*, p. 205, n. 31), that here Luther flatly sets up an antithetical relationship between the two concepts. On the one side is the hidden God as a logical consequence of the idea of faith, and yet, on the other side, is a sharp disjunction between the hidden God and the revealed God. How is this contradiction resolved?

It seems to me that the idea of the hidden God in the latter context is not exactly the same as in the former. The hidden God in the area of faith—if I may put it that way—reminds us altogether of the hidden God in the Heidelberg Disputation. There the character of hiddenness is associated with revelation, here it is associated with faith. As revelation or faith is posited, hiddenness is also posited. The hidden God and the revealed God are completely identical.

The faith character of the knowledge of God is preserved by uniting revelation and concealment as two inseparable aspects in one and the same act. In the explanation of the Ezekiel passage this is accomplished by warning against an all too confident arguing with God's thoughts, as Erasmus does. Here the idea of the hidden God demonstrates that also in the revealed God there are secrets which we cannot penetrate. The dualism between God hidden and revealed, clothed in mythological form, does not exist for faith. It is precisely because of the revealed God that faith knows about the hidden God. Revelation addresses itself to faith, not to sight,[27] not to reflective reason. Reason can only establish a dualism. Faith presses through the revealed God to the hidden God, and yet does not meet a second God behind or beside the former.[28] But this is something only faith can achieve.

On the other hand, faith needs the idea of the hidden God for its own sake. This thought is a constant reminder that it is risky to believe in the revealed God.[29] Thus, the idea of God's love dare never become a general truth. Only by means of this constantly repeated consummation is faith what it is. Hence there is also here an inner connection between the idea of the hidden God and the concept of faith. It is precisely for the sake of faith that Luther must here undertake the apparently rigid metaphysical separation between the hidden God and the revealed God. The difference between the two lines may be summarized in this way: In the former the idea of the hidden God means that revelation in principle is possible only in concealment; in the latter it means that also in the revealed God secrets remain. Both lines intersect in the concept of faith.

If Luther had not been familiar with the idea of the hidden God from the perspective of his view of faith, he would probably not have used it polemically against Erasmus. But in the process the idea has shifted somewhat for him, as we have observed. Before we determine how this shift is to be evaluated, we will pursue further the development of this thought in Luther.

C. Lectures on Isaiah

In his lectures on Isaiah (1527-1530) Luther explains Isaiah 45:15, "Truly, thou art a God who hidest thyself," as follows:

> These are the words of the prophet, who had already predicted these words of consolation. Now he is snatched into a trance of the Word of God, as if to say, 'Dear God, how strangely You deal with us!' It is a matter beyond comprehension to which reason cannot attain. Is this not a wonderful deliverance, that restoration is promised to Jerusalem, the temple, etc.? There the flesh sees nothing and concludes: Nothing produces nothing. Nevertheless, we see that in this Nothing all things will come to pass through the Word of consolation. Thus we observe God and His incomprehensible plans. So today we see in the Word the progress of the church of God against the force and the schemes of all tyrants. Since faith is the

conviction of things not seen, the opposite must appear to be the case (LW 17, 131f.; W. XXXII, 2, 364, 21ff.).

What is the meaning of the hidden God here? Unfortunately, the concept is not formulated very clearly at this point. The whole discussion of *The Bondage of the Will* is not referred to. Here the hidden God signifies a wonderful, incomprehensible God, whose works are inaccessible to reason. God's activity takes place in concealment. The flesh sees none of that. Only faith, as the conviction of things not seen, recognizes God's ways in the opposite. This is a thought which Luther never tires of repeating from his earliest days onward.

If the interpreter of this passage offers us nothing new, the Genesis lectures of 1535-1545 [30] are a particularly rich mine presenting the thoughts of the old Luther concerning the hidden God. Here Luther consciously refers back to *The Bondage of the Will*. In the pertinent Genesis explanations we have good guidance for understanding the thoughts developed in the tract. It could be that his Genesis interpretation is colored by historical and polemical concerns, making its value questionable. It must never be forgotten that everything that Luther said was spoken in a very specific situation. The question whether the old Luther interpreted himself correctly can be answered only after further investigation.

On the subject of the hidden God, we find in the lectures on Genesis also the same two lines we distinguished above in *The Bondage of the Will*. There is therefore no basis for the oft-repeated claim that in his later years Luther no longer adhered to his idea concerning the hidden God, but rather warned against it. This claim overlooks the double track on which this idea runs for Luther. Let us proceed to the documentation.

God cannot be comprehended without a covering (LW 1, 14; W. XLII, 11, 28ff.). Such coverings are "word" and "works" (LW 1, 13). Again we have the familiar thought that if God wants to reveal himself, he must hide himself.[31] For Luther it is part of God's essence to reveal himself. But if he cannot do this without concealing himself, then this, too, belongs to God's essence. This is the meaning of Luther's words that "God is the One who is hidden. This is His peculiar property" (LW 6, 148; W. XLIV, 110, 23ff.). Yet stronger than the thought that God is concealed under the cloak of the word is the other thought that he is hidden in his works. Word and works were mentioned as the two coverings that

God uses. The "hidden in suffering" of the Heidelberg Disputation here receives a rich concrete interpretation. God's "proper work" becomes visible to us as "alien work." "Therefore the prophet (Isa. 45:15) calls him 'a God who hides Himself.' For under the curse a blessing lies hidden; under the consciousness of sin, righteousness; under death, life; and under affliction, comfort" (LW 4, 7; W. XLIII, 140, 28ff.).

God is so deeply hidden that he appears to us a pure nothing. "For this reason nothing in the world seems more uncertain than the Word of God and faith, nothing more delusive than hope in the promise. In short, nothing seems to be more nothing than God himself. Consequently, this is the knowledge of the saints and a mystery hidden from the wise and revealed to babes (Matt. 11:25). The pope and the Turk believe easily, because they have experienced such great successes, and because they are flourishing with such great power, with wisdom, with the outward appearance of saintliness, and with their religion, to the point that there is nothing beyond this" (LW 4, 355f.; W. XLIII, 392, 16ff.). "God is utterly incomprehensible and is nobody in all His works" (p. 360; W. XLIII, 395, 18ff.). Nor does God make an exception in the case of one who prays. He hides his face from him (LW 6, 259; W. XLIV, 192, 27ff.). God appears to us under the mask of a devil. "Therefore we should know that God hides Himself under the form of the worst devil" (LW 7, 175; W. XLIV, 429, 24f.).

A similar explanation appears in the story of Joseph's temptation by Potiphar's wife. Evil triumphs and Joseph is cast into prison.[32] But why does God hide himself so thoroughly? Why are his ways in such opposition to all human thinking? We shall receive a complete answer only in the "light of glory." For the present we know that it is the "wisdom of the saints," to believe contrary to appearance.[33] So that we may learn what it means to believe and finally bid farewell to our reason in these matters, God withdraws himself from our eyes (LW 4, 360; W. XLIII, 395, 13ff.).

All these thoughts are such as we have found in Luther from the beginning. Now, however, they appear somewhat modified. The simultaneous relationship of being hidden and revealed has become one of succession. This may perhaps be best demonstrated by the term "the back parts of God" (posteriora Dei; LW 31, 52). This same term was used already in Thesis 20 of the Heidelberg Disputation. The picture is derived from Exodus 33:18ff. No mortal may see the face of God. Even Moses can only look upon God from

behind. In literal terms, man cannot have a direct knowledge of
God. He knows nothing at all if he is not content with an indirect
knowledge. This is the meaning of the term in the Heidelberg
Disputation. Knowledge of God means knowledge of the "back
parts of God." This is the true vision of God.

The question whether there is also something like the "fore parts
of God" is not raised at all. The theologian of the cross does not
ask about it. For him the being of God is disclosed in cross and
suffering. In the lectures on Genesis the term appears again a number of times. There it is found with reference to the suffering and
trial of the godly man. "When there is affliction, we see God from
behind" (LW 3, 71; W. XLII, 599, 29ff.). "This is the view from
behind, when we feel nothing but affliction and doubts" *(ibid.)*
This seeing of God from behind is necessary for the godly, as will
be shown in more detail in connection with Luther's views on spiritual trial.

Let no one imagine he has experienced anything of God if he
has not stood over against these "back parts of God." Luther can
still insist that the "back parts" are basically God's true counte-
nance. "When the trial has passed, it becomes clear that by the
very fact that God has showed Himself to us from behind He has
showed us His face, that He did not forsake us but turned away
His eyes just a little" *(ibid.)*. Hence a simultaneous relationship
exists between the "fore parts" and the "back parts." In the main,
however, Luther, in his Genesis lectures, regards the relationship
as one of succession.[34] " 'You shall see My back' (Exod. 33:23),
the Lord says to Moses when he asked that His face be shown to
him; that is, 'You will see My thoughts after the deed has been
done' " (LW 8, 30; W. XLIV, 601, 18ff.).[35]

We may observe exactly the same thing as we investigate the
question concerning the relationship between the hidden and revealed God. Just as Luther in the Genesis lectures still unites the
"back parts" and the "front parts of God," so the knowledge of the
hidden God can coincide with the knowledge of the revealed God.
"God is the One who is hidden. This is His peculiar property. He
is really hidden, and yet He is not hidden, for the flesh prevents us
from being able to look at Him. . . . But in faith, in the Word,
and in the sacraments He is revealed and seen" (LW 6, 148; W.
XLIV, 601, 23ff.).

Yet here, too, the successive relationship predominates. "If you
believe in the revealed God and accept His Word, He will gradu-

ally also reveal the hidden God" (LW 5, 46; W. XLIII, 460, 26ff.). And if we persevere in prayer and do not doubt God's promise, even though we perceive no sign of being heard, "in this perseverance in prayer and faith God becomes a visible God . . . comforting us and doing what we wish" (LW 6, 259; W. XLIV, 192, 27ff.).

From all this it should be clear that Luther did not surrender the idea of the hidden God in the period after 1525. In fact, he could not surrender it without also surrendering his concept of faith. For this concept demands a hidden God—in spite of, indeed because of, the significance Christ has for him. Also in the Genesis lectures, his last major work, Luther is determined to maintain the hidden God of the faith line. Alongside the simultaneous or identity relationship between concealment and revelation of a hidden and revealed God has now come the successive relationship. But this changes nothing in the essential significance of the doctrine concerning the hidden God for the concept of faith. However, there are also other statements which reject the idea of the hidden God in every form. These rejections are clear, blunt, and to the point. How are they to be interpreted?

In connection with his interpretation of Genesis 26 the old Luther speaks in a prophetic tone to his young students and indicates how he wants his tract, *The Bondage of the Will*, to be understood.[36]

> After my death many will publish my books and will prove from them errors of every kind and their own delusions. Among other things, however, I have written that everything is absolute and unavoidable; but at the same time I have added that one must look at the revealed God, as we sing in the hymn: *Er heist Jesu Christ, der HERR Zebaoth, und ist kein ander Gott*, "Jesus Christ is the Lord of hosts, and there is no other God"—and also in very many other places. But they will pass over all these places and take only those that deal with the hidden God. Accordingly, you who are listening to me now should remember that I have taught that one should not inquire into the predestination of the hidden God but should be satisfied with what is revealed through the calling and through the ministry of the Word (LW 5, 50; W. XLIII, 463, 3ff.).

Luther warns against a brooding preoccupation with the idea of the hidden God. It should be carefully noted that he does not with a single word recant the doctrine concerning the hidden God.

He only warns against speculations about the hidden God. The
same is true of the numerous other pertinent passages. Speculation
on the high majesty of God is repudiated as a dangerous, even
devilish activity, and, instead of that, Christ is extolled as the only
sure way to the Father. For man the "nude" God is a consuming
fire, and his works are "terrifying." Christ is the "way to God." If we
are unwilling to travel this way to God we shall fall into despair. (So
in his lectures on Isaiah, LW 16, 54f.; W. XXXI, 2, 38, 21ff.).[37] In his
1531 commentary on Galatians Luther goes all out in pointing to
Christ as the only mediator of revelation. "God in his own nature"
cannot be endured by man. In our thinking about God we must
therefore begin at the manger (LW 26, 29; W. XL, 1, 77, 11ff.).
Christ is the "lovely picture" in which we see God (LW 26, 30;
cf. p. 39 and 396; W. XL, 1, 79, 20; cf. 93, 23ff. and 602, 20ff.).
Finally, we rediscover the same thoughts in the Genesis lectures.
Luther recalls an old tale which warns against theological speculation. In that connection Luther speaks a sharply critical word
against monastic contemplation and meditation.[38] The true speculative life is something entirely different. It renounces reason and
imagination and lives solely by the Word of God (LW 6, 261; W.
XLIV, 193, 37ff.). Luther therefore draws from Genesis 6:5 the
teaching that one should "avoid as much as possible any questions
that carry us to the throne of the Supreme Majesty" (LW 2, 45;
W. XLII, 293, 29ff.)

Thus in all these statements Luther opposes a view of God that
is separated from faith and has been gained by speculation. The
"naked God" is the god of the philosophers (LW 4, 145; W. XLIII,
240). Instead of this God Luther sets forth the concept of the revealed God. In this Luther is entirely consistent. We have already
established the anti-speculative trend of the theology of the cross.
And we have seen that this trend reaches its climax in the idea of
the hidden God. In his Genesis lectures Luther rejects all brooding
over the hidden God as "altogether devilish" (LW 5, 44; W. XLIII,
458, 36ff.). From the standpoint of the theology of revelation, such
brooding cannot possibly aid the understanding of the concept of
the hidden God, as we have encountered it in the theology of the
cross of the Heidelberg Disputation and in the idea of faith in
The Bondage of the Will. On the contrary, in these passages the
hidden God must be equated with the naked God, the God in his
own nature.

With that we have already implicitly answered the question why
Luther now warns against the idea of the hidden God, an idea he
himself had introduced in *The Bondage of the Will*. Does he, then,
admit that he had at that time allowed himself to be pushed on the
wrong road in the heat of polemics? Hardly. We have already seen
that he does not renounce the idea itself. He only warns against a
misuse of it. In our investigation of *The Bondage of the Will* we
have seen that also the hidden God of the second line must be
understood from the concept of faith. However, the passage in
question (LW 33, 139; W. XVIII, 685) does not make this clear.
The passage is open to misinterpretation, especially if it is lifted
out of the context of the tract. In that case it is no longer clearly
seen 1) that the concept of the hidden God is posited precisely for
the sake of faith, and 2) that in *The Bondage of the Will* both lines
intersect in the concept of faith, and that, consequently, the concept of the hidden God does not appear by accident, but in substance belongs together with central aspects of Luther's theology.
One is the more easily seduced into ignoring these connections because the concept appears by name in only this one passage (and
here only twice!). As a result, one arrives at the metaphysical distortion of the concept, to which the misunderstanding of the
enslaved will corresponds.

Luther himself must have sensed that the passage could lead
to such misunderstanding. This alone explains how he can list
The Bondage of the Will among his best writings and yet warn
against the idea of the hidden God at the same time. The antithesis
between the God hidden and revealed can too easily be twisted
into the metaphysical. In that case the tension between the two
statements about the one God, within which the movement of
faith takes place, would become a rigid side-by-side relationship of
two hypostases. Luther's later polemics is fully justified in opposing this. For nothing less than the well-understood idea of the hidden God (Heidelberg Disputation; the "faith line," LW 5, 46; W.
XLIII, 460, 26 ff.; LW 6, 148; W. XLIV, 110, 23 ff.) is at stake here.
For the sake of the hidden God Luther must assail the idol, "hidden
God." We must therefore evaluate the relationship of the two lines
in *The Bondage of the Will* as follows: The second line, taken by
itself, is subject to misunderstanding; it must continually be criticized and validated by the first line. Luther demonstrates this pro-
cedure in the pertinent expositions of the Genesis lectures.

We have attempted to understand the idea of the hidden God in connection with Luther's view of faith. To our knowledge Kattenbusch was the first to do this.[39] His thesis reads: "We must rate Luther's idea of the hidden God altogether as a unique and positive idea of faith, or else we shall not do it justice" (p. 183). To that we can only agree, as our explanations have shown. Kattenbusch has definitely moved the debate concerning the hidden God onto a new basis.

Albrecht Ritschl's interpretation [40] is not generally accepted today. In his view the idea of the hidden God represents a relapse into nominalism.[41] He claims that Luther in his polemics against Erasmus took refuge in the Occamistic God of pure arbitrariness, the *Deus exlex,* the God bound by no law. But any attempt at explanation that contents itself with merely showing up contradictions and inconsistencies in the thoughts of a great man is never quite adequate even as a working concept. In this case, however, it is also substantively impossible. Kattenbusch (p. 196) is quite right in pointing out that the sentence, "He is God, and for his will there is no cause or reason" (LW 33, 181; W. XVIII, 712, 32), has additional words that dare not be overlooked. For God's will there is no cause or reason "that can be laid down as a rule or measure for it." Then the sentence does not mean that God's activity is purely arbitrary, but only that it need not submit to any norm imposed from without. Thus God's freedom is safeguarded.

Luther never conceives of this freedom as ethically indifferent. The fact that God is righteous, even when he condemns the innocent and elects the guilty, we can now grasp only in faith; in the light of glory God's righteousness will reveal itself to us in its full brightness. The assertion that "it is not because he is or was obliged so to will that what he wills is right, but on the contrary, because he himself so wills, therefore what happens must be right" (LW 33, 181; W. XVIII, 712, 35ff.) need not be interpreted nominalistically. It can also be understood (cf. Hirsch, l.c., p. 24) "as a strong expression for the certainty of faith" in God's goodness, even when it is completely hidden "under the appearance of the opposite." Above all, according to Heim's penetrating explanations,[42] what is new in Luther's view consists of the paradoxical synthesis between the transcendence of God's salvific will and the subjective experience of the incalculable double will on the one hand, and the transcendence of the absolute double will and the subjective experience of the unconditional salvific will on the other hand. If, with Ritschl, one excludes from Luther's basic view the one line of thought as nominalistic, then the other line of thought, the objectification of God's isolated will of love, becomes a repetition of medieval thoughts, as maintained, for example, by Abelard.

If Ritschl's views are then quite generally rejected,[43] the position of Theodosius Harnack,[44] his contemporary and opposite number, can still rightfully claim a high degree of consideration. Harnack spreads a rich store of sources before us, on the basis of which he undertakes to carry through his thesis concerning the hidden God for the whole of Luther. In a somewhat modified form it is also the basis for Seeberg's treatment in his history of dogma.[45]

Harnack distinguishes a twofold knowledge of God in Luther. The one follows from reason and is therefore a natural knowledge of God. Luther can also label this a knowledge through the law. For him the law of Moses and reason belong together on the side of natural man. But this knowledge only understands God as creator of the world. Besides, men have misused this knowledge, and consequently it has become the source of all idolatry. Even the devil possesses this knowledge. For that reason it cannot be a saving knowledge; for it knows only about the majesty of God but has no inkling of his mercy.

It is, however, just the latter that concerns sinful man. To this knowledge apart from Christ which has proved itself to be inadequate, though not objectively untrue, is opposed the knowledge of God in Christ which brings the consolation of forgiveness. This twofold knowledge corresponds to the double relationship in which God stands toward the world—as its creator and its redeemer. In this double relationship Harnack finds the basic design to which Luther's entire theology may be traced back. The doctrine of the hidden God and revealed God is inserted into this design. The hidden God is God in his creator-relationship, while the revealed God is God as the redeemer. The hidden God is God "apart from Christ," while the revealed God is God "in Christ." Concretely stated, with reference to sinful mankind, this means distinguishing between the God of wrath and the God of grace. Yet the identity of God must be maintained in this distinction since it is only a matter of two different relations (p. 94).[46]

One can of course have his misgivings about Harnack's distinction between creator-God and redeemer-God. For Luther, faith in the creator-God was by no means an extra-Christian preliminary step for the true faith in God (W. XIII, 439f.). He can find the whole Christian knowledge of God comprehended in the faith of the creator. He can even say:

> If they (the pagans) had stayed with this feeling and had said, 'Look, we know this: Whoever this God, or this Divinity, may be whose nature is to be immortal and powerful and able to hear those who call upon Him, let us worship and adore Him, let us not call Him Jupiter and say that He is like this or that image, but let us simply worship Him, no matter who He is (for He must have being),' then without a doubt they would have been saved, even though they had not recognized Him as the Creator of heaven and earth or taken note of any other specific work of His hands (LW 25, 158; W. LVI, 177, 18ff.).

Therefore we must not exaggerate the difference between creator-God and redeemer-God. In any case it proves itself unsuitable as a basis for the doctrine of the hidden and revealed God. In the Heidelberg Disputation Luther specifically contrasts the God manifest in his works, hence the creator-God, with the God hidden in suffering, and this hidden God is for him the revealed God. Harnack, too, was struck by the fact that Luther "designates the revealed God himself again as the hidden one" (W. X, 1, 1, 44, 5ff.). But this observation did not bother him very much. Here Luther "does not have the content but the form of revelation in view, and thus the contradiction at once resolves itself automatically" (p. 110).

It is true that here the form of revelation is involved first of all. But can one distinguish so simply between form and content? Is the form of revelation perhaps accidental, or is it not to the highest degree characteristic for the content of revelation? Is Christ somehow only an indifferent form of revelation? Is not the "what" of revelation to a considerable degree contained in the "how"? The insufficiently reflected distinction between form and content of revelation would lead to conclusions about the doctrine of the person of Christ that Harnack would emphatically reject. It is all the more surprising that Harnack here passes so quickly over this problem, since he himself can say (p. 95), "God as the revealed one is the hidden one, so that he may nevertheless be and remain God, and be feared and adored as such by us. And as the hidden one he is the revealed one, so that he might be our God and be grasped as such by faith." From here it is just one step to the insight that the idea of the hidden God must be associated with Luther's concept of faith.

Harnack himself takes this step when he says (p. 103) that God, if he were not also the hidden and absolute one, "not only could not be feared by us," but that then also "neither faith nor hope nor love would take place in us." That is to say, we would then "be and live without God" anyway (W. V, 175, 4ff.). But instead of pursuing these thoughts, he immediately (p. 86) subordinates the hidden God to his basic design of creator-God and redeemer-God, and thus denies himself insight into the relevatory character of the hidden God.[47]

Seeberg does this even more decisively.[48] According to him the doctrine of the hidden God furnishes only the general metaphysical and scientific frame for the Christian idea of the love of God. In his view Luther here simply allies himself with the combination established by scholasticism, in which the Christian idea of divine love is placed in the center in a general metaphysical frame (p. 148). What is new in Luther is that he "sharply lifts out the specifically Christian element of the positive revelation of love and ascribes all religious power and significance to it alone" (p. 148). Here we see plainly how the road from Harnack leads back to Ritschl again.[49] If Harnack's interpretation were correct, then the idea of the hidden God could not be justified theologically. Ritschl would still be right. The idea of the hidden God can be maintained only when it is understood as a positive idea of faith. We have uncovered indications in that direction in Harnack, but they remained indications. In the last analysis the hidden God belongs to natural theology after all.[50]

We believe, on the contrary, that we have shown that Luther's theology of the cross is the real native soil for this concept. From here a way must be found to understand the special formulation of the concept in *The Bondage of the Will*. It will then be seen that it is not meant in a speculative-metaphysical sense, although it is open to such an interpretation. For that very reason Luther later warns against this idea, while at the same time it remains a basic perspective of his theological thought. In order to safeguard the true concern of the idea, he warns against the speculatively misunderstood hidden God. Thus Luther remained true to his original views.

We were able to document a slight shift of the original thought in connection with the concept of "the back parts of God." But this minor reshaping is always carried out on the basis of the theology of the cross. Hence we may already establish the fact that Luther's theology of the cross must not, as Otto Ritschl insists, be regarded as a preliminary stage of Luther's theology, but rather that it constitutes an integrating aspect of Luther's entire theology.

II.

Luther's Doctrine of Faith

We have shown how Luther's idea of the hidden God grows out of his views on revelation and faith. God permits his true nature to be seen in opposition to what human wisdom calls divine and eternal. God hides himself under the appearance of the opposite. He can arrive at his proper work only by way of his alien work. Revelation cannot simply be discerned from history. This view of God is foreign to the theology of the cross. Although God is the Creator of the world, he nevertheless stands in sharp contrast to all that is called world. For this world is dominated by sin. God's holiness militates against it. Consequently, where there is a confrontation between God and this world, a radical reversal of all existing orders of precedence and relationships takes place. And as the Creator of the world God demonstrates himself to be the one who rules over this world in sovereign freedom. There are no laws by which we could obligate God (W. XVIII, 712, 32f.; LW 33, 181). We cannot make any "deals" with this God.

Also in the revealed God there remains an ultimate secret whose veil will be lifted only in the light of glory. The reference to this light of glory, in which faith is to be turned into sight, is finally the ultimate concern in *The Bondage of the Will*. The God who is hidden under the opposite, the God who as the absolutely free one eludes all calculation, this is the God of the theology of the cross.

We have already said that the two ideas of God we uncovered in

The Bondage of the Will, which are not completely identical, come together in the idea of faith. But what is the meaning of "faith"? Difficult questions are hidden behind this simple term. Can anything in man correspond to such an idea of God? Does the God who as the revealed one is the hidden one still permit himself to be grasped in any way? Can there be some kind of mechanism within man that can comprehend this God even though he stands in opposition to all that is called world? Is there anything human that need not be considered as belonging to the world? Here, indeed, are basic questions for every serious religion, questions that have received classic expression in Christendom by Augustine in his *Confessions.*

The innermost problem here is not the question of how the finite can share in the infinite, or how the creature can be a vessel for the divine content. The basic question is whether in man there can be a point of contact for the activity of that God who stands in such a contrary relationship to the world. How is it possible to continue to ascribe the character of reality to faith, if the crucified God *(Deus crucifixus)* signifies the great *No* to reality? Obviously faith must also be a negation of all human ideas about God, but where, then, is its place? How, on the part of man, can a counterpart to the "under the appearance of the opposite" in the idea of God be fashioned without thereby surrendering every claim to reality? If the concept of faith can only be defined negatively, how do we escape the danger of religious nihilism? And yet, according to the theology of the cross, there is no direct way from any human quality to God. If the theology of the cross represents the surrender of every human position, how can we still arrive at positive statements concerning the relationship between God and man? But without such positive statements theology ceases to be theology. Here we see the point at which the question concerning the possibility of faith and the legitimacy of theology intersect.

Having treated the idea of the hidden God as the decisive idea of God in the theology of the cross, we now pose the question: How does man fit into this system? With what does man respond to the revelation of the hidden God? How may we more fully describe the response of faith—for there can be no other response? We shall do this, in the first place, by delimiting the question, secondly, by searching out its positive aspects, and finally, by asking whether a comprehensive theological category may be found for it.

A. Critical Delimitation of the Concept of Faith

1. Faith and Synteresis

Is there in man a point of contact for the divine? Scholasticism explicitly established such a point in its doctrine of *synteresis* (conscience). Since also Luther for a time held to this doctrine, we must deal with it briefly.

Its origin has not yet been sufficiently clarified.[51] But we are less concerned about its origin than its content. Jerome describes synteresis as the "spark of conscience which was not extinguished in the breast of Adam even after he was expelled from paradise, and by which . . . we know that we sin." The Bible would also call this ability "spirit" (Rom. 8:26). With this description the term *synteresis* as meaning *preservation* fits quite well, if we accept the reading simply as correct, as scholasticism did. In that case synteresis seems here to be distinguished from conscience by calling the former "a spark of conscience." In this direction the history of the concept was developed further. Over against conscience, synteresis is understood as *ethical consciousness*. This view has been accepted since the time of Alexander of Hales. Man retained the synteresis, the ethical consciousness, also after the fall. Man knows what is good and bad. Of course, errors arise in individual acts.

Thomas considers synteresis as *habit*, while he labels conscience as an act since it applies to individual activity. "Wherefore the first practical principles bestowed on us by nature do not belong to a special power, but to a special natural habit, which we call synteresis. Whence synteresis is said to incite to good, and to murmur at evil, inasmuch as through first principles we proceed to discover and judge what we have discovered. It is therefore clear that synteresis is not a power but a natural habit" (I, qu. 79, art. 12; *The Summa Theologica* of St. Thomas Aquinas, London: Burns Oates & Washbourne Ltd., 3rd ed., 1938, Vol. 4, 119). "But synteresis does not regard opposites, but inclines to good only. Therefore synteresis is not a power" *(ibid.).* Synteresis is practical intellect. "Synteresis is said to be the law of our mind, because it is a habit containing the precepts of the natural law, which are the first principles of human actions" (II, I, qu. 94, art. 1; Trans. Vol. 8, p. 4).

Conscience on the contrary, is an act. The following sentence shows its relationship to synteresis: "Now all the habits by which conscience is formed, although many, nevertheless have the efficacy from one first principle, the habit of first principles, which is called synteresis" (I, qu. 79, 13; trans. Vol. 4, p. 121). As the first principle of conscience, synteresis is also called conscience itself. "And for this special reason, this habit is sometimes called conscience" *(ibid.).*

According to Gabriel Biel, synteresis, though not an "act or habit in the will," is nevertheless an infallible moral ability of knowledge. "Synteresis is something that at all events necessarily directs in general toward a just and right activity" (Collect II, dist. 39, quaest VII, art. 2, concl. 1). For him, too, synteresis is an "inextinguishable spark that necessarily inclines toward the good" *(ibid.).*

According to this doctrine there is present in man a capacity for the divine. Man is in principle capable of recognizing and desiring the good. He needs only produce the acts corresponding to this aptitude. Even though this does not always succeed in individual cases, the principle still holds. Man is indeed fallen, but he has retained the ethical consciousness, the inclination toward the good. The corruption of inherited sin is thus considerably weakened; it is not located in man's center but on the periphery. Thus the doctrine of synteresis is solidly semi-pelagian. It is also characteristic for the theological style of scholasticism.

At the outset decisive things are conceded to man, the inclination toward the good is ascribed even to fallen man. But it is also conceded that individual acts are not without their faults. In spite of that, the original position is maintained without the least scruple. In this way one is protected on both fronts, and every radical statement is very cautiously avoided. This ambivalence however, basically reveals a bad conscience. (See, for example, also the doctrine concerning the "merit of congruity and the merit of condignity." cf. WA XVIII, 769ff.; LW 33, 266). Against these cleverly devised distinctions, by means of which an objective decision has in truth been pushed aside, we can appreciate Luther's derision and rage (cf. W. XVIII, 769ff.; 617ff.; also LVI, 382, 21 to 383, 24; LW 33, 266f.; 33, 40f.; 25, 372).

Clearly Luther had to reject the doctrine of synteresis because of its semi-pelagian implications. It does not fit with the idea of the theology of the cross. "Through the cross works are destroyed," as we heard. Man does not possess true knowledge as the result of an aptitude, but only as one "who has been reduced to nothing through cross and suffering." In spite of this, Luther did not at once rid himself of this doctrine but labored to combine it with his new insights.

We frequently find the concept in the *Dictata super Psalterium,* 1513-1516.[52] Synteresis is a natural inclination in man. This concreated yearning for the good, for God, cannot be extinguished, even though it is often enough crowded out by other impulses (W. III, 238, 11ff.; LW 10, 197). Even the most reprobate, despite his distance from God, can still pray because the spark of the synteresis still glows in him. Luther illustrates this by means of the parable of the prodigal son (W. III, 617, 25f.). The synteresis will not permit man to be at ease; he cannot permanently ignore its admonishing voice (W. III, 94, 13ff., 21ff.; LW 10, 99; W. III, 624, 32). Hence in this case synteresis is equivalent to conscience.

In those trials when man despairs of God, the synteresis experiences purification and strengthening (W. III. 93, 35; W. III, 44, 17ff.; LW 10, 49). The natural longing for God is increased through the spiritual testing, through the apparent distance from God. In all this Luther is still solidly Catholic. The passages offer us nothing new. But Luther could not permanently hold to these teachings without getting into difficulties. We are now in a position to observe this more closely.

Luther dealt with the synteresis most thoroughly in the sermon "Concerning one's own wisdom and will," a monastery sermon which the Weimar edition dates December 26, 1514 (W. I, 30-37). It is very interesting to see how the old and the new in Luther's thought are here side by side and press for a solution.[53]

Luther's remarks on the synteresis in this sermon may be organized in a fourfold way.

1. Man does in fact possess this ability. By nature he wants to be saved, he hates condemnation. This will always remain so. The synteresis is a remnant of man's original nature as created by God and was not lost even after the fall. It is directed toward a good and blessed life (W. I, 32, 2), just as the synteresis of reason is directed toward the knowledge of the good, the true, and the right. Thus it may be compared with the spark that glows beneath the ashes, and needs only to be fanned into flame again, or with the seed that rests under the earth and yet encloses in itself the germ of new life, or also with the matter that only awaits the form through which it arrives at its goal (W. I, 32, 1ff.). If the synteresis had not been preserved for man, nothing at all of his original nature would be left. "If the Lord had not left us a seed, we should have been like Sodom" (Isa. 1:9). This passage is interpreted in a moral

sense: "Unless he (the Lord) had preserved the synteresis and the remnants of nature, it would have perished altogether" (W. I, 32, 10f.). Thus the synteresis is the point at which the continuity between the fallen man and the created man becomes visible.

2. But it is difficult to demonstrate this continuity in a practical way. Actually the natural ability of the synteresis is not expressed in corresponding acts and so there is nothing to indicate that this ability has been preserved. The problem arises with the practical application of what is known. There is no disagreement between God and man regarding the goal, but there is regarding the way to the goal. "There is total conflict concerning the means to the end" (W. I, 30, 31ff.; 32, 39f.). The original will toward the good planted in man does not come to fruition; the wisdom of the flesh prevents it (W. I, 32, 36ff.). Hence one must distinguish sharply between the synteresis of the will and the will itself, as well as between the synteresis of reason and reason itself. Between the synteresis of the will and the will of God there exists the same conformity as between the synteresis of reason and the wisdom of God, while there is an acute contrast between man's will as such and God's will, between human reason and divine wisdom. Although, because of the synteresis, man's will and reason are "organs" for the apprehension of the invisible and hidden things of God, they nevertheless prove themselves to be unusable for that purpose, in fact they are in opposition. And this is true of reason and will as one whole; no parts remain in them that are excluded from this rule. Thus synteresis and will are not related as higher and lower wills but the synteresis is opposed by the total will or the total reason (W. I, 36, 11ff.).

3. Hence the synteresis proves itself to be unfruitful in practice. The inclination toward the good is indeed given with it, but is not realized. But then the reality of the synteresis becomes questionable. It may be compared with the phenomenalistically understood "thing of itself," except that here the appearance is in intrinsic contradiction to the hypostasized thing in itself. As a result, the synteresis has finally become nothing more than a postulate. This view is supported by the cited passages in which the synteresis is compared to the seed, tinder, and matter. From this Luther concludes, "Consequently nature is capable of being revived" (W. I, 32, 14). Grace finds a point of contact in man.

Here Luther regards such a point of contact as necessary. He employs the picture of a sick man. The sick man is indeed not well, but he still possesses the "synteresis of soundness." The powers of nature have not been fully extinguished in him. They are present and would like to exert themselves but are for the moment unable to do so. If this synteresis of soundness were no longer present there would be no prospect of recovery (W. I, 37, 3ff.). This comparison shows that Luther regarded a "seed of nature to be revived and restored" as necessary, if God's grace is to be able to do its work in man. In this Luther sees the positive significance of the synteresis. On the detour via the quickening power of God's grace the synteresis does became active in the will and reason of man. They are in a mutually conditioning relationship: the synteresis is the condition for the effectiveness of grace, and grace is the condition for the effectiveness of the synteresis. But the effectiveness of both aims at the proper effectiveness of will and reason. Thus the circle is closed (W. I, 36, 37ff.).

4. The synteresis is a condition for the effectiveness of grace, but it may also be a hindrance to that effectiveness. What we have considered thus far turns against itself. The synteresis becomes a disaster for man the moment he takes any credit for himself because of it. If man wants to leap out of the synteresis-grace-good will circle at any point, he has lost all three. It will not do to pit the synteresis against grace. Yet this is done by those who rely on their synteresis (W. I, 32, 14ff.). One who possesses the synteresis of soundness is far from being well for that reason (W. I, 37, 7ff.). As soon as man builds on the synteresis, he puts an obstacle in the way of grace. Stated pointedly: We can reckon with the reality of the synteresis only if we do not reckon with it at all.[54] It has then actually lost every practical significance.

Luther goes even farther. Not only can the synteresis lead to man's destruction when he places his confidence in it, hence in his own quality instead of in grace, but the synteresis also raises misgivings for Luther. For he identifies the good will with the will of salvation (W. I, 32, 29ff.). Because of the synteresis man desires to be saved and hates condemnation. Therein consists the true torment of hell that even there man is not rid of his synteresis [55] which longs for salvation and yet has in fact been delivered up to condemnation and torment.[56] But what about this longing of man for salvation that is inherent in the synteresis? May it really be affirmed without qualification as man's highest ability? Here Luther makes a discovery by means of which the whole Catholic system receives the deathblow.[57]

Our human longing for salvation may be in conflict with God's will. We flee punishment and seek rest and salvation, but perhaps God's will for us is punishment and suffering. Here Luther does not yet break through to his later formulation that salvation is willing what God wills, but the break with the popular Catholic view of salvation is plain. Understood in this way, our synteresis turns out to be our damnation. Then our punishment consists precisely in the will which God has also for us, namely the will to salvation, because we have failed to understand that salvation is not the fulfillment of our desires, but the union of our will with God's will, which also includes a joyful affirmation of punishment and trouble (W. I, 32, 28ff.).

These are Luther's thoughts on the synteresis as they confront us in this sermon. We saw that Luther attempted to adhere to the doctrine of the synteresis, since it corresponds to Augustine's ideas. At that time Augustine's conversion, as depicted in his *Confessions,* was Luther's model.[58] It is therefore natural that Luther clings to the doctrine of the synteresis not only out of an outward loyalty to the church, but also because he has an inner relation to it. Yet at the same time insights were developed in Luther which would eventually come to maturity during the Reformation, namely the realization of the radical corruption of human nature and the sufficiency of grace. Where these insights have once taken hold the doctrine of the synteresis can no longer flourish.

Thus we see here a conflict between two unreconciled ideas. On the one hand Luther emphasizes the reality and value of the synteresis, but on the other hand he makes it inoperative in practice, and even uncovers the hidden motive of selfishness that slumbers in this indestructible inclination toward the good. In the final analysis this does away with the whole doctrine. Yet Luther still shrinks from drawing this conclusion, and this accounts for the contradictions. Luther does not want to give up the doctrine at its starting point, but the more detailed exposition destroys the force of this starting point. For that reason we hear no more of this doctrine from Luther. But as a result of this investigation we may already establish the following:

For Luther the synteresis cannot have the significance of a divine attribute in man. Such a thing is unthinkable within the framework of a theology of the cross. The "reduced to nothing" is taken seriously, more seriously than in mysticism. For precisely when he has become nothing the mystic discovers in his inner self something extremely positive, namely the spark of the soul. In this sense the theology of the cross knows of no such spark of the divine. Also for this theology man is not completely indifferent to all that God wants to accomplish in him. Man is actually grasped by the grace of God and recognizes a religious experience. Luther would never think of denying the "Thou hast made us for Thyself." The theology of the cross concedes two things:

1. Man is created for fellowship with God, and

2. The knowledge of God and faith have a psychological side. Nothing that affects our inner self can evade psychological mediation.

However—and to emphasize this is more important for the theology of the cross—this predisposition is never something given that man can simply insert in his dealing with God. It is not only a gift but also an accusation. It is not the rock on which our house could be built. Rather, it really has to do with a destroying, a radical demolition and a complete reconstruction of the foundations. And because the doctrine of the synteresis has obscured this, it has no place in the theology of the cross. In all seriousness the watchword must be *turning around,* not *turning inward, beyond,* not *inside.*

To come immediately to the second point, the turning around is also mediated psychologically, but the psychological serves only a technical function. Because the doctrine of the synteresis in the last analysis proclaims the "direct way," it is repudiated by the theology of the cross.[59]

2. Faith and Understanding

In Luther's early theology the concept of understanding is in an especially close relationship to the concept of faith. That raises the question whether faith may not after all be defined as a function placed in the human consciousness. What is the meaning of understanding? Is it perhaps the desired vehicle by which man may lay hold of the divine? The principal sources for this investigation are the *Dictata super Psalterium* of 1513-1516 and the lectures on Romans of 1515-1516.

The question leads us at once into a larger context. What about Luther's "Neoplatonism"? As is known, Hunzinger[60] posed this problem. He thinks that Luther's theology in the *Dictata* can be understood only on the basis of a Neoplatonic ontology. Statements that one would initially be inclined to take as religious-ethical were in fact intended to be metaphysical. In his view this Neoplatonism is historically to be traced back to Augustine. Augustine's influence on Luther during this period is firmly established (cf. the marginal notes on Augustine's *Opuscula* in W. IX). Augustine never discarded this Neoplatonic leaven as long as he lived.

The basic insight which Luther takes over from Augustine's Neoplatonism is the separation of two worlds. On the one side is the world of things invisible, spiritual, understandable, interior, and on the other side the world of things visible, physical, subject to the senses, external. Both worlds stand in sharp contrast to each other. To be sure, this contrast is not taken in a dualistic sense, but as established by creation. The clinging to the idea of creation is the thin line that separates this two-world theory from pure Neoplatonism. Characteristic of the world of invisible things is its unversality, its simplicity, its indivisibility, and its immutability, while the world of visible things is characterized by its isolatedness, its multiplicity, its separatedness, and its mutability. This antithesis already makes clear that God will belong on the side of the invisible things, even though he confronts them as their Lord. This bifurcation is explained by the fact that the idea of creation is not given up, but on the other hand, the philosophical concept of God as pure Being is also maintained: "Thou art the same, forever immutable, Thou dost not pass away, but Thou simply art" (W. IV, 146. 8).

Man—and this leads us to our theme—stands between these two worlds. He belongs fully to neither of the two, but he participates in both. In him spirit and flesh, soul and body, are joined together. With his higher nature he belongs to the world of the invisible, with his lower nature to the visible. But to his lower nature is assigned not only the physical organism but also the whole realm of the lesser abilities of the soul, hence also the knowledge that is based on sense perception. With his lower nature man is oriented toward the visible; to the extent that his urge for knowledge is active only in the visible it does not belong to man's higher nature. Knowledge of the supersensory, the invisible, is accorded man only insofar as he is spirit.

Into this context belongs the concept of understanding. Understanding and will, including memory, constitute the two higher abilities of the soul. This understanding brings with it knowledge of the invisible. Accordingly, this understanding is also the seat of the knowledge of God.[61] This would, then, give us the view that man can know God by natural powers; for the understanding is created in man together with his higher nature. But here we must be careful. Man is by nature equipped with understanding, but his entire higher ability of the soul (understanding and will) has been seriously weakened by original sin. This is the nature of sin, that man has turned away from the invisible to the visible. Thereby the ability of the understanding to know the supersensory has been corrupted. It can be restored only by grace. So for a second time Luther breaks through the Neoplatonic design at a decisive point.

Understanding of the invisible is possible only where faith is. But faith points back to grace. To the extent that the understanding belongs together with faith, it moves from the purely ontological sphere into a religious one. For that reason Luther sharply distinguished it from philosophical knowledge, and even placed it in opposition to all natural knowledge in general.[62] Understanding has a theological function. Only one who has the Spirit of Christ attains to knowledge of the invisible. Christocentric theology and universally ontological ideas are brought into a curious mixture. "So then, to understand concerning Christ is to have knowledge about the invisible things in him, things that are not in any other man" (W. III, 230, 25f.; LW 10, 190). Knowledge of the invisible depends on the knowledge of the person of Christ. Knowledge of the universals flashes up at this contingent point of history. "Therefore the understanding is from the Lord alone, as he says, 'They will all be taught by God.' Therefore this understanding, by which we speculate about the invisible, is not philosophical or natural, but theological and freely given, enabling us to contemplate through faith things not seen" (W. IV, 324, 1ff.).

Philosophy also has to do with the invisible, but only in the form of speculation, not of contemplation. Here it must be borne in mind that Luther—also in his lectures on the Psalms (despite Hunzinger!)—is philosophically an Occamist. There is no such thing as purely abstract knowledge apart from observation. All thinking must proceed from observation. But observation always has to do with concrete individual phenomena. To the extent that philosophy arrives at abstractions nevertheless, it can do so only through inference from observations, hence not directly, as in the old ontological philosophy of an Augustine and an Anselm, by "savoring" or "attaining." [63] "For philosophy always speaks about what is visible and apparent, or at least what is deduced from the apparent, whereas faith is not a matter of appearances nor of things deduced from the apparent. Indeed, it is from heaven, since what is deduced from appearances is always rather that which is contrary to faith, as is clear" (W. III, 508, 1ff.; LW 10, 452). Philosophy arrives at a knowledge of the invisible only by a process of deduction, while theology sees the invisible. This is expressed by the distinction between "speculating" and "contemplating."

We see, then, that understanding and faith belong together. What follows are further aspects of this relationship.

1. Faith alone enables the understanding to comprehend the invisible. The concept of understanding is subject to change. It is basically a concreated ability of man's higher nature, but has been weakened by sin to the point of impotence. In conjunction with faith, however, it definitely becomes a religious ability created by grace. Without faith there is no understanding of the invisible. For that reason Luther emphatically endorses the axiom, "Faith precedes understanding." "Knowledge does not come into being except on the basis of a pre-existent faith" (W. IV, 289, 15). Hearing is to be preferred to seeing (W. IV, 95, 1f.). Faith as hearing precedes knowledge as seeing.[64]

Of course Luther is here thinking not of the hearing of the external word, but the hearing of the internal word (W. IV. 10, 28ff.). Hence the way to the understanding of the invisible is to turn to one's own inner self (W. IV, 11, 1). It is beyond the scope of this work to investigate how, in spite of this view of the inner word, Luther can still maintain that the external word and the internal word belong together, and into what kind of difficulties this led him. It is enough to establish that the ability to understand the invisible is made to depend on faith. This is a clear assertion in the otherwise opaque confusion of disparate lines in the *Dictata super Psalterium*. Faith is the precondition for knowledge.

2. Faith is at the same time the means to knowledge. The purpose of faith is knowledge (W. III, 172, 19); "through faith" one arrives at "understanding." As the way to understanding, however, faith is both precondition and means to the goal. This formulation, "through faith" occurs frequently.[65] Also the passage in W. IV, 94, 33, "there is need for understanding, which faith bestows," well shows how faith is both precondition and means to knowledge.

3. The intellectual side of faith is also strongly emphasized.

Therefore we are not surprised to find that faith, although based in the will according to its subjective psychological side (cf. Hunzinger, p. 62), is finally also equated with knowledge: faith equals understanding. If the formula "the understanding of faith" (W. III, 176, 3; LW 10, 147; W. IV, 149, 33; 290, 21), designates the faith character of understanding, so, conversely, the character of faith as knowledge is confirmed by the sentence, "faith . . . is not a sensual knowledge nor one proceeding from the sensual, but a solely intellectual one from above" (W. III, 474, 14ff.). Understanding and faith are frequently used indiscriminately (e.g., W. III, 367, 34ff.; LW 10, 310; W. IV, 81, 12ff.). An explicit equation of faith and understanding is found in a large number of passages.[66]

The material from the lectures on Romans, 1515-1516, which was not yet available to Hunzinger, does not offer anything essentially new. We again find the equation of understanding and faith [67] (W. LVI, 238, 28ff.; LW 25, 224). We see furthermore that understanding is a specifically religious function. It is expressly stated that it has to do with "what a man cannot know by himself." But here the invisible is further defined as "wisdom incarnate and thus hidden" W. LVI, 237, 20ff.; LW 25, 222f.)—and this perhaps represents an advance over the *Dictata*. Thus the metaphysical concept of the invisible is equated with the theological concept of wisdom incarnate. Here mysticism and theology of revelation collide.[68] We find the following interesting parallel: "wisdom was made incarnate and is thus hidden and unapproachable except by understanding, just as Christ cannot be known except by revelation" (*ibid.*). On the one side this is pure mysticism (even the term, "approach" used by the old Franciscan school appears), on the other side there is an appeal to revelation. A certain two-sidedness (in the sense of Heim) does pervade medieval theology, but it is noteworthy that this passage is most clear and needs no further investigation. From it we learn how Luther takes these Neoplatonic mystical terms, which at the outset bear a purely ontological stamp, and unexpectedly gives them a strictly theological sense, thereby making something quite different out of them, only to drop them entirely later on. This is a phenomenon we shall have occasion to observe frequently. The precondition for the understanding is revelation. Therefore understanding is attained neither by those who cling to the world of the external senses nor by those who rely on their own mental ability.[69] This understanding is precisely the understanding of faith.[70]

Now two questions arise. First, what about Luther's Neoplatonism? This question leads to the second one: Is man's understanding his link to the divine? The answer to the first question will determine the direction for the answer to the second.

1. What about Luther's Neoplatonism? It is Hunzinger's achievement to have recognized this problem. In his *Studies in Luther* he reduces the whole world of thought in the *Dictata super Psalterium* to the common denominator of Neoplatonism. Later he more carefully distinguishes four facets of it.[71] First, Augustinian Neoplatonism, second, Augustinian teaching on sin and grace, third, scholastic semi-pelagianism, fourth, Bernardian monkish theology. In fact, in spite of the value of posing the problem, the thesis concerning Neoplatonism [72] must be rejected as one-sided. Hunzinger overlooks, or at least obscures three factors:

a) that at many points there is, in fact, a relationship between Neoplatonic statements and those of the New Testament;

b) that nominalism, too, never rid itself completely of ontological elements, which Luther then took over together with Occamism, and which were strengthened in him by his reading of Augustine and Bonaventure; [73]

c) that in the adoption of ideas that seemed close to him Luther proceeded more nonchalantly than the historically trained modern theologian would do (see also Schmidt, op. cit, p. 211, n 2). So, for example, the antithetical pair of flesh and spirit is good New Testament usage. But also the concept of the invisible things is native to the New Testament. We know that Hebrews 11:1 remained for Luther the basic definition of faith also at a time when even Hunzinger no longer asserted Neoplatonic influence. Describing God as pure Being is, indeed, to be traced back to Augustinian Neoplatonism, but on the other hand, the idea has permanent value beyond its Neoplatonic limits as expressing the ineffable majesty of God.

In any case one can here vacillate as to which is decisive, the New Testament idea or its metaphysical dress. Luther himself appeals to Dionysius the Areopagite (W. III, 124, 32; LW 10, 119). However, in the course of our investigation we have already met with statements in which such vacillation is no longer possible. We have seen that the knowledge of the invisible is bound to the knowledge of Christ (W. III, 230, 25ff.; LW 10, 190; W. III, 285, 36). For that reason the understanding of the invisible is sharply distinguished from every philosophical insight. "Philosophy discloses the invisible world, theology contemplates it" (Hunzinger, op. cit., p. 47). Even Hunzinger has trouble with this assertion, for it, in fact, calls for a severe correction of his thesis. "It may legitimately be questioned whether the contrasting of both kinds of knowledge accords fully with Luther's ontological principles. Meanwhile, the more precisely he draws the boundaries between them, the more he approaches a purely religious view of understanding. This is not to say, however, that Luther arrived at such a view within the present line of thought" *(ibid.)*. But Luther did arrive at such a view (W. III, 376, 3ff.). The concept of understanding as here presented bursts through the metaphysical frame. With that we have come to the second question.

2. Does the understanding provide us with man's link to the divine? Is man's understanding his potential for reaching into the divine? Are we dealing here with a forerunner of the "intellectual view" of Idealism? Is it an unmediated participation in the absolute Spirit? Is the quiescent point of unity between the being of God and that of man? In a summary way these questions may be answered as follows:

a) If Hunzinger were completely correct in his thesis, then we would certainly have to grant that Luther at that time did not yet hold the insights of his theology of the cross. In Neoplatonism the higher ability of the soul of man is in itself a divine power. The direct way to God from a competence in man would be open. In the concept of understanding we would be dealing with theology of glory.

b) But we have seen that Neoplatonism was broken through at a decisive point. Not the understanding as such, but only the understanding of faith attains to the true knowledge of God. But this presupposes an about-face *(metanoia)* in the strict sense, something totally different from mere backward reflection. Faith points back to revelation. With that something entirely new appears on the scene, something that is simply beyond the sphere of human possibility. The concept of the understanding of faith belongs within the realm of the theology of the cross.

Thus we see two things: First, faith maintains itself in man's reality. It is not only the negation of human possibility, but its realization as well. Faith leads to knowledge. But second, the faith character of this realization dare never be overlooked. That means, this "being realized" cannot be made the starting point of a self-contained system. For as surely as one must in all statements constantly reckon with revelation whose correlate is faith, so little may one "reckon" with it, because in that way it would be deprived of its epochal character. The understanding is indeed potentiality, but this does not yet mean that it will become power. For it is not the understanding as such, but only the understanding of faith that proves itself as faith's vehicle of knowledge.

3. Faith and Reason

The two concepts of synteresis and understanding play a role only in Luther's early period. He soon recognized that they were untenable in the plan of his theology and dropped them. The *sola fide* cannot be shaken by them. It has become superfluous for Luther to deal with them any further. Yet the problem they posed continues in some form. It is present in Luther's conflict with reason. In the question concerning "believing and knowing" all that we have treated above is brought once more to a point. The place of reason remains a permanent problem not only for Luther but for theology in general. The whole of medieval theology is concerned about the relationship of authority and reason, and cannot be understood apart from this question. The same problem continues in Protestant scholasticism which reverted to the old scholastic methods in dealing with it The problem is presented anew by rationalism and idealism to an orthodoxy mired in antiquated philosophical premises. This also forces a theology, which only with great difficulty still maintains the connection with contemporary philosophical currents into the ruts of an occasionally dubious apologetic. Not even a theology that is no longer merely on the defensive can permanently avoid coming to grips with this question.

In this respect Luther stands at the end of a long development. In the Middle Ages the question of authority and reason had been subjected to the most sagacious investigations. Luther's contribution to these has been variously evaluated. In order to reach our own evaluation we must understand Luther's philosophical position. Since the Catholic scholar Denifle pointed to the significance of Luther's medieval presuppositions, much work has been done in this area by Protestant scholarship as well. Here we must confine ourselves to emphasizing a few basic aspects and then determining what may be gathered from them for our specific area of inquiry.

Luther came out of the school of Occamism. His theology must therefore be understood and evaluated on the basis of Occamism. Recent attempts to deny this have presumably proved to be untenable.[74] Stange *(Theologische Aufsätze,* No. 8) thinks that Luther's remarks about the best known representatives of nominalism, especially Occam and Biel, were "so preponderantly couched in the tone of extreme polemics that one can hardly think of bringing him into a positive relationship to the school of Occam." This view is opposed by the undisputed fact that Luther received his philosophical training in Erfurt by means of the *via moderna.*[75] Furthermore, Luther's polemic against Occamism does not imply a blanket condemnation. What Luther, on the basis of his insights gained from Augustine and Paul, attacks in Occamism is its doctrine of sin and grace. Philosophically he remained an adherent of the *via moderna* as long as he lived. Even in the years of bitterest conflict with Rome and the scholastic doctrine, he is quite serious when he claims membership in the Occamist party, even though he says it in a joking manner (W. VI, 195, 4; 195, 7; 600, 11). According to Stange, Luther's theological development is to be explained on the basis of Augustinian theology. The determinative influence here came from Gregory of Rimini (died 1358). From him Luther is said to have learned both nominalism and the Augustinian doctrine of sin.

In response two things need to be said: First, philosophically Gregory was also an adherent of Occam. Luther would be an Occamist even if the line of tradition ran directly through Gregory whom, incidentally, he could have learned to know also from the citations in Biel's commentary on the *Sentences.* Second, Stange cites a number of passages in which Luther expressly mentions Gregory and assigns him a position of priority over all other dogmaticians. But these passages do not go back beyond the year 1519. Hence Luther probably read Gregory only at this time. By then, however, he was already so far advanced that Gregory could not possibly have had a decisive influence on him.[76] Consequently Stange's investigation changes nothing in the fact that in his scholastic orientation Luther is an Occamist.

What is the nature of the problem of "faith and reason" in Occamism? To understand this we must clarify the position Occamism occupies in the history of medieval philosophy. Usually the development of scholasticism is viewed as follows: After a short ascent it reached its zenith in Thomas, and then quickly declined in Duns Scotus, coming to an end with Occamism in an arid logical formalism. But this picture, maintained by Catholic scholars for good reason, undoubtedly needs correction.[77] But it remains true that over against both Thomism and Scotism, Occamism represents a consistent further development. Hence there can be no talk of apostasy; at most we can say that the difficulties that were latent in the Thomistic system became manifest in Occamism. The Neoplatonic-Augustinian elements of Thomism have been almost totally deleted in Occamism in favor of Aristotelian elements.

Over against Scotism the principal advance of Occamism consists in dropping the questionable entity of the "intelligible form" *(species intelligibilis)*. According to Scotism the acting understanding reaches the real object of knowledge, the intelligible form, from the individual object by means of abstraction from its individual determinations. Occam deletes this intermediate thing between the universal and the matter. Only in this way does a neat separation between intuitive and abstract knowledge become possible. All knowledge comes from sense perception; what is perceived is the individual thing. The universals (to which, by the way, as individual things in the mind reality need not be denied) function only as terms in the decision. Thus the logical decision, which alone is entitled to scientific value, presupposes perception by the senses. What follows from this for the knowledge of God?

Since the universal is involved only as an ingredient of the decision, universal existence may no longer, as in the past, be ascribed to God. Instead of Supreme Being we must now speak of God as the most individual entity *(singularissima res)*. Now, however, the intuitive basis for the knowledge of this most individual entity is lacking. Where there is no intuitive knowledge, no abstract knowledge is possible either. Strictly speaking, a knowledge of God would then be excluded altogether. Yet Occam (as well as Biel) draws this conclusion only in view of the *certainty* of the statements concerning God, while clinging to a rational substructure of theology, in contradiction to his epistemological presuppositions. In spite of this substructure, however, the statements of faith concerning God become logically incomprehensible. For all statements concerning God are combinations of terms; the reality presupposed by these terms is not intuitively supplied.

But the less reason is able to know God, the more urgent is the need for authority. This is provided in the positive revelation. Already Duns Scotus had strongly emphasized the authority of Scripture in connection with the knowledge of God. In the case of Occam we can speak directly of a Scripture principle.[78] For him the authority of Scripture and the authority of the church are brought together, not merely in theory, but in practice. This authority cannot be logically demonstrated; the infused faith is the supernatural inclination to accept revelation. In practice, however, this supra-logical assumption of the infused faith recedes behind the acquired faith, the authoritative acceptance of the truths of faith revealed in the Bible. Thus, on the one hand, we have arrived at the most pointed expression of the supra-logical character of the certainty of faith, but that very fact leads, on the other hand, to the proclamation of a crass faith in authority. This is the solution to the problem of authority and reason which Occamism was able to provide.

Luther belongs to the Occamist school. Also in the question of faith and reason he will not have denied his orientation. But now the question arises whether Luther was philosophically well trained. Heim denies this. Yet there are statements of Luther in which he expresses pride in his specifically Occamist training.[79] We also know that already as a student Luther was feared because of his debating skill. Even in his later disputations he deftly makes use of the formulas learned in school. He never repudiated his Erfurt education. It will therefore not do to regard Luther as a layman in philosophy. Yet it is indeed true that the center of gravity of his interests never rested in philosophy. This is evident already in his famous letter to Braun in the year 1509 (W. Br. I, 17, 42ff.). And later on he has nothing but ridicule for the mental chisel work of scholasticism.[80]

Why does Luther combat philosophy, and why does he regard Aristotle as the greatest corrupter of Christendom? [81] What sounds through these accusations is not anti-intellectualism; but it is a passionate protest against a theological pursuit in which the primary matter has been made secondary and the secondary primary. In its pursuit of philosophy theology lost sight of revelation. Philosophy crowded out the Bible. Philosophy wanted nothing to do with the way of God; it is offended at the cross of Christ, the great no to all human endeavor, to all opinions of one's own. For that reason philosophy does not speak about this (W. V, 107, 5ff.). For that reason also Luther declaims against the "seat of the scornful" (W. V, 32, 6ff.; LW 14, 293). He considers it is his divine mission to fight this battle against philosophy on behalf of the Bible. For this he is especially qualified as a philosophically trained theologian. He thinks the great turning point in time has come: Turn away from philosophy and turn to Christ the Crucified! (W. LVI, 371, 17ff.; LW 25, 361).

This means turning away from the theology of glory and turning to the theology of the cross! For it is precisely the characteristics of the theology of glory that are the distinguishing marks of churchly philosophy. This kind of thinking presents the delusion of self-righteousness in thought and deed and teaches man to flee and to despise the cross of Christ as something directed against himself and his self-security (W. V, 107, 5ff.). This philosophy is as unconcerned as the theology of glory about the deep cleft that runs through creation.

In this passage (W. LVI, 371ff.; LW 25, 360ff. on Rom. 8:19) Luther gives his opinion about what a sacred philosophy should look like. Paul appears to him to be a true philosopher. True philosophy would, of course, be a complete reversal of the hitherto existing kind. While the accustomed philosophy occupies itself with the *being* of things, this appears to the "apostolic philosophy" as a foolish approach. For the true being of things does not lie in their existence and condition, but in their final purpose. Therefore the apostolic philosophy is thoroughly eschatological (W. LVI, 371, 1ff.; LW 25, 360f.). Such a philosophy is suitable for theology (W. LVI, 371, 7ff.; LW 25, *ibid.*).

But secular philosophy does not reckon with the "expectation of the creation." For that very reason it does not attain to a grasp of the true reality. In its knowledge of the world, philosophy is like a clumsy apprentice in the shop of a tentmaker; he sees the individual pieces but has no idea of how they should be put together and what purpose they are to serve (W. LVI, 371, 28ff., 32ff.; LW 25, 361f.). Philosophy has no ear for the groaning and sighing that run through nature. How could it? It knows nothing of a need for deliverance. It has the view of "moral man" through and through. Just as the theology of glory prefers works to sufferings, glory to the cross, power to weakness, wisdom to foolishness, so philosophy would rather investigate the essences and actions of the creatures than listen to their groanings and expectations (W. LVI, 372, 22; LW 25, 362). It is completely unaware of the fact that the things themselves suffer under their own essences. Philosophy's pride of scholarship stands in curious contrast to the yearning for deliverance existing in the creaturely world (W. LVI, 372, 7ff.; LW 25, 362). Genuine metaphysics would have to proceed from the principle that creatures are creatures which dare not be absolutized in their being. They are not self-contained. Philosophy overlooks this. It is blind to genuine reality (W. LVI, 372, 18ff.).

Here Luther's thoughts are especially profound. It is to be regretted that he did not develop them further, as far as I know. This whole way of thinking might well be considered dilettantish. Philosophy can never do without the "view of things that are there." But for that reason Luther's comments are to be taken seriously. It depends on what is expected of philosophy. If one really looks to it for ultimate knowledge, one will not be able to ignore Luther's thoughts. In fact they sound most timely to us. For eschatology has moved into the center of theology. On the other hand, the desire for a sacred philosophy becomes more and more insistent.

The two extremes of present-day theology have here been united by Luther into a synthesis. Eschatology has been placed into the service of philosophy. But at this point Luther does not reflect on the way this sacred philosophy can be implemented in practice. All too easily it becomes in general the exact opposite of eschatology. Conversely, a strong eschatology has up to now always shattered the boundaries of a "holy philosophy." Do we really have a synthesis here? This seems to me to be the great question addressed to our current religious and theological situation.

Luther obviously regards such a synthesis as possible. This is the ultimate meaning of his comments on Romans 8:19. But this passage is isolated. We have only this starting point. Luther did not develop it further, and we can only say, alas! For over against the flagging interest of our Reformation-based theology stands an equally lively interest in these questions on the part of heterodox elements in the history of theology. Thus we find ourselves today in the curious position that in this question we are able to look back on systems that command our reverence, but find in them the surrender of important reformation insights, while on the other side we see these same insights preserved, but without yielding any results in this question. It is only in the last generation that this situation is perhaps beginning to change.

How, then, may we summarize Luther's attitude toward philosophy?

1. According to his training Luther is an Occamist. He did not repudiate this school even in his later years. There is no cogent reason to question the thoroughness of his philosophical education.

2. However, from the beginning Luther's interest is not in philosophy but theology. In spite of this, his polemic against philosophy does not mean a blanket rejection, but only a setting of limits for it. In the same way we must also understand his very dissimilar evaluations of Aristotle.[82] The idea of a "sacred philosophy" is found only as a passing suggestion.

Having thus briefly sketched Luther's attitude toward philosophy, we may turn to the question which is really our concern here: How does the problem of faith and reason look to Luther in the context of his theology of the cross? This question at once divides itself into two sub-questions which we must keep separate for the sake of clarity:

1. What is the Occamistic contribution to the faith-reason question?

2. Does Luther have anything of his own to say, and if so where might his contribution be found?

Hermelink (p. 98) had emphasized that "the key to the systems of Occamism" is "to be sought in the precise delimitation of the realms of faith and of knowledge." Although the sentence thus formulated is not correct, it remains true that this strict separation of realms is characteristic of Occamism. We have already developed the manner in which it arrives at this. We must now draw the inferences and show how Luther is a good Occamist in this regard. If the two realms are to be so sharply separated, it is clear that in matters of faith reason has no authority. At this point the validity of logic has been abrogated. The statements of faith are rooted in supra-logical bases. To reason they appear unreasonable. But since they are founded on positive revelation and hence must be true, it follows that logical rules must here be dispensed with.

Luther knows this too. He aligns himself with the strictest tendency of Occamism as he sets up the following theses in his disputation in 1517 against scholastic theology:

Thesis 46: "In vain does one fashion a logic of faith, a substitution brought about without regard for limit and measure."

Thesis 47: "No syllogistic form is valid when applied to divine terms."

Thesis 49: "If a syllogistic form of reasoning holds in divine matters, then the doctrine of the Trinity is demonstrable and not the object of faith" (W. I, 224ff.; LW 31, 12).

Hence we cannot get at the statements of faith by means of syllogistic logic. This thesis must be viewed entirely in connection with the Occamistic problem of knowledge. It is not modern irrationalism that finds expression here, but rather a philosophical criticism operating with the most precise tools of logic. In these theses Luther brings nothing new; philosophically he contributes nothing to the problem of reason and faith.

If, however, we consider the manner in which Luther usually expresses himself about reason, we receive a completely different impression. His railing against "harlot reason" does not seem to have been guided by philosophical considerations. Luther's statements can create the impression that he wants to have nothing to do with philosophy at all.[83] Then again, we meet with passages in which he unhesitatingly appeals to reason. He does this, for example, in the famous response without horns at Worms. Or in *The Bondage of the Will* (W. XVIII, 718, 15; LW 33, 189) he can refer to God's all-inclusive activity as something demanded by reason. How are we to understand these differences in his judgment of reason?

In his investigation of the formula at Worms,[84] Preuss has worked out a threefold usage of the term reason in Luther:

1. Reason as a process of logical conclusions.

2. Reason as a cultural factor, as the mind that is active in secular matters, as presupposition for all human cultural endeavor.

3. Reason in the metaphysical religious sense as the principle of a world view.

In this third sense reason is harshly rejected. Here it belongs in the same category with the law. Law and reason are both a human activity. But this activity wants to glory in itself in opposition to God's work. Luther's battle is directed at reason insofar as it claims to be the principle of a world view. As a cultural factor Luther accepts the validity of reason. He was no despiser of human culture. In this connection even the "pagan" Aristotle is given his due. Finally, with respect to reason as a process of logical conclusions, Luther employs it without hesitation. (Cf. the documentation in Preuss, pp. 74ff.) In this sense we must understand the formula "authority and reason" in Luther. Reason does not come beside authority as a second foundation, but as a formal process of drawing conclusions it teaches how to make proper use of authority and shows how one must build on this foundation. For this undertaking reason proves itself altogether useful and must be permitted to function. This threefold meaning of reason explains Luther's dissimilar judgments, according to Preuss.

However, Heim (p. 239, n 1) has called attention to the fact that at times Luther also refused to accept the role of reason in the process of drawing conclusions.[85] Luther knows of cases where the premises are correct and yet the formally correct conclusion leads to a false result. In the disputation of January 11, 1539, on John 1:14, we find the following statements:

Thesis 18: "This common syllogism is good: The Father is the entire divine essence; the Son is the divine essence; therefore, the Son is the Father."

Thesis 19: "But again the premises are true and the conclusion is false; and this is not a case of truth agreeing with truth."

Thesis 20: "This is indeed not because of the defect of the syllogistic form but because of the lofty character and majesty of the matter which cannot be enclosed in the narrow confines of reason or syllogisms."

Thesis 21: "So the matter is not indeed contrary to, but is outside, within, above, below, before, and beyond all logical truth."

Thesis 26: "In these and similar statements the syllogism is a most excellent form, but it is useless with regard to the matter itself."

Thesis 27: "Therefore, in articles of faith one must have recourse to another dialectic and philosophy, which is called the word of God and faith."

Thesis 28: "Here we must take a stand, and the arguments of philosophy drawing the opposite conclusions must be regarded as the vain croaking of frogs."

Thesis 42: "In articles of faith, the disposition of faith is to be exercised, not the philosophical intellect" (W. XXXIX, 2, pp. 3-5; LW 38, 239-242).

What is here questioned is the validity of logical conclusions in statements of faith, even when both premises are true. Therewith reason is rejected also in that third sense. Theology and philosophy are two separate realms which must not be intermingled. What applies in philosophy need not apply in theology, and vice versa. Thesis 4 explicitly condemns the Sorbonne's assertion that "truth is the same in philosophy and theology." [86] If philosophy contradicts theology it must be regarded as the croaking of frogs. Hence there is an area in which contradictions may be dispensed with, and in which "clear reasons" have no significance.

How can Luther abrogate the rules of logic here? He bases his action on the loftiness and majesty of Scripture. Here, it seems to me, lies the difference between Luther and the Occamists. It is therefore necessary to see this point quite clearly. In the net result Luther coincides with strict Occamism, but the starting point is different for both. The Occamists arrive at theology by way of critical reflections on knowledge, while Luther becomes critical of the means of knowledge by way of theology. The Occamists engage in the most subtle investigations of man's ability to know and, by way of philosophical reflection, conclude that knowledge of God in the strict sense is impossible. Luther, on the contrary, stands entirely under the overwhelming impact of the content of Scripture. This, not philosophical reflection, is primary for him. The matter is too great to be squeezed into the narrow rules of human reason. Luther is then able to express this insight in the formulas of Occamistic scholasticism. Luther could use this readily available Occamistic terminology for his own purposes, realizing full well that these same terms were also used to further interests altogether different from his own. Ultimately this should also be said once more against Ritschl concerning the use of the formula "the hidden God."

In our day some like to strip Luther's theology of all paradoxes, considering them elements retained from his scholastic years. In opposition to this view we must emphatically stress:

1. Even if Luther simply borrowed these paradoxes from tradition, they still constitute an important ingredient of his theology, no less important than that which may be termed "the line of experience" in him.[87]

2. We must seek to understand these paradoxes out of the innermost reaches of his theology. For that, ultimately, is their origin, not philosophical reflection. In other words: We attempt to grasp these thoughts of Luther as the expression of his theology of the cross, and we believe this is methodically more correct and provides more fruitful results than a Luther research which in part is still under the influence of A. Ritschl.

Research that ends in reducing the thought world of a great man into disparate historical elements cannot be methodically satisfactory, however penetrating it is in detail. Thus, as surely as Luther was historically influenced by Occamism with regard to the problem of reason and faith, so it is equally sure that we cannot rest once we have established that fact. The doctrine of the theology of the cross has proved itself as a heuristic principle already in the presentation of Luther's view of God. In connection with this doctrine we must attempt to see also the problem of reason and faith.

We have heard how the profoundest sense of God's dealing with the world becomes manifest for the theology of the cross at the cross of Christ and of the Christian. At the cross every fictitious conception of God is destroyed. The cross puts everything to the test. The cross is the judgment upon all of man's self-chosen thoughts and deeds. In view of man's actual situation this means the radical reversal of all human assumptions. What is foolish is wise, what is weak is strong, what is disgrace is honor, what appears hateful to man is to be desired and loved in the highest degree. Does it not follow as a matter of course when we are told that lack of understanding is the true understanding before God (W. I, 171, 29f.)? When we plunge into lack of understanding, then we go the way of the cross. How is this equation to be explained? We are not dealing here with anti-intellectualism. It is not at all a matter of the contrast, intellect-feeling, or intellect-will. Reason is valid in its domain, but reason is a human work, and therefore judgment is pronounced upon it. For the cross is the judgment upon all human glory. The way of the cross means the surrender of human glory and a plunge into foolishness. One who has caught something of the wisdom of the cross knows that reason is a "dangerous thing" (W. IX, 187, 5ff.).

But does not this wisdom of the cross run into conflict with faith in God the Creator? Has not God created reason in man, and is it not reason that distinguishes man from other creatures? Is there not a light of nature which shows man the right way to knowledge? Indeed, says Luther, "nature" knows about God. It knows about the existence of a divine being.[88] But this does not yet provide a true knowledge of God. Reason plays blind-man's buff with God. In its blindness it gropes this way and that, and misses God who it merely knows exists (W. XIX, 207, 3). Compared to the light of grace the light of nature is darkness. It will not do simply to appeal to God's order of creation, because the fall stands between it and us. This fact cannot be evaded. And the light of nature stands in close relationship to it. It was the serpent that said, "You will be like God" (W. LVI, 356, 18ff; LW 25, 346). Hence an appeal to the light of nature is no help. The conflict is not introduced into the order of the creation by the theology of the cross, but it is already there because of human sin. But the theology of the cross lays it bare.

Reason is about as helpful in leading to God as the law. The inner kinship between the way of speculation and the way of works righteousness has already been demonstrated. Reason and law are the two foundation pillars which support the theology of glory. Both are toppled by the theology of the cross. Therefore there is "in the whole world no one that fights more against the cross than they" (the wise), (W. I, 164, 19f.). For the cross is the judgment upon the pride of wisdom. No self-glory can maintain itself in the presence of the cross (W. II, 613, 37ff.; LW 27, 404). Wisdom [89] and righteousness stand together as the abilities that man believes are exempt from God's judgment. Paul thinks otherwise; it is the purpose of his letter to the Romans to destroy that delusion (W. LVI, 157, 1ff.; LW 25, 135). As in Christ's death the divine *kenosis* reached its lowest point, so we too must put off the form of God (W. II, 606, 10ff.; LW 27, 393; W. LVI, 171, 8f.; LW 25, 151), and not seek "a wisdom and a righteousness apart from Christ" (W. II, 113, 26; LW 42, 59).[90] Our own wisdom is a wisdom of the flesh which resists the will of God (W. I, 32, 36). Our wisdom is in love with itself. It is like a sick person who refuses the doctor's help (W. LVI, 217, 8f., 28ff.; LW 25, 202f.).

Our wisdom is offended at God's Word; it is scandalized by the cross of Christ. But Luther knows that it must be so (W. V, 263, 15). If the church's proclamation is no longer a rock of offense to the people, this is a sign that it has betrayed the gospel (W. II, 601, 25; LW 27, 387). The cross of Christ vehemently opposes natural understanding (W. III, 367, 36ff.; LW 10, 310). For nothing but lowliness, disgrace and shame are to be seen there, unless we recognize the divine will, yes, God himself under this cloak (W. V, 108, 1ff.). It is generally true of divine works that reason does not know what to make of them and tends to despair because of this (W. V, 615, 17ff.; W. XIX, 195, 31ff.). Thus the gospel becomes a rock of offense, a scandal. But in that scandal lies the power of the gospel. "The gospel is itself an offense, not just offensive" (W.

XXXI, 2, 500, 9ff.; LW 17, 311). We see that the incompetence of reason in spiritual things is based chiefly on the idea of the offense. Reason refuses to come to terms with the paradoxical character of the divine activity.[91]

In summary, the following may be said about the problem of reason and faith in Luther:

1. Because of his Occamistic training the sharp separation between believing and knowing, between faith and reason seemed to Luther a matter of course.

2. But Luther's statements concerning reason do not seem to be based on philosophical reflections.

3. In fact they cannot be explained adequately on the basis of his philosophical training. Rather they grow out of his concept of the authority of Scripture.[92] Not Luther's Occamism, but his theology of the cross is the compelling motive in his fight against reason.

4. This is confirmed by the significance the idea of offense has in Luther's theology. But this idea stands in the center of the theology of the cross.

5. Accordingly, in our treatment of the problem of faith and reason we cannot be content with establishing historical dependence, but we must attempt to evaluate it as an essential concern of Luther's theology. Here too, as already in the doctrine of the hidden God, the theology of the cross proves its value as a heuristic principle.

4. Faith in Opposition to Experience

Thus far we have drawn the limits of faith over against the synteresis, the understanding, and reason. Faith is something different than the innate ethical consciousness. It is in tension with every natural capacity for knowledge. It stands as the absolutely new over against all givens. It is precisely what consciousness is not. In Luther's sense it would be misleading to define faith as "unity of experience." [93] Faith repeatedly bursts through the unity of experience, but it also creates that unity. We have already said that setting reason and faith in opposition has nothing to do with anti-intellectualism. We find this indirectly confirmed as we now must attempt to show how the same opposition also exists between faith and feeling, in fact between faith and experience in general.

That pious experience and blissful feeling may not be made the standard of faith is already evident from a glance at the outward signs for the genesis of faith. One may speak of faith in a person when he has renounced everything that he possesses, when he has abandoned everything in the presence of God. A stance of faith means that man perceives the impossibility of his stance before God, even though it may appear ever so irreproachable in the eyes of men and to his own conscience. The first step faith takes, (a step that must be taken again and again) is the negation of ourselves, the thoroughgoing demolition of all our own glory (W. III, 282, 29ff.; LW 10, 233; W. XLIII, 209, 23ff.; LW 4, 103). "Disaster" must "stare man in the face" (W. I, 160, 12; LW 14, 141), if he wants to experience God's help and rescuing hand. To believe means to undertake to die. "Christ says in John 3:7, 'You must be born anew.' To be born anew, one must consequently first die and then be raised up with the Son of Man. To die, I say, means to feel death at hand" (W. I, 363, 35ff.; LW 31, 55).

In his Epiphany sermon of 1517 Luther identifies complete self-surrender as the tropological sense of the gift of myrrh. We must become nothing to the same degree as we were nothing before creation (W. I, 123, 38ff.). This is Luther's "short way," that is, the way of the cross. There is no other way out for us but to live "in the bare confidence in his mercy" (W. I, 357, 3; LW 31, 44). If we wanted to appeal to anything of value in ourselves, we would thereby make the hopeless attempt of wanting to steal a march on God (W. IV, 375, 31ff.). But we are to know or have nothing but God alone, "and in no other way than in faith" (W. XVIII, 484, 16ff.; LW 14, 146). For that matter, what could we have in ourselves for which we could take any credit? There is "no form or beauty in us, but our life is hidden in God (i.e. in the bare confidence in his mercy), finding in ourselves nothing but sin, foolishness, death, and hell" (W. I, 357, 3f.; LW 31, 44).[94] It must be so. To conclude from our qualities whether they are pleasing to God would not be faith. Faith must experience negation. For in matters of faith all affirmation is hidden under negation.

In language that is at least influenced by mysticism Luther gives expression to this basic idea of his theology of the cross in a passage of his lectures on Romans (W. LVI, 392, 28ff.; LW 25, 382f.). Of course, such a renunciation on the part of faith is not easy (W. V, 446, 1ff.); but one who does not reject himself will be rejected by God (W. XVIII, 504, 17ff.; LW 14, 172). To confess oneself guilty is the first thing faith does. "For confession is the principal work of faith" (W. LVI, 419, 21ff.; LW 25, 411). But confession means dying and self-denial. For that reason the new life of faith is a life of the cross, that is, of death, and this only in its most shameful form (W. V, 444, 26f.).

Thus the new life arises out of the experience of the old life. Faith does not begin with the elating experience of God's nearness but with terror because of God's remoteness. Hence faith is kindled by a contrary experience. But what is the relationship between faith and experience now that faith is growing and maturing? Is this tension between faith and experience permanent?

It was, in fact, Luther's view to the end of his life that faith and experience are often mutually exclusive. Seeing and believing stand in sharp contrast. What we can see or what we can verify by natural means cannot be an object of faith. In its essence the object of faith must be hidden and dare not be accessible either to sense perception or to rational thought or to any psychic empathy, if it is not to cease being an object of faith. This is clearly expressed in the already cited famous definition of faith in *The Bondage of the Will* (W. XVIII, 633, 7ff.; LW 33, 62). Luther expresses the same thought in countless variations. Especially in his earlier writings it appears on almost every page. We shall confine ourselves to a few of the chief passages.

Already the *Dictata super Psalterium* emphasizes that faith stands in sharp contrast to sense perception (cf. W. III, 474, 14ff.). This does not mean, however, that faith is denied the soul's lesser capacity of sense perception and assigned to a higher intellectual capacity. We have already made this clear. Rather, faith comes directly from heaven and hence can in no way be anchored psychologically. Therefore the knowledge of faith comes into constant contradiction to the other methods of knowing. In its nature it is not only completely different from them, but it also comes to insights which they must regard as absurd (W. III, 508, 1ff.; LW 10, 452). This is connected with the fact that not visible but invisible things are the objects of faith. For Luther Hebrews 11:1 is the classic definition of faith. Here faith does not deal with a reality *(res)*, but only with "evidence of things that do not appear," just as in this life in general we do not have in hand the reality itself but only the witness of things (W. III, 279, 30ff.). The concept of faith is therefore strongly eschatological. The invisible things are, to be sure, the things we do not possess, which we do not see, of which we have no control, which are not yet present. Thus, in distinction from knowing, the proper domain of faith is the future, not the present and the past (see section 5). Faith and hope almost become synonymous. And again the strict faith-knowledge contrast manifests itself (W. IV, 322, 20f.).

Similar amplifications recur in Luther's lectures on Romans. Faith is directed to the "hidden things" and is explicitly delimited in relation to feeling and experience. In this way faith is the behavior appropriate to this life, while experience and feeling receive their warrant only in the life to come. For only faith deals not with visible things but with the Word. The correlation of faith and Word, already found in the *Dictata*, becomes clearly evident here (W. LVI, 424, 27ff.; LW 25, 416). Repeatedly we find the definition of faith according to Hebrews 11:1 set forth in its most detailed and most extensive form in W. LVI, 409, 8ff.; LW 25, 399. As the evidence of things that do not appear, faith draws the believer away from all that is visible; as the assurance of things hoped for it directs him to eternal things, which are, however, not present but future.

This is what makes faith hard and difficult, so that it proceeds in opposition to all appearance (W. LVI, 48, 18ff.; LW 25, 41) and is content with the word of God above (W. LVI, 231, 14; LW 25, 215). In this way it differs from the wisdom of the world which deals with visible things (W. LVI, 453, 13ff.; LW 25, 446), as well as from reason (W. LVI, 356, 18f.; LW 25, 346; W. LVI, 465, 3; LW 25, 457) and science (W. LVI, 440, 11f.; LW 25, 432). True knowledge is therefore to be found where one knows that he knows nothing (W. LVI, 414, 8ff.; LW 25, 405). One must be zealous for God "in pious ignorance and mental darkness," "without understanding, without feeling, without thinking" (W. LVI, 413, 22; LW 25, 404) one must wait upon God's activity. For faith is an expectancy, not a possession upon which a person can relax, not an opinion upon which he can insist. The "condition of this life is not that of having but of seeking God" (W. LVI, 239, 14f.; LW 25, 225. W. LVI, 441, 15ff.; LW 25, 433f.). Thus everywhere one finds the opposition to an objectification of faith!

Even the love to God is strictly delimited over against all experience. For it rises above all that is visible and embraces the God who cannot be experienced or comprehended (W. LVI, 307, 4ff.; LW 25, 294). Holl (Luther [2], p. 136, n. 2) has pointed out that the weight of such statements cannot be historically eliminated by the negative judgment that we are here dealing with mysticism,[95] but rather that in the language of mysticism Luther presents material of his own. We believe, however, that our conception of the hidden God provides a somewhat different elucidation for this and similar passages than that offered by Holl. On the basis of Luther's theology of the cross it is quite understandable that also in these expressions of mysticism he expresses his own positive ideas of faith. With that we are not trying to say anything about the historical origin of such formulas (which are found in great number in the *Operationes in psalmos*), but only to gain an understanding of their appearance in Luther's theology.[96]

This isolation of faith from every kind of observation, as in the lectures on Romans, we find in a sermon for St. Andrew's Day, Nov. 30, 1516. Not to see anything, not to feel anything is presupposition for the existence of faith. For Luther the suspension on the cross becomes a parable for faith: a stance in which a confident foothold on the earth is excluded. We call attention to this passage because of this unique picture; in substance it offers nothing new (W. I, 102, 39ff.).

The idea of a blind faith is strongly emphasized in the exposition of the penitential psalms of 1517. But while the previous statements were couched in more formal tones, they now receive a very definite coloring by means of concrete application. In this first German work of Luther's, in which he addressed himself not to the learned but to his "unlearned Saxons," [97] we hear everywhere the pastoral note that would soon make him a man of the people. Here he does not speak in general terms about the invisible things to which faith is to direct itself. On the contrary, faith stood the test quite practically in its reliance on God's providence. In this instance faith has ample opportunity to prove itself as the evidence of things that do not appear. Although God does guide our life, we so often notice nothing of this guidance. As a result it is necessary to induce the faith that sees nothing to walk the dark way and not prefer to follow the light of reason (W. I, 217, 8ff.; LW 14, 201). Otherwise we are like the horses and mules (Ps. 32:9) that find the right way only when they feel the hand of the driver (W. I, 122, 20ff.).

The great exemplar of faith is Abraham, who abandons his own knowledge and yields to God's knowledge and so is led on the right way like a blind man (W. I, 171, 29ff.; LW 14, 152). God's eyes are always directed to the godly; therefore they must close their eyes (W. I, 172, 10ff.; LW 14, 152). The fact that, from the world's point of view, this faith is an impossible stance which can be understood, strictly speaking, only eschatologically, is given expression in the powerful picture Luther presents to us in connection with Psalm 102:

> But to wake is to hold fast and to look to, and long for, the eternal good. But in this he is alone, and no one is with him; for all the others are sleeping. And he says, "on the housetop" as if he meant: The world is a house in which all men are enclosed and are sleeping. I alone am outside the house, on the roof, not yet in heaven and still not in the world. The world is below me and heaven is above me. I hover between the life of the world and eternal life, lonely in the faith (W. I, 199, 1ff.; LW 14, 181).

Luther's *Operationes in psalmos* of 1519 to 1521 is an inexhaustible gold mine for his view of faith. If, in the judgment of Hirsch *(Luthers Gottesanschauung,* p. 4), Luther "himself never surpassed the clarity and liveliness with which he speaks about God in that commentary," it may perhaps also be said that Luther is here employing particularly bold words concerning faith. For this exposition is the work of a man who suddenly finds himself removed from the quiet of the monastery and placed into battle with the world and must daily be prepared for martyrdom. He is doing theology in the face of death. All props that do not stand firm in the presence of the ultimate have been dropped. Hence we are not surprised that faith is ardently opposed to all human feeling and all human observation (W. V, 86, 33ff.). It must be considered a temptation of Satan when man judges on the basis of what he feels within himself. Faith does not ask about that; it is simply "insensibility" (W. V, 623, 36ff.). Of course it is a great miracle that man who feels nothing but his God-forsakenness may still believe in the gracious God. But faith lives in this miracle (W. V, 270, 17ff.), for the "words of faith fight against appearance" (W. V, 137, 37). In this lies the power of faith that it turns away from appearance toward God and clings to him without wavering (W. V, 53, 31ff.; LW 14, 321). These are therefore two mutually exclusive ways of looking at things, whether I look at something within the present situation or in faith (W. V, 36, 31; 252, 35; LW 14, 299). Here, too, the knowledge of faith is distinguished from philosophical knowledge.

> However, this is not the wisdom for which the philosophers seek; it is faith itself, which in prosperity or adversity can see things that are not seen. Therefore he does not show wherein

they should be instructed; but he says absolutely: "Be wise," that is, take heed that you are wise, be concerned that you believe. That which is understood by faith has neither name nor category. . . . Faith unites the soul with the invisible, ineffable, unutterable, eternal, unthinkable Word of God, while at the same time it separates it from all visible things. This is the cross and the Passover of the Lord, in which He preaches this necessary comprehension (W. V, 69, 20ff.; LW 14, 342f.).

This comprehension of faith can therefore, strictly speaking, have no object with it that has a name, for the sole objects of faith are the invisible things. But this comprehension of faith is "the entrance into darkness, where everything that the feeling, reason, mind, and understanding of man is able to grasp will be dissolved." Here again Luther uses the language of mysticism. The "entrance into darkness" is an image taken from mysticism (cf. W. V, 45, 30; 507, 7ff.; LW 14, 309).

The question must indeed be raised whether Luther is here not simply to be judged a mystic, and therefore rejected in substance.[98] Listen, for example, to the following passage from the *Operationes,* in which not only the entrance into darkness is mentioned, but where also the formula for the specifically mystical experience of leading and snatching occurs.

> Finally, the other virtues have to do with crass physical things outwardly, while those have to do with the pure Word of God inwardly, by which the soul is grasped, but does not grasp, that is, it is divested of its robe and shoes, of all things and fantasies, and is snatched by the Word (to which it clings, yes, which grasps it and leads it in a wonderful way) into the desert, into the invisible, into its bed chamber, into the wine cellar. But this leading, this snatching, this cleansing torments it wretchedly. For the way is hard and narrow, to forsake all visible things, to be stripped of all senses, to be led out of all accustomed things, indeed, this is what it means to die and descend into hell. It seems to it as if it were being destroyed down to the ground, where it is deprived of everything on which it relied, with which it had to do, to which it clung; it touches neither earth nor heaven, it feels neither itself nor God, and it says, "Tell my beloved that I languish with love" (Song of Sol. 5:8), as if it were saying, I have been reduced to nothing and I did not know it. Having entered into darkness and blackness I see nothing; I live by faith, hope, and love alone and I am weak, that is, I suffer, for when I am weak, then I am strong (W. V, 176, 16ff.).

Surely this looks like unadulterated mysticism. But it only seems so. This passage is particularly instructive because, on the one hand, Luther here achieves the strongest terminological approximation to mysticism to be found in the *Operationes,* but on the other hand, takes an explicit though cautious stand over against mysticism. He continues: "This 'leading' the mystical theologians call 'going into darkness,' rising above being and non-being. But I do not know whether they understand themselves when they attribute this to elicited acts, and not rather believe that this denotes the sufferings of the cross, of death and hell. The cross alone is our theology" (W. V, 176, 29ff.). Hence Luther believes he understands the mystics better than they understand themselves. This means, of course, that he interprets them in his sense. He reinterprets them in accordance with his own conviction and finds his own ideas confirmed thereby. He reads the mystics with the eyes of a theologian of the cross and finds there much that is congenial. But he solemnly commits himself to the theology of the cross—"The cross alone is our theology." As surely as the theology of the cross stands historically under the influence of mysticism, so certain it is, on the other hand, that Luther interpreted mysticism in the sense of his theology of the cross. But the point at issue is to take seriously what Luther had in mind with his program of the theology of the cross and not overlook the substantively decisive new material, while being concerned with the historical relationships. We are convinced that Luther's concept of faith certainly echoes mystical formulas but cannot be adequately explained by them.

What is the real objection to mysticism in the passage before us? Luther objects to a piety that turns the entrance into darkness into a technique, a self-chosen religious exercise. Thereby it is robbed of its ultimate seriousness. It is then man's work and remains under the judgment of the cross. The entrance into darkness that the theology of the cross has in mind means to be drawn into the event revealed to us in the cross of Christ. Thus it is not self-chosen activity, but it comes upon us as God's activity in us. It is not slanted toward timelessness but is oriented to a history. It is certainly not a theology of glory but a theology of the cross.

We have investigated thus far individual statements of the young Luther regarding the nature of faith, as opposed to all experience. It is now regarded as almost settled that Luther, matured by his battles for the gospel and enriched by experiences, traded in this negatively defined concept of faith for a positive one and began to stress in connection with faith, the present possession rather than the expectancy of future blessings. The quietistic elements of faith give way to the activistic, the world-shunning elements give way to those that shape the world. The object of faith is no longer simply the invisible, but concretely the Word. It is alleged that in place of the Catholic royal road of the Christian who maintains the proper middle-ground between fear and hope there is now the calm, joyful certainty of the forgiveness of sins.

This reversal is explained chiefly by the inner growth of the reformer, who in his conflict with opponents freed himself inwardly from his Catholic opinions more and more. But with regard to the concept of faith attention is also called to a very definite fact which is of great interest. We know that Hebrews 11:1 retained for Luther the value of a definition of faith as long as he lived. But he did later change his exegesis of this passage, which he had gained from Jerome, because of a philological clue supplied by Melanchthon. Luther reports this himself in his commentary on Galatians of 1519.[99] While faith was identical with hope earlier, he now sees its essence in faithfulness to God's promise. We may say that the eschatological aspect has receded over against the soteriological. The Word has taken the place of the invisible.

This shift in emphasis has undoubtedly taken place. How is it to be evaluated? With our modern orientation toward eschatology we may perhaps find the "young Luther" more attractive and feel ourselves closer to him. But must this not make us dubious about our modern orientation? Do we really have the right to remain with the young Luther, or does perhaps our modern "reformation" renewal in fact bear a pre-reformation stamp? The Luther of the lectures on Romans may in many respects be bolder, more charming, even more learned, but the more mature Luther is certainly the Luther of the commentary on Galatians. Some things may have become narrower with the post-1525 Luther (cf. Steinlein, *Explanation of the Third Petition*). Nevertheless, for our recapturing of the reformation position it is of decisive importance whether we can take the step from the young Luther to the mature Luther. This is not a plea for a Luther renaissance. Only when we are able to understand the gradual change in Luther, will we refrain from useless questions. As mistaken as A. Harnack's criticism of Luther's "Catholic remnants" may seem in our present situation, the consideration we give the period of Orthodoxy as a matter of course must also be applied to Luther in a larger measure than is now the case. Only it dare not take the form of playing off the "young" Luther against the "mature" Luther.

Perhaps we make the contrast between the early and the later Luther greater than it is in reality. Let us look at our specific question. We have said that a shift is taking place. While Luther at first defines faith more as opposition to experience, he is later on more interested in the content of faith than in a formal definition. Over against the clinging to the invisible, the trusting in the promise moves into the foreground.[100] But it is nevertheless only a matter of degree. As from the beginning the correlation between faith and Word is present with Luther, so on the other side the negation of all objective experience continues as an essential element of the concept of faith to the very end. Faith can only direct itself to the invisible; since the papal church is visible, it cannot be the true church, which can only be believed (W. VI, 300, 37ff.; LW 39, 75). Thus invisibility is the first requirement for the object of faith, and this is true even now. Therefore faith stands in a more intimate inner relationship to suffering than to works.

This note is sounded in the *Treatise on Good Works* and may not be ignored especially there. In suffering we are dealing with the hidden God. But the idea of the hidden God has disclosed itself to us out of the idea of faith (W. VI, 208, 6ff.; LW 44, 28). Not feeling but believing—this is also the contrast expressed in the exposition of the Magnificat (W. VII, 586, 11ff.; LW 21, 340). When we feel and sense nothing of the love of God we are ready to despair. But God's "arm" must be discerned by faith. Therefore "our sense and our reason must close their eyes" (W. VII, 587, 8ff.; LW 21, 341). Faith dwells in the darkness.

Luther compares man in his spirit, soul, and body to the three sections of the old tabernacle.[101]

> In this tabernacle we have a figure of the Christian man. His spirit is the holy of holies, where God dwells in the darkness of faith, where no light is; for he believes that which he neither sees nor feels nor comprehends. His soul is the holy place, with its seven lamps, that is, all manner of reason, discrimination, knowledge, and understanding of visible and bodily things. His body is the forecourt, open to all, so that men may see his works and manner of life (W. VII, 551, 19ff.; LW 21, 304).

Again the delimitation of faith over against every kind of empirically psychological and verifiable experience. But also in the sermons of this time—in which Luther generally speaks more "positively" than, for example, in his lectures—we have the very same view (W. X, 3, 130, 34ff.). And in the *Church Postil* the life of faith is depicted entirely in the style of the "Neoplatonic" *Dictata super Psalterium.* "Thus our eyes are closed to worldly and visible things and direct their hope to eternal and invisible things; grace does all this through the cross into which the divine life, which is insupportable to the world, brings us" (W. X, I, 1, 43, 18ff.).

How little one may isolate from each other the two lines indicated above or play them off against each other is shown in a passage from the famous sermon about the Canaanite woman. In it the Word to which faith confidently clings has precisely the sense of setting us free from our feeling and thinking. Here both lines, the negative and the positive, so to speak, are joined together. As faith here clings to the Word, it renounces the given objective and embraces the invisible (W. XVII, 2, 203, 29ff.). A passage from the lectures on Isaiah makes quite clear that alongside its substantive meaning the Word does in fact also have the meaning just indicated (W. XXXI, 2, 445, 33ff.; LW 17, 238. In the same place it is said: "This is what it means to place appearances beyond sight. And this happens only by the Word"). To entrust oneself with closed eyes to the guidance of God on an unknown path, this is what it means to believe (W. XXXI, 2, 320, 26ff.; LW 17, 76). And so we are not at all surprised to find these thoughts expressed quite frequently and with full precision also in Luther's last great work, his lectures on Genesis. In them also blind faith is called for, and that in a twofold respect: both in his practical attitude over against providence and in the reception of the highest articles of faith. In both cases an attempt at proof is inadmissible (W. XLIV, 378, 3ff.; LW 7, 106). If the story started with having our eyes opened, then our whole endeavor must be to make this originally misdirected development retrogressive (W. XLII, 672, 12ff.; LW 3, 173).

There is, of course, a certain justification in that first eye-opening. We have actually been created for the purpose of arriving at sight. But the time when this will be granted us is in God's hand. Man cannot snatch it for himself. The nature of the satanic temptation is that man takes for himself what God wants to grant him, and precisely thereby fails to get it. Faith, on the contrary, does not want to encroach on God's activity. It knows that it has not yet become sight, but rather that it is in diametrical opposition to sight (W. XLIII, 393, 9ff.; LW 4, 357). Hence faith, which is here too defined according to Hebrews 11:1, is a high art. Nevertheless, one who has not learned it and thus has not achieved the confident nay to all experience and observation, or rather does not continue to achieve it, is no Christian (W. XLIV, 751, 36ff.; LW 8, 236). This concept of faith becomes for Luther the key to the history of the patriarchs. From this point of view he develops a powerful picture especially of the figure of Abraham. The Pauline "hope against hope" is the background against which all details are viewed (W. XLIV, 655, 1ff.; LW 8, 103).[102]

Here, too, faith and experience form a strict contrast: either faith or experience. But alongside this disjunctive relationship we very frequently find a successive one especially in the Genesis lectures. Thus the concept of faith becomes analogous to the view of God, as we demonstrated it in connection with the "rear parts of God" in the Genesis lectures. There, too, we were able to demonstrate this idea of succession as being peculiar to the Genesis lectures; and here we meet with it again. Alongside the exclusive contrast between faith and experience we have the temporally conditioned one. What is at first contrary to all experience, accessible only to faith, is later proved to be true also in relation to experience. God's action penetrates the contrast; as long as it remains in the contrast it is a matter of *sola fide*. It becomes intelligible only after the event (W. XLIV, 300, 3ff.; LW 6, 401). The way to exaltation is only through humiliation (W. XLIII, 567, 36ff.; LW 5, 202). To wait means not to have in hand, to be unable to appeal to any experience, and yet to have a sense of waiting.

It may be said that by this idea of "waiting for God," which corresponds to the view of the "rear parts of God," Luther's position has not been surrendered in either instance.[103] For the waiting faith is relevant precisely where experience is lacking. But as for the positive significance of the idea itself, two things need to be said:

1. Luther's theology always has a pastoral cast. Considered in the light of pastoral care, this idea is extremely valuable.

2. In his theology Luther never becomes frozen into a design. All too easily the faith-experience contrast can be turned into a design that lacks all concreteness. To prevent this from happening, the idea of "waiting for God" is especially valuable. Luther's theology is not a dialectical game with absolute opposites, but the expression of being addressed by the living God in a thoroughly concrete way.

5. Faith and Hope

We saw how sharply Luther delimits faith from all objective experience. This leads us to a final consideration. We can say that Luther's concept of faith has a strong eschatological character.[104] It is always thus: the more I understand theology as a description of human conditions, the less room is in it for an eschatology. Conversely, the more sharply I draw the lines of separation between theology and psychology, the more eschatology gains in significance. If the "essence of religion" can be abstracted from the psychological functions of the religious subject, then eschatology is excluded. If theology sees its task in a descriptive psychology, it does not get to deal with the empty space which all of our theological statements must leave open. Conversely, the more I come to realize the inadequacy of a psychological description of the function of faith and the more I sense the tension between that which is called faith and the empirical condition of "believing man," the more of an eschatological ring will my theological statements assume by themselves. Hence we should not be surprised to hear this ring in Luther.

In the earlier Luther this is given without further ado in the definition of faith that is determinative for him on the basis of Hebrews 11:1, as he then understood that definition. If faith is in the first instance a not-seeing, then it finds its goal *(telos)* in seeing; but this is part of the light of glory. Faith is geared to this *telos*, and thus, in opposition to sight, it is oriented eschatologically. The antithesis is stressed for the sake of the synthesis. For that reason faith and hope, are almost identical for Luther in the first period. For also faith is in the first instance directed to the future; therein lies its difference from knowledge which has to do with the present (W. IV, 323, 20f.). But it is distinctive of hope that it stands in contrast to the reality surrounding us. Hope *(spes)* and physical reality *(res)* are two members of a disjunctive relationship (W. III, 301, 11f.; LW 10, 249).[105] This is expressed very clearly in the Romans lectures (W. LVI, 520, 5ff.; LW 25, 515f.).

Another passage in which the God of hope as the true God is set in opposition to the false gods, the gods of material things, shows in what measure hope is constitutive for the whole estate of being a Christian (W. LVI, 522, 9ff.; LW 25, 518). Hence in this hope, this bare hope, the first thing to be emphasized is not the positive, but the negative element: hope is not material reality. This reality, which surrounds us, and hope are in conflict with each other

(W. LVI, 465, 9ff.; LW 25, 457). As with faith, so with hope the positive element is certain about the future blessings (W. IV, 332, 27ff.). In a certain sense we may already speak of a possession of the future blessings: "Through hope we dwell in heaven" (W. III, 389, 34). What is proclaimed here is not nihilism, in spite of its radical attitude toward reality. What is placed in opposition to the espousal of reality is not a flight into nothingness but faith in another, a higher reality which is the genuine reality. Christians are only seemingly "idealists," in truth they espouse a "higher realism" (W. IV, 355, 29ff.). Nevertheless, the negative element in hope dare not be forgotten. In fact it is emphasized much more strongly than the positive. It must, of course, be said that none of us has this pure hope; for we all still put our confidence somehow in creatures; we are not ready to risk it with God alone (W. I, 359, 20ff.; LW 31, 48).

Hence the eschatological character of Luther's concept of faith can be traced to his early years; it is given with his understanding of Hebrews 11:1. But even after the change in Luther's understanding of this passage had taken place, as described above, the eschatological thrust did not disappear. We must not overestimate this change in its significance, even though it was certainly neither accidental nor without effect. There were a number of shifts in accent, but Luther never gave up his theology of the cross. We demonstrated the truth of this assertion in the doctrine of the hidden God. We found it confirmed in the individual points of our critical delimitation of the concept of faith, and now we see it again. Following Otto Ritschl, we will now set the turning point in the time of the 1519 commentary on Galatians and not around the year 1525, as we did earlier. But with what justification we may speak of a turning point will become clear as soon as we turn our attention to the individual items.

In the *Operationes in psalmos* we again find the characteristic joining together of faith and hope. It is their task to leave all creatures behind. Faith and hope grant citizenship in heaven. There is a grasping of God, but, as is immediately added, only through faith and hope. This grasping does not mean the exclusion of eschatology (W. V, 54, 9ff.; LW 14, 322). For that reason hope remains a "difficult matter." For hope, in the strict sense, is always a matter of waiting for the opposite and is always in contradiction to the reality that surrounds us (W. V, 589, 5ff.).

That Luther could not give up this element in his ideas of faith becomes clear also from his understanding of justification. This is not the place to pursue it in detail. Nor is it of decisive significance for our question on which side we stand in the controversy regarding Luther's doctrine of justification. For both in the view of grace as making righteous and in the view of grace as declaring righteous, the process of justification is incomplete without the idea of hope. This part of the theology of the cross is too intimately entwined with Luther's central thought ever to be given up. "Thus our righteousness does not yet exist in fact, but it still exists in hope" (W. XL, 2, 24, 6f.; LW 27, 21). In this formulation the contrast between hope and reality certainly persists. In this way the eschatological idea keeps its place in the middle. Over against this it is not so much theological significance but rather the expression of a mood in the expectation of Christ's return that later becomes ever more prominent in Luther (cf. W. XL, 1, 646, 35ff.; LW 26, 428). The idea that righteousness and hope belong together forms the specific eschatological thought of the later Luther.

At this point the great tension between the invisible and the visible, which cannot even be fully removed through Word and sacrament, always remained clear to him. Thus we find it expressed also in the great Genesis lectures (W. XLII, 147, 22ff.; LW 1, 197). But even the more general idea of hope that is practically identical with the faith that sees nothing is found. As already indicated, Abraham is the great exemplar of such a faith and such a hope. For Luther the stories about Abraham are illustrations of the idea of faith (W. XLII, 463, 12ff.; LW 2, 281). We may therefore conclude also in this last point that Luther never abandoned the decisive insights of his theology of the cross in spite of a number of shifts in emphasis. The Abraham of the Genesis lectures is the same as the Abraham of the lectures on Romans.[106]

B. Positive Realization of the Concept of Faith

We have completed the first part of our investigation of the concept of faith. We endeavored to show how this concept must be critically delimited. For Luther faith is not simply a function of the soul, and this is true in a twofold respect.

1. Faith does not have its origin in any of the given abilities of the soul. This was shown in connection with the concepts synteresis, understanding, and reason. They proved not to be the desired

point of contact. No direct way from any of these intellectual functions to the act of faith could be found.

2. Also with regard to its condition faith cannot be classified with the rest of the psychic functions. It contains in itself a contrary element against all substantive experience. It stands in permanent conflict with perception. Its object is nothing perceptible, nothing visible, but their very opposite. And, as we have seen, it is precisely that which gives faith its eschatological character.

This negative, critical fixing of the concept of faith corresponding best to the idea of God, or rather, the idea of the hidden God is intelligible only on the basis of the concept of faith. Both together constitute the foundation pillars of the *theology of the cross*. The concept of this theology of the cross, as set forth in the Heidelberg Disputation and the Resolutions, finds its development in the idea of God and in the concept of faith.

But questions will now be raised: Is the presentation of the concept of faith given thus far complete? Is it not a monstrous distortion of what faith means for Luther? Is not the picture that has been sketched highly one-sided? Does it not all too clearly betray the influence of the most recent theology and is therefore not able to claim historical credibility? Are we perhaps dealing with a forced construction for which also a corresponding number of supporting passages may naturally be culled from Luther?

We must certainly consider these questions. Especially where there is live interest, it is easy to draw a caricature. Two things must be said:

1. We are convinced that too little attention has been given to what we have presented in the critical delimitation of the concept of faith. The older confessionally oriented Luther research (perhaps apart from Th. Harnack who, however, could not yet be aware of our modern questions) was not yet able to deal with this. For one thing, decisive documents from Luther's early period had not yet been discovered. And this research viewed Luther far too much as being in the line of orthodoxy, with such a sizeable element of the theology of glory in it that it could not emphasize Luther's theology of the cross. But the research begun by A. Ritschl suspected Catholic remnants in the things that did not fit into its own contemporary dogmatics.

We have already seen that Occamism was believed to explain Luther's view of God, while for the concept of faith mysticism was claimed to be the explanation. By means of historical classification the seriousness of the idea was evaded. Our investigation is based on the conviction that this dare not be done in spite of all genetic questions of detail. And we do not disparage such questions. Our position could be undermined only if it could be shown beyond objection that the negative definition of faith, as outlined above, was present only in Luther's early years. But we believe we have clearly demonstrated that this is no more the case than the alleged disappearance of the idea of the hidden God after 1525. But these thoughts of the theology of the cross may no longer be ignored, even if, as is the case, they do not appear later in the same degree as earlier.

2. But the negative definition of faith is inadequate. This is not meant to weaken in any way what was said in the previous paragraph. The critical delimitation of the concept of faith must be carefully kept in view as we now proceed to demonstrate its positive elements. For these can be established only after the critical substructure has been erected. Only in the light of the critical approach can they be correctly evaluated. If this approach is overlooked, we get a completely false impression. Then arises that unfortunately still popular picture of Luther as the man who thumps the Bible and whose faith is not essentially different from true German defiance. But this picture is false. We dare never forget the dark and grave background of Luther's statements. But it would be equally wrong if we were to suppress the positive elements of his concept of faith. We must now proceed to present them. By way of introduction it should be stated that it cannot be our concern here to pursue questions of detail—a very impressive investigation could, for example, be undertaken concerning the question of faith and Word—but we are here concerned with placing in a supplementary way the positive elements in their principal features vis à vis the negative delimitation of the concept of faith.

1. Faith as Experience

a) It is not at all true that faith excludes every kind of experience. Faith is not a hypostasis floating in the air but a reality. *I believe:* only in this subjective reference can we speak of faith. But this presupposes some kind of experience. If faith is to be achieved as an act in the subject, it cannot be something purely trans-subjective. For the moment we shall leave undecided what the nature of this experience is. It is certain that already in the early writings of Luther faith and experience appear as a pair that belongs together, for example, in the lectures on Romans (W. LVI, 246, 16ff.; LW 25, 232). Exactly the same classification is found in the *Operationes in psalmos* (W. V, 36, 15ff.; LW 14, 299), where experience appears as almost identical with faith. There Luther knows of a "tasting" of the objects of faith. But "tasting" is the old term for an unmediated awareness (W. V, 285, 29ff.). Hence there is an experience of that which cannot be experienced. Luther can even promote a "feeling" (W. V, 387, 40ff.). It is possible to "experience and feel" faith (W. VI, 217, 25ff.; LW 44, 39). The grace of God "can be felt and experienced; it is hidden, but its works are not hidden" (W. X, I, 1, 115, 4ff.). From faith "a most sweet stirring of the heart" results (W. VI, 515, 29ff.; LW 36, 40). Hence the love which follows faith (sic!) is seen here under the aspect of faith capable of being experienced. The faith that carries through in experience is love.

This "line of experience" (Bohlin) runs through all of Luther's writings. It is expressed ' with especial clarity in Luther's most beautiful piece, his explanation of the Magnificat. Here experience is called the school of the Holy Spirit. "No one can correctly understand God or His Word unless he has received such understanding immediately from the Holy Spirit. But no one can receive it from the Holy Spirit without experiencing, proving, and feeling it. In such experience the Holy Spirit instructs us as in His own school, outside of which nothing is learned but empty words and prattle" (W. VII, 546, 24ff.; LW 21, 299). The antithesis is clear: The emphasis on experience is directed against a faith that is solely a concern of the mind.[107] Experience means that the whole man has been effected sympathetically. But we will save an evaluation of these thoughts until later and for the present continue with presenting the material. We learn to know God only through the Holy Spirit. But the Holy Spirit uses experience as his school. Consequently experience is the legitimate way of getting to know God. Experience brings the affection with it. Holy Spirit, experience, affection move into one line (W. VII, 548, 4ff.; LW 21, 300f.). Where there is genuine personal faith, there experience must follow. Experience practically becomes the criterion for faith.

But does Luther no longer know at this point that faith dwells in the Holy of Holies and reigns in the deepest darkness? Indeed he does. Luther knows of a faith that does not concern itself about seeing and experiencing anything of God's nearness. The true bride of Christ praises and loves God's goodness whether she experiences anything of it or not. But then Luther immediately adds that this is impossible. There is no genuine faith which permanently sees itself face to face with nothing (W. VII, 557, 28ff.; LW 21, 310).

In the exposition of the prophet Jonah (1526) Luther speaks about the prayer of petition. A serious prayer will soon experience something of God's love (W. XIX, 222, 12ff.). The prayer of faith must feel that it is "reaching" God (W. XIX, 224, 23ff.). For, according to the famous definition of faith in the Galatians commentary, faith is not "an idle quality or an empty husk" (W. XL 1, 228, 31; LW 26, 129). That is to say, it wants to succeed. But with that he enters into the realm of experience. Here belongs also the formula Luther so often uses: "To the extent that you believe this, to that extent you have it" (W. XL, 1, 444, 14; LW 26, 284).

Faith is something positive throughout, not an impotent negation; faith produces experience, it creates possession. It may indeed take a long time until experience arrives, but it will not fail for one who is able to persevere (W. XLIII, 367, 35ff.; LW 4, 321). In opposition to speculation, only experience is competent to learn to know God's goodness and power (W. XLIV, 429, 24ff.; LW 7, 175). In all these cases the fact that faith and experience belong together is made evident. While we had to establish a sharp antithesis between faith and experience earlier, we here meet with their juxtaposition, and at times even their equation.

b) Also the definition of faith as *trust* points in this direction. There is of course also a trust that does without any basis of experience; but the warmer note that sounds here shows nevertheless that with this idea we are moving on the "line of experience." The rigid paradoxes recede. A strong personal fulfillment crowds out the sharp formulations of faith as non-seeing, non-feeling. Everywhere we sense the warmth of experience coming through. The subjective reference of faith finds beautiful expression especially in the idea of trust. While through the critical delimitation of the concept of faith the main emphasis was, in the nature of the case, placed on faith as that which is believed *(fides quae creditur)*, here faith as an activity *(fides qua creditur)* is given its full due. The subjective element of faith demonstrates itself as trust. To the extent that faith as antithesis to all objective experience desires to show itself efficacious in the subject, it assumes the concrete form of trust. In trust we have the point at which faith and experience intersect.

We need not prove Luther's view of faith as trust by means of extended documentation. Everyone knows the explanation of the First Commandment in both the Small and the Large Catechism. Sufficiently known are also the famous words concerning the "sure trust and firm acceptance in the heart," as found in the large commentary on Galatians (W. XL, 1, 228, 31ff.; LW 26, 129). The exposition of the First Commandment in the *Treatise on Good Works* corresponds almost verbatim to the Large Catechism (W. VI, 209, 27ff.; LW 44, 30). For, as stated in the explanation of the Penitential Psalms of 1517, "God wants us to have a true, simple faith and firm trust, confidence, and hope" (W. I, 172, 15ff.; LW 14, 152).

c) When the subjective reference of faith is given expression, we must not be surprised to hear of different *grades* of faith. Of course, faith is faith. As such it meets man's other functions as something absolutely new. With regard to faith there is no more or less, but only an either-or before God. But if I look at faith from the perspective of the subject, I may speak of different grades of faith. In this case very distinct differences in degrees of loftiness come into view. The fact that Luther also considers this situation shows that for him faith has an empirical element in it. For such a way of looking at it is possible only if this is granted. Thus some people manage only a puny, unformed faith that remains ineffectual in life and which Luther deplores (W. III, 490, 26ff.; Luther still does not hesitate to use the term "unformed faith"; cf. W. III, 495, 14; LW 10, 435). Others, as for example the martyrs, demonstrate their faith in Christianity "in a heroic manner" (W. IV, 286, 36ff.).

In his sermon on John 4:46ff. (1516), Luther distinguishes three degrees of faith (W. I, 87f.), the inchoate, the progressing, and the perfect. The first is faith directed to signs and wonders, the second is deprived of these props and directed only to the Word, and the third, the perfect faith, is no longer dependent on the external Word but is a constant inner readiness to do God's will. And yet there is a difference between the faith which Luther recommended to the little woman of Torgau (W. XLIII, 460, 15ff.; LW 5, 46) and the faith of the highest grade, which is fixed on the hidden God and is able to grasp God's proper work in the alien work (W. XVIII, 633, 10ff.; LW 33, 62; cf. W. XLIII, 367, 33ff.; LW 4, 321). The highest and most difficult test of faith is when God in his activity not only delays but even conceals it under the opposite appearance.

d) To the extent that faith proves itself in experience we may also speak of a possession of faith. What I experience I possess. As something enters my consciousness it becomes my intellectual possession. Since faith has a specific content, that content becomes my possession. And as faith is seen in the sense of hope, this possession will also be a possession of future blessings. In this form we find this thought mainly in Luther's early years, for example, in his first lectures on the Psalms (W. IV, 271, 29ff.). Here the concept of possession is dialectical. It has to do with a possession, and yet again a possession of things that we do not possess. The idea is different in the gloss on Romans 5:4 (W. LVI, 50, 16ff.; LW 25, 44). Here a possession, though hidden, of, for example, patience and experience is given together with faith. The look toward the future is not involved. We are dealing here with the latent possession of present blessings, while in the former reference it is a matter of possessing things in hope. The development moves in this direction. As you believe, so you have. This is now the formula (W. V, 578, 38ff.; W. XL, 1, 444, 14; LW 26, 284). Thus together with faith a genuine possession is given. It is of course a possession only for faith, but a possession nevertheless. These thoughts therefore belong to the "line of experience."

e) Faith as possession enters into experience. It can therefore manifest itself as a *power*. The life of the reformer is the best illustration of this idea, and can be traced through his writings, from the earliest to the latest.[108] But it should once more be pointed out that this idea will not be subjected to abuse if it is viewed against the background of the negative definitions about faith.

f) Finally, faith may be defined in this context as the basic stance out of which all true expressions of Christian piety proceed. Faith is the point of unity for their multiplicity. To that extent faith may be taken as "ego-unity." [109] But this ego-unity is not a psychological given; it cannot be recognized objectively. Faith as such eludes objective experience, but it asserts itself in acts that are accessible to experience. Faith is the invisible point of unity that holds together the visible multiplicity. It is neither equal to the sum of its expressions, nor can it be equated with any one of them, but it is their all-pervasive point of reference. Hence, while the individual expressions may be grasped psychologically, faith can be grasped only indirectly because it is never identical with them. Faith *is* not experience, but it *is experienced*. But of course, only in a broken

form! In the language of Luther: Works proceed from faith, but
no work is in itself a proof of faith. No direct identity between faith
and works takes place, and hence there is no unbroken experience
of faith. Conversely, there is no faith that is not related to experience. Faith always calls for assertion and formation; but this formation belongs into the realm of experience. For that reason we
consider faith as "basic stance" toward the "line of experience" in
Luther's theology, not as if it could itself be interpreted in psychological terms, but because of its assertion in the area of experience.

But let us hear Luther himself! Already in the *Dictata super
Psalterium* we find this thought expressed allegorically but clearly
(W. III, 532, 13ff.). Faith itself is a work and a power of God and
therefore never a psychological given. Ultimately its subject is not
man at all, but God himself ("in faith, where it is not man who
sees, but God," W. III, 542, 34f.). However, as this ungraspable,
non-objective power faith creates all powers, but in the process it
does not coincide with any of these separate powers, but rather
as the work of God, forms the element of reference in every power.
This same view is found in the *Operationes in psalmos* (W. V,
395, 9ff.).[110]

Luther discussed the connection between faith and works most
beautifully and profoundly in his *Treatise on Good Works*. The
explanation of the first three Commandments given there belongs
to his most valuable writings. We are already familiar with its basic
thought. Everything revolves around the central statement: All
works must proceed from faith, but faith itself is no work. Faith
also is more than the mere total of good works (W. VI, 215, 13ff.;
LW 44, 37). Consequently it cannot be eradicated even by a big
minus. It retains its strength under all circumstances. As surely as
it wants to prove itself true in the realm of experience, so it does
not depend on experience. For it is the "before" *(prius)* of all experience (W. VI, 206, 18ff.; 204, 25; 204, 31f.; LW 44, 23ff.). Works
that have been separated from their invisible point of unity are,
like all things related to experience, subject to criticism, in this
case, judgment. Therefore all activity must proceed from this center
(W. VI, 206, 8ff.; 4ff.; 217, 34ff.; LW 44, 25).

Faith alone is the ground on which good works are made possible.
Hence works are dependent on faith, but faith is not dependent
on works (W. VI, 207, 12f.; LW 44, 26). Therefore faith must not
be lost sight of for one moment. All multiplicity is based in this
unity (W. VI, 212, 32ff.; LW 44, 34). Hence the "first, highest, and

most precious of all good works is faith in Christ" (W. VI, 204, 25ff.; LW 44, 23). But the last thing that Luther has to say concerning these relationships he expresses at the close of his explanation of the Third Commandment as he looks back once more on the first three Commandments (W. VI, 249, 11ff.; LW 44, 79). We will have to come back to this passage in another connection. What is most important for us at the moment is the statement: "Thus faith goes out into works and through works comes back to itself again, just as the sun goes forth to its setting and comes again at its rising. This is why the Scriptures associate the daytime with peaceful living in doing works, the night with a life of suffering and adversity. And so faith lives and works in both; it goes out and returns in both" (W. VI, 249, 33ff.; LW 44, 79f.).

Thus in this movement the starting point and goal is faith. In the works faith arrives at itself. Works are the self-realization of faith. Faith is no idle quality, no isolated quality that takes its place beside other qualities. But faith would be this if in its definition one would remain simply with the critical delimitation. It is precisely when I set faith into a purely negative antithesis to experience that I miss the goal that I have in mind. In this way I only put it on a level with objective experience after all. I will achieve a positive delimitation only when I place it above experience in the manner just indicated, as the ground and principle of all experience. Experience flows from faith and flows back into faith.

g) From this point of view an addendum is necessary for the problem of faith and reason. We have shown that a sharp tension exists for Luther between faith and reason. Faith and knowledge diverge as two realms that are different in nature. We have traced this understanding back to Luther's theology of the cross. What was said above remains valid and is not to be weakened in any way. But we would not have a complete picture if we were to say nothing about the other side of the matter. Also in connection with this problem the line of experience can be established. Luther knows of a Christian *gnosis* (knowledge). But not much is made of it. The theme of faith and works is entirely in the foreground, while the analogous faith and knowledge remains a torso. The analogy is carried through only in the antithesis.

With the same vehemence as works, also knowledge in the sense of natural reason is opposed. But while the new synthesis of religion and morality now forms the high point of Luther's world of thought, we do not find such a synthesis in the question of faith and knowledge. As is known, Richard Rothe saw the decisive short-coming of Reformation theology in this fact. We shall be more cautious in this matter. Obviously the gnosis of Rothe is no longer a theology of the cross. The connection between faith and gnosis is not as close as the connection between faith and love. Hence a simple analogy of the problems will not suffice. Luther himself offers us too little material to enable us to draw clear lines.

There is no question about the problem of gnosis emerging twice in the course of Luther's theological thought. The first time it is the gnosis of natural man, who has not yet been touched by reve-lation. As such it is "wisdom of the flesh," that means, in the plain language of the lectures on Romans, sin (W. LVI, 359, 1; LW 25, 348). Against this gnosis is directed the theology of the cross. Also the speculative reason of the theology of glory falls under the judgment of the theology of the cross, as we have seen. But the problem of gnosis appears again at another place. Faith is also knowledge and demands knowledge. How is it with the knowledge of faith? Luther did not bypass this question altogether. We have already been able to observe suggestions in this direction. Here belongs the concept of the understanding of faith, as well as the profound discourse on apostolic philosophy in connection with Romans 8:19.

By way of supplement we offer a few more passages in which we can likewise note a positive evaluation of a Christian gnosis. Thus "wisdom" (prudentia) can be used in a sense in which it is nothing else than an insight into God's dealing with man (W. LVI, 379, 17ff.; LW 25, 369). But above all it is wisdom (sapientia, cf. n. 89) which is frequently claimed along with understanding (intel-lectus) as an organ of knowledge for faith (W. LVI, 262, 22; LW 25, 249). True wisdom is possible only where one's own wisdom is renounced (W. V, 250, 30ff.). Hence perfect humility is perfect wis-dom (W. LVI, 346, 19ff.; LW 25, 335). This makes clear that such wisdom cannot be found in natural man. "Perfect wisdom is per-fect spirituality" (ibid.). The wisdom of the spirit and the wisdom of the flesh stand in unreconciled opposition to each other (W. V, 545, 10ff.). There is indeed a reason "enlightened by faith" (W. XL, 1, 442, 12), but the wisdom of the cross remains a wisdom hidden in a mystery for the perfect (W. XVIII, 638, 24ff.; LW 33, 71).

What we have to work with here is limited to some scanty allu-sions. They carry no weight in relation to the sharp antitheses that we had to set forth above. But they do indicate that here too we must guard against an abridgement, just as in connection with the question of faith and experience in general.

2. The Substantive Definition of Faith

To the positive element in the concept of faith belongs, in the second place, a determination of its content. Faith is not merely a negation but rather lives by its very specific content. For Luther the faith by which one believes is inconceivable apart from the faith which is believed. Echoing Kant's famous formula, we could say in the sense of Luther: The faith by which one believes is empty without the faith which is believed, and the faith which is believed without the faith by which one believes is blind. Faith is not only concerned with the "that" of revelation but also with the "what." The determination of content is essential for the concept of faith. We may speak of it in a twofold respect. According to Luther, the following belong together:

a) faith and Word

b) faith and Christ [111]

Here, too, we must be brief. Both of these do not strictly belong to our theme, but could not be entirely omitted for reasons already mentioned.

a) We have seen that the definition of faith as "the evidence of things not seen" does not exclude the thought of its relationship to the Word. On the contrary, it is emphasized already in the *Dictata super Psalterium*. Hunzinger's thesis cannot overthrow the facts of the case. In his early years Luther knows of a clinging to the Word, even a becoming one with the Word (W. IV, 695, 34ff.). In this case Luther's development is the safest refutation of Hunzinger's one-sided thesis. Luther's entire development is oriented to the Word. In the Word there arises for him the strength to believe contrary to his experience (W. VI, 519, 12ff.; VII, 785, 3ff.; LW 42, 183f.; W. XVIII, 495, 36ff.; LW 14, 160). The experience of God's love is kindled by the Word. For Word is gospel. But this Word is true only for faith (W. XL, 1, 217, 6ff.; LW 26, 122), which is more, however, than merely regarding something as true (W. X, 1, 71, 3ff.). Historical faith does not justify, but special faith does (W. II, 458, 20ff.; LW 27, 172).

How is special faith distinguished from historical faith? Historical faith keeps its distance from its object, and does so in a double respect: It does not leap over the historical chasm that is between us and the time of Jesus, and it views these events purely as a spectator. Special faith, however, receives these accounts for their effect, that is, it is not neutral over against them, but feels itself participating in them to the highest degree. This faith knows that "this concerns me." For this event, to which faith is directed, is not historical in the sense of an event that is closed and lies behind us, but one that is new every day through faith (W. XL, 1, 523, 30ff.; LW 26, 340). Hence it may be said that in distinction from historical faith special faith contains an element of experience. For to the extent that the ego-reference is emphasized here, it is inevitable that the ego is involved. But every involvement of the ego produces an emotion. Insofar as the special faith is accented with respect to the emotion, it bears an element of experience in it. For that reason it was proper to make mention of it in this connection. But we must add immediately: This experience is the experience of faith and hence always in a certain tension with natural experience. The element of experience in special faith does not make this easier but more difficult. For precisely in that way man is placed before the decision and is snatched away from his spectator attitude (W. XL, 1, 86, 2ff.; LW 26, 33f.; W. XL, 1, 484, 2ff.; LW 26, 311). The experience of special faith is a special kind of experience.

This, however, brings us a step farther in our understanding of the relationship between faith and Word. We have observed the belonging together of faith and Word from the viewpoint of the line of experience. But as in the presentation of the idea of special faith we were made aware of the two-sidedness of the problem of faith and experience, so it is also with the theme of faith and Word. We may consider it from this viewpoint: Faith is not empty; experience arises in the Word. Or as we have already intimated, we can take the Word precisely as the element of inability to experience. By the fact that faith is directed only and alone to the Word —"we have the Word alone"—the renunciation of all experience, rather, all objective experience, is proclaimed. It is precisely the significance of the Word, for example, in time of trial, that through the Word we are freed from all anxious self-observation, freed from attaching value to our own pious feelings and experiences, freed ultimately from our own empirical self. The Word proves to be the sharp, two-edged sword, that cuts through all the bonds that would tie faith to our empirical condition. As surely as it is improper in Luther's sense to define faith in a purely formal way as a not seeing, as the antithesis to all experience, and as surely as the content relationship to the Word must be accented, so little dare we delude ourselves about the fact that this relationship to the Word means abstraction from all objective experience and that this realization of content bears an exclusive character.[112]

We therefore maintain: Faith and Word belong together. Faith is not a negation but a realization. It does not live by saying no but by saying yes. Since faith is directed to the Word, it does not remain an empty slate. On the other hand, the Word isolates faith from all objective experience. The Word enters into opposition to the realities that surround us. It is precisely the realization of content on the part of faith that allows it to negate other contents. The determination of content of faith by means of the Word thus makes the above antithesis of "faith in opposition to experience" and "faith as experience" doubtful. There is something in this antithesis that does not seem to jibe. The problem of faith and Word makes it clear in which direction our investigation will have to proceed.

b) But first we want to linger a moment with the second determination of the content of faith: Faith and Christ belong together. Luther cannot speak of faith without thinking Christ. As little as the idea of God can be seriously achieved apart from Christ, so little does Luther know of a faith whose content is not determined by Christ.[113] Christ is the ground and content of faith.[114] Both "through Christ" and "through faith" must be said. Neither may be separated from the other (W. LVI, 298, 21ff.; LW 25, 286; W. LVI, 299, 17ff.; LW 25, 287). Hence we cannot come before God *sola fide*. On the contrary, faith has its origin in Christ (W. VI, 216, 26ff.; LW 44, 38). These thoughts received their consummate development in the large commentary on Galatians. There the relationship of faith and Christ is described in a threefold gradation.

i. Christ is the only object of faith. Faith may also direct itself to other things; but it either has Christ in mind in them, or it is not "in its proper function" (W. XL, 1, 164, 7; LW 26, 88). For in Christ alone there is comfort for the troubled conscience (W. XL, 1, 164, 10ff.; LW 26, 89). Hence the eminent significance of *propter Christum* ("for Christ's sake," W. XL, 1, 576, 1ff.; WL 26, 378). This *propter Christum* is the foundation for our being God's children. But it is also the only source of certainty for the person who has been accepted by God (W. II, 497, 15ff.; LW 27, 231; W. XL, 1, 408, 2f., 15f.; LW 26, 260). It has in fact epistemological significance. Faith and Christ cannot be torn apart (W. XL, 1, 233, 2ff., 16ff.; LW 26, 132f.).

ii. The significance of the *propter Christum* urges us to formulate the relationship of Christ and faith still more precisely. Christ is not only the principal object of faith but also the ground for making it possible. This already points beyond the mere reference to the object. Christ is also the entelechy of faith. Christ is related to faith as form to matter. The matter arrives at its definition only by means of the form, faith has its goal in Christ (W. XL, 1, 228, 30.[115] LW 26, 129; W. XL, 1, 229, 9; LW 26, 130). Without Christ faith cannot become what it should be in line with its object. Therefore Christ and faith belong together.

iii. But Luther goes a step farther. The connection between faith and Christ is so intimate that for its presentation neither the subject-object model nor the teleological relation of matter and form are adequate.[116] Rather, with faith the presence of Christ himself is posited. "Christ is the object of faith, or rather not the object but, so to speak, the One who is present in the faith itself" (W. XL, 1, 228, 34ff.; LW 26, 129). This does not express identity between Christ and faith, but reduces their belonging together to its most acute form (cf. W. XL, 1, 546, 3ff.; LW 26, 356). Every formula that expresses the relationship of two antithetical entities is inadequate here.

Thus we have to do with an indwelling of Christ in the believer. Luther describes this in pictures which may best be summarized under the catchword "union with Christ." Christ and the believer grow together into one person.[117] But it is a unity in diversity. In this union the ego of the believer is not erased. No mystical identicalness takes place between Christ and the soul. It is true, "it is not the righteous man himself who lives, but Christ lives in him." In what way? "Because through faith Christ dwells in him, and pours His grace into him, through which it comes about that a man is governed, not by his own spirit but by Christ's" (W. II, 502, 12ff.; LW 27, 238). Already at this point the question arises whether the union is something that goes beyond the relationship of faith and Christ, or whether it is only a second description of the same relationship. But we will lay it aside for the moment and continue with a presentation of the material. By faith we become "as one person" with Christ (W. XL, 1, 285, 5; LW 26, 168; cf. W. XL, 1, 443, 23ff.; LW 26, 283f.), we have "all things in common" with him (W. II, 504,

6ff.; LW 27, 241; cf. W. I, 364, 23ff.; LW 31, 56; cf. W. I, 539, 19ff.; LW 31, 104). In details Luther describes this union with Christ in pictures that were familiar to him from Paul and mysticism.

1. Faith means to put on Christ (W. II, 535, 24f.; LW 27, 289; W. II, 592, 30ff.; XL, 1, 540, 2ff.; LW 26, 352).

2. Luther employs the illustration of the body and its members (W. II, 531, 11; LW 27, 281f.; W. XL, 1, 282, 21ff.; LW 26, 166f.).

3. But most frequently we find the picture of marriage. Here the question becomes especially acute once more: Does not Luther forsake his theology of faith by using the concept of union? That Luther for a while actually moved in the thought processes of bridal mysticism (Song of Solomon!) is clear, for example, from a passage in his lectures on Romans (W. LVI, 379, 1ff.; LW 25, 368). Luther retains at least the images of bridal mysticism extensively, as in the familiar passages from the *Freedom of a Christian* (cf. W. VII, 25, 26ff. and 37ff.; 26, 6ff.; LW 31, 351, 352). We find them again exquisitely drawn in the large commentary on Galatians (W. XL, 1, 241, 1ff., 12ff.; cf. also 214, 2, 14ff.; LW 26, 137. cf. 120). But of course this image also proves to be inadequate for the "insolent and unprecedented phrase" which Paul uses in Galatians 2:20. For the union of Christ and faith has a more intimate relationship than that of husband and wife (W. XL, 1, 285, 12ff.; 286, 6f.; LW 26, 168).

Two questions arise for us from this presentation.

1. Does not the idea of the union lead beyond the relationship of "faith and Christ"?

2. How does the determination of content of faith through Christ agree with the above stated critical delimitation of the concept of faith?

Regarding the first question, we may indeed speak of a Christ mysticism in Luther.[118] But we must be sure to ask what the expression means. The union comes into being through faith. In connection with the union, faith can never be omitted. The union does not do away with the distinction of persons ("as if one person"). A "blessed exchange" takes place between Christ and the believer. Such a thing exists only between two different persons. Luther was always conscious of the difference between Christ and us. It cannot be shown here in detail but may be presupposed as familiar, how Luther never forgets about the Christ outside of us *(Christus extra nos)* when he talks about the Christ in us *(Christus intra nos)*.

Hence the union with Christ is in no case a quiescent identity, but it can be consummated only in the movement of faith. If in some of the cited statements Luther seems to have gone beyond this, it can be understood in its context only as a particularly emphatic expression of the fact that faith and Christ belong together. Oneness with Christ is always the *Christus extra nos*.[119] Hence we may say that in the statements about the union with Christ the one side of the concept of faith, namely its determination of content, receives its strongest expression. "In faith itself Christ is present." There is no such thing as a union apart from faith. "Christ and faith must be altogether joined together." The thought of union does not lead beyond the relationship of faith and Christ but forms its climax.[120]

On the second question, already in connection with the point concerning faith and Word we saw that the determination of the content of faith in no way stands in opposition to its critical delimitation. On the contrary, the latter was demonstrated precisely in connection with the determination of content. It is to be expected right from the start that we will here arrive at a similar result. Also the question concerning faith and Christ may be considered from the double point of view established earlier. We may just as well assign it to the "line of experience," as we may regard it a special case of critical delimitation, and vice versa. For the fact that Christ and faith belong together clearly shows, on the one hand, that faith is not a leap into a vacuum. It perhaps gropes in the darkness—and precisely there runs into Christ. It moves away from all experience and experiences Christ. And Christ is the firm possession of this faith. But just then—and this is the other side—as it looks away from all other objects, it arrives at this object.

The fact that Christ and faith belong together makes clear the exclusiveness of faith just as does the fact that faith and Word belong together. This constitutes the scandal of Christianity. From it follows the rejection of natural theology. Through its relationship to Christ Christianity is sharply delimited against all other religions. Expressed practically: Faith is oriented toward Christ, hence not to something that belongs to objective experience. To the extent that Christ, as a fact of history, is accessible to objective experience he is the object of "historical faith." But we are concerned with "special faith." In it, not in historical faith, Christ is "present." Being oriented to Christ means removal from all objective experience. All that had to be said in the first part of this chapter about "blind faith" applies here too. The fact of Christ is not a "dull fact."

When Luther speaks of Christ, he is thinking of the cross. But the cross is revelation in concealment. The theology of the cross is the background against which the doctrine of the union with Christ must be viewed. Union with Christ is consummated only when we, on our part, are "destroyed and rendered formless" (W. II, 548, 28f.; LW 27, 308).

Thus with regard to our problem the view of "faith and Christ" presents an exact parallel to the view of "faith and Word." In both we are dealing with the consummation of the content of faith. For that reason we treated it in connection with the "line of experience" in Luther. However, in both the negative delimitation of the concept of faith has not been surrendered, but has rather been retained as their presupposition. That this is not a construction on our part, or a disparateness of which Luther had not become aware, is clear from the famous definition of faith in the large commentary on Galatians, where both sides are allowed to stand unreconciled side by side.[121] Accordingly, this definition shall form the close of this discussion.

> Therefore Christian faith is not an idle quality or an empty husk in the heart, which may exist in a state of mortal sin until love comes along to make it alive. But if it is true faith, it is a sure trust and firm acceptance in the heart. It takes hold of Christ in such a way that Christ is the object of faith, or rather not the object but, so to speak, the One who is present in the faith itself. Thus faith is a sort of knowledge or darkness which sees nothing. Yet the Christ of whom faith takes hold is sitting in this darkness as God sat in the midst of darkness on Sinai and in the temple (W. XL, 1, 228, 31ff.; LW 26, 192f.).[122]

C. The Unity of the Two Definitions of Faith

As we have seen, the two definitions of faith as to content—"faith and Word," "faith and Christ"—cannot be fully covered either by the negative delimitation or by the positive definition of the concept of faith. But this is not the only observation that urges us to consider the question whether these two definitions are in fact mutually exclusive. Quite apart from this question it would still have been our obligation to pursue the matter further. We cannot possibly be satisfied with having established two opposing lines of thought. We must try to view the two opposites together in a higher unity.

Not because we love attempts at harmonization. We have no interest in them! But it would be an evasion of the problem before us if we were to content ourselves with the juxtaposition of thesis and antithesis. If we have thus far presented the two opposing definitions, each by itself, this was done purely for the sake of clearly tracing the two lines. But in what manner is the unity of both lines to be conceived? Can we find a superior category for the two definitions of the concept of faith? To the task of investigating this possibility we now turn our attention.

1. A surprisingly simple observation gives us the first help. Are we in both cases dealing with the same thing when we speak of experience? In the first section we took experience as a collective term for mental and sensory perceptions, hence as the epitome of man's natural capabilities of receiving the phenomena of the intellectual and sensory world. This concept of experience is in direct opposition to faith. Faith must be delimited against every natural ability if its peculiarity is to be preserved. To this extent the contrast between faith and experience is fully justified. In the second instance, however, we are dealing with an experience that is qualified by faith, as already the ranking of faith and experience side by side shows us (cf. W. LVI, 246, 14ff.; LW 25, 232). Faith asserts itself in experience understood in this way. Experience does not stand alongside faith but is a consequence of faith (W. XLIII, 367, 35ff.; LW 4, 321).[123] For that reason its degree depends on the degree of faith. "To the extent that you believe this, to that extent you have it" (W. XL, 1, 444, 14; LW 26, 284; cf. W. V, 578, 38). Experience is the organ of faith, and for that reason at times also takes the place of faith (W. XLIV, 429, 24ff.; LW 7, 175). The life of faith is "the life of experience" (W. II, 499, 21; LW 27, 234).

Without doubt the emphasis on experience in faith is directed against the scholastic idea of "unformed faith." Hence experience is nothing more than the emphatic reference to the existential element of faith. But since faith is certainty only in its existential attitude, experience denotes also the element of certainty on the part of faith in opposition to the Catholic authorities, the pope and the council.

Hence we may say: In the one case we are dealing with natural experience, in the other case with the experience of faith.[124] But now we have this difficulty: Is not "the experience of faith" a contradiction in terms? If faith posits an experience, is it not stripped of its character as faith? Or rather, conversely: What kind of experience must it be to be conformable to faith, an experience that does not transform faith into sight? Obviously this experience must meet a twofold condition:

a) It must really be an experience, capable of being established psychologically in the subject.

b) In spite of that, it may not for one moment be isolated from faith, it may not be posited beside faith as something autonomous and thus abridge its special character.[125]

We started with the contrast, "faith as experience," and "faith as the reverse of experience," and sought to find a superior unity for it. We established, first of all, that a different concept of experience is at the bottom of both formulas. But we must not imagine that we have now solved the problem. The difficulty has now been shifted to another area. It does not lie in the fact that at times Luther puts faith into the sharpest contrast to experience, and at times views faith and experience together, but it lies in the unique concept of the experience of faith. For when it is analyzed in its constituent parts, the result in a more sharpened form is precisely that doubleness which made the problem clear to us in the first place. There would, of course, be no problem if we could simply operate with the concept of "religious experience." Where the critical delimitation of the concept of faith is not taken altogether seriously, no difficulty is noted.[126] We must ask, on the contrary: How is an experience of faith conceivable in spite of the critical delimitation of the concept of faith? This again confronts us with the question concerning a higher unity of the two lines, a category which does justice to both sides of the matter.

2. Luther himself tells us in what sense he wants to be understood when he speaks about an experience (W. VII, 546, 24ff.; LW 21, 299). Experience is called the school of the Holy Spirit. The experience of faith is a work of the Holy Spirit. He has been the teacher wherever we have experienced something of God's goodness and love, wherever a holy joy has filled our hearts.[127] Thereby the "supernatural" character of this experience is clearly expressed. For the significance of the Holy Spirit can be considered from the point of view that precisely by regarding something as the work of the Holy Spirit, it is withdrawn from a purely empirical causality (W. IX, 189, 32ff.). Hence Luther frequently puts reason (but also sense) in opposition to the Spirit (Cf. W. LVI, 185, 26ff.; 186, 1ff.; LW 25, 167; W. XVIII, 489, 15ff.; LW 14, 152; W. XXXI, 2,

500, 9ff.; LW 17, 311). Not reason but the Spirit teaches who is the true God (W. XIX, 207, 3ff.). The true wisdom comes from elsewhere than from us; it, too, is a gift of the Spirit (W. LVI, 158, 10ff.; LW 25, 136).

The same contrast exists between what sensory perception shows us and what we see with the eyes of the Spirit (W. LVI, 445, 21ff.; LW 25, 437). Hence we must understand the Bible passages as spoken "in the Spirit," while they contradict appearances step by step (W. V, 30, 16ff.; LW 14, 291; W. V, 42, 27ff.; LW 14, 305; W. V, 178, 29ff.). "In the Spirit" is therefore equivalent to "hidden" (W. III, 150, 27ff.; LW 10, 125; W. V, 41, 27ff.; LW 14, 304; W. V, 286, 31ff.; cf. also W. V, 58, 38; LW 14, 327f. and W. V, 63, 28ff.; LW 14, 335). Here we find again all the critical delimitations that we applied earlier in connection with the concept of faith.

But this would not make clear in what respect the thought of the Holy Spirit should prove to be the desired category under which we want to place the concept of the experience of faith. However, as is known, the Holy Spirit is the creator of the new life. This surely requires no further elaboration.[128] But the experience of faith is a part of the new life. It is the realization of faith in reality. This, too, is the new life, and so Luther at times designates the new life as the creation of the Holy Spirit and at times as the effect of faith. To the extent that the experience of faith belongs to the new life, it is a work of the Holy Spirit. But the new life is a reality.

In this way the concept of the Holy Spirit proves to be the desired category.[129] In it the critical delimitation of the experience of faith over against all other experience is solidly fixed on the one hand, and, on the other hand, the character of reality in the experience of faith is also given expression in it. The experience of faith is experience in the Holy Spirit. That is to say, this experience is in no way to be derived empirically and yet it makes the claim of being a real experience (W. XVIII, 605, 32ff.; LW 33, 24). This remarkable doubleness is characteristic for the entire new life created by the Holy Spirit. More on this in the next chapter. At this point we shall attempt only to summarize the net results of this chapter.

We began with the question whether in the theology of the cross it is still possible to speak of a relation of the subject in religion at all. If it is the great no to every attempt to ascend to God from the naturally given, can it still arrive at the formation of a concept of faith? For faith, too, is a function of the religious subject. Does not the reality of the religious life, the life of faith, slip away, if God's activity always takes place only under the opposite appearance? Is it possible to speak of faith in view of the hidden God? If revelation is present only in concealment, if the proper work can be accomplished only by way of the alien work, must not then faith also appear under the opposite appearance? But how is that possible? What about its reality?

To answer this question we first had to undertake a thorough critical delimitation of the concept of faith. It is certainly in line with the theology of the cross to say first of all what faith is not. We would be justified in a sense to call the theology of the cross a negative theology. If the concept of faith is to have a place in the theology of the cross, it is necessary for once to hear the negation that is contained in the word faith. We saw and we emphasize it once more that this concept of faith is not just a part of the pre-reformation stage of Luther's theology; on the contrary, these negations remain in force even in Luther's late writings. But alongside this negative definition of the concept of faith we had to place a positive one. Faith comes to fruition in experience, faith is accomplished through experience. We saw that the existential element of faith is given expression in this way over against an intellectualistically misunderstood concept of faith.

Our question was how the negative and positive definitions of the concept of faith are related to each other. We discovered the idea of the Holy Spirit as a superior category. In it both are fixed with equal force: delimitation against all empirical causality and also the claim of the experience of faith to reality.

From this it follows, however, that the so-called line of experience within the theology of the cross need not at all have the effect of an explosive charge. For what is intended is always "experience in the Holy Spirit." [130] Experience and the "sweet feeling" are not religious feelings as the highest stage of human self-consciousness, but gracious operations of the Holy Spirit. This is of two kinds. The "from elsewhere" in opposition to the given is intended when something is designated as an effect of the Holy Spirit. The concept of the Holy Spirit is the vociferous protest against a psychological deduction of faith. One may argue about the form of this protest.[131] but we dare not fail to hear the real concern in it. Wherever in theology the Holy Spirit is taken seriously into account, we are not dealing with the theology of glory but with the theology of the cross.

III.

Life under the Cross

We have unfolded the program of the theology of the cross in the presentation of the idea of the hidden God and of the concept of faith. Both correspond to each other. We have sought to understand the view of the hidden God as a positive idea of faith. This automatically led us to an investigation of the concept of faith.

But our picture of Luther's theology of the cross would not be complete if we would stop here. The impression could remain that the theology of the cross has to do essentially with a theoretical affair. The criticism could be raised that the theology of the cross proves to be remote from life. If it is in principle suspicious of every psychologizing of religion, does it not then forfeit its concrete claim on life? Where is it to intervene in the everyday affairs of life if it bids us turn our eyes away from all that is visible? With its strong eschatological character, can it arrive at an ethic at all? In the theology of the cross, are we not dealing with a monkish theology which has not yet been exposed to the harsh atmosphere of reality? Do not the ideas of the hidden God and of blind faith remain a theory about which one may speak profoundly but according to which it is impossible to live?

It would be a complete misunderstanding of the theology of the cross if this is what we concluded. This very theology is eminently practical. It is distinguished from the theology of glory precisely because it leads a person out of his spectator stance and propels him into the decision of faith. Luther's battle for the hidden God against Erasmus, Luther's defense of the "scandal" against all invalid claims of reason to authority, his almost tiresome repetition of the statement about blind faith—aim at nothing else. But the same goal is in view in Luther's emphasis on experience. As we saw, experience gives expression to the existential element of faith. The concept of the existential, which in our time is almost hounded to death, provides the key to the understanding of what we must now consider. The doctrine of the cross, which has decisively determined the concept of God and of faith, will be understood only in a life under the cross.

We have already demonstrated the ambiguity of "cross." The cross of Christ and the cross of the Christian belong together. The meaning of the cross does not disclose itself in contemplative thought but only in suffering experience. The theologian of the cross does not confront the cross of Christ as a spectator, but is himself drawn into this event. He knows that God can be found only in cross and suffering (W. I, 262, 28f.). For that reason he does not, like the theologian of glory, shun suffering, but regards it as he would the holy relics, which are to be embraced devoutly. For God himself is "hidden in sufferings" and wants us to worship him as such. If the footprints of God in our life are all too visible before us, we have no need of faith, and then faith does not come into being. Therefore faith stands in a closer relationship to suffering than to works. If we are serious about the idea of God and the concept of faith in the theology of the cross, we are faced with the demand of a life under the cross.

And Luther was in deadly earnest about it! We dare never forget that Luther's theology of the cross cannot be dismissed as the brooding product of a lonely monk, but it proved its worth for him when he stepped forth into an unprecedented battle. Luther practiced this theology in the face of death. Here every sentence is soaked with his heart's blood. If anywhere, then in Luther's theology of the cross "doctrine and life" are in agreement.

Before we present the details, we would say two things by way of introduction.

1. In this chapter we do not propose to offer something like an ethic of Luther. This concerns us as little as a complete dogmatics did earlier. We take the theology of the cross as having an impact on his entire theology. And it is those elements of his theology that clarify this impact that we want to show here, nothing more. Hence we are consciously desisting from a full-scale portrayal in this chapter. It will then, of course, make no sense to attack our presentation

by pointing out that, after all, Luther "also said some other things." We are aware of this self-evident fact. But at this point we are concerned with exposing certain little-noted ideas of Luther which permit the impact to be seen clearly.

2. It has already been indicated as an essential trait of the theology of the cross that in it life and doctrine may well be distinguished but not separated. Hence we must not expect to meet completely new thoughts in this chapter. If this were the case it would not be a good omen for what we presented before. In both instances we must deal with the same basic thoughts. On the other hand, this frees us from the obligation to trace extensively at this point all the details back again to the basic thoughts. We shall rather be as brief as possible and seek to avoid repetition as much as we can. We cannot of course avoid repetition entirely, for this lies in the nature of the case.

A. The Hiddenness of the Christian Life

1. God is a hidden God, faith is the evidence of things that do not appear, the life of the Christian is hidden. These three statements belong together in the most intimate way. One follows from the other. Here we are interested in the third one. Why is the life of the Christian a hidden one? Very simply because it is a life of faith. The Christian life can be demonstrated in an empirical-psychological way as little as faith itself. What was said about the critical delimitation of the concept of faith applies in an analogous manner also to the Christian life. The Christian life can never be fully identified with the empirical life that we lead. The Christian life is an object of faith and, as such, it is hidden. What we see is never the real thing; only God and faith see this innermost core. As little as revelation is possible without concealment, so little can the Christian life surrender its incognito. Our life is like the treasure hidden in a field (W. LVI, 393, 3ff.; LW 25, 383). Everything positive in it is hidden under negation. By means of this hiddenness the faith-centered character of the Christian life is to be safeguarded (W. I, 543, 25ff.; LW 31, 104; W. LVI, 392, 28ff.; LW 25, 383).

But this hiddenness is so deep that the saints themselves are not aware of their own most personal life. They have no idea about the adornment in which they stand before God (W. IX, 191, 3ff.; I, 486, 15ff.). For this Luther appeals to the statement in the psalm, "The Lord knows the way of the righteous" (Ps. 1:6). The original meaning of the word is that the righteous will receive the reward for their good works. Luther cannot use it in this sense. But by an unconscious stroke of genius he reinterprets the passage and is able to find one of the most profound ideas of his theology of the cross expressed in this verse. The Lord knows the way of the righteous, the Lord alone; not even the righteous man himself can know it, since it is the way of dark faith. On the other hand, the senses and reason remain captive to the empirical.[132] Being a Christian is not externally perceptible like differences in race or sex (W. VI, 295, 34ff.).

It must not be supposed, however, that such thoughts appear only in the young Luther. Luther did not drop the idea of the hidden life of the Christian any more than he gave up the view of the hidden God. The one corresponds to the other, and both are united in the concept of faith which Luther never surrendered. Thus we find the idea in the "Beautiful Confitemini" of 1530 (W. XXXI, 1, 91, 4ff.; LW 14, 58) as well as in the lectures on Isaiah (W. XXX, 2, 562, 21ff.; LW 17, 387).[133] We have in part already given the pertinent passages from the lectures on Genesis in another connection. It will suffice here to refer you to them once more.[134]

2. In speaking of the Christian life we must speak of a contrast between perception and reality. The hidden life of the Christian is a reality but it is not perceived. The new life is not the object of empirical experience, but often enough is in opposition to it (W. IV, 476, 26ff.). Sin and righteousness in the Christian are in the same relationship as reality and hope. His righteousness consists in God's imputation (W. I, 148, 35ff.). Here reality confronts reality (W. I, 177, 4ff.; LW 14, 152). Accordingly, the question: Who belongs to the ungodly? cannot be decided simply according to outward appearance. This decision would have to be made "in the spirit" (W. V, 44, 31ff.; LW 14, 308; W. V, 55, 11ff.; LW 14, 323). God's judgment on man, which alone has ultimate reality (W. V, 293, 24ff.), is hidden from us. We must not anticipate this judgment with our assertions.[135] In the judgment of God the contrast is bridged between perception and reality (W. V, 359, 19f.). But this judgment of God is manifest only to faith, not to direct perception (W. V, 270, 17ff.). Luther can also express it thus: It is true in Christ. In Christ the reality God has broken into the reality of the world. Both realities are in conflict with each other. Luther's view of justification is to be understood in this perspective. In Christ the sinner is righteous.[136] The reality of Christ is stronger than the

reality of sin (cf. the repeated *re vera*, "in reality"). But it is a reality of faith, a hidden reality. In this point Luther's doctrine of justification is a concrete application of his theology of the cross.

3. The life of the Christian presents itself in this hidden way as a spiritual life. This says both things at once: its reality and its hiddenness. We remind ourselves of what we said earlier about the view of the Holy Spirit. For when we are here speaking of a spiritual life, we are thinking of the Holy Spirit, not the Neoplatonic dualism between lower and higher abilities. Spirit and flesh cannot psychologically or physiologically be delimited from each other, but are two different aspects of the same thing (W. II, 589, 1ff.; LW 27, 367). "In reality and in spirit" the ungodly do not belong to the believers, no matter how much it appears so. Like the reality of Christ, the reality of the Holy Spirit is a hidden reality.[137] The spiritual man is buried with Christ, he has died to the world and the world to him (W. LVI, 324, 4ff.; LW 25, 311f.). Instead, he understands that which the world can never comprehend: "The cross is very useful, but only to the spiritual" (cf. W. XXXI, 2, 445, 23ff.; LW 17, 238), since with a perfected spirituality he also receives perfect wisdom (W. LVI, 346, 18ff.; LW 25, 334).

4. Since the spiritual man always remains the empirical man— and as such is carnal man—we may speak of a double life of the Christian. This very fact again expresses the hiddenness of the Christian life: the old man stands beside the new man. For if man were unequivocally spiritual man, we could not speak of a hiddenness. But now the new man is always hidden under the old. The "under the contrary appearance" applies here too. Beyond his empirical life the Christian leads still another life. The doubleness is frequently expressed by means of the contrast of old man and new man,[138] or spirit and flesh.[139] Luther has the same thing in view when he deals with the Pauline distinction between the "outer" man and the "inner" man.[140] But Luther expresses his very own insight when he calls this higher life in us Christ.[141] A passage in the large commentary on Galatians makes particularly clear once more how the new life stands in hiddenness. The "inherent holiness" is not enough. We may not be called saints because of an inherent quality. For then all too easily there could be confusion between the old and the new man. The new man is hidden, and yet an obvious psychological quality lies open to view. Christ takes the place of the "inherent holiness." Christ is the new life (W. XL, 1, 197, 25ff.; cf. 198, 1f.; LW 26, 109).

5. This double life cannot be definitive. The tension demands a resolution. The hidden life must one day come out into the open. Thus we again meet the eschatological character of the theology of the cross. Just as the contrast between the hidden God and the revealed God will come to an end when faith is permitted to attain to sight, so also the Christian life will one day shed its hiddenness. The old man then will submerge, the conflict between flesh and spirit will cease, and the "Christ lives in me" can be said without reservation. But here and now our life is that of a foreigner (W. II, 535, 32ff.). For as Christians we are always only in a state of beginning. To use the familiar expression, it is rather "a becoming than a being" and thus points beyond itself.[142] Also the prayer to the Father shows us that we are pilgrims and guests on earth (W. II, 83, 25ff.; LW 42, 23). We are in "wretchedness," as Luther impresses upon us also in connection with the second petition of the Lord's Prayer (W. II, 95, 35ff.; LW 42, 37). Our true home is in heaven; here everything is but a shadow of that which is to come. There alone true praise of God sounds forth; even though we praise God already here, our praise is hidden with our life in God (W. V, 252, 30ff.).

Thus Luther here expresses the exquisite thought that the miracle of prayer and praise really bursts through our existence and points to a form of existence in which the limits that are now drawn for us will fall away. Prayer is the beachhead through which eternity breaks into time. But now we are still in a foreign land. Only at the last day will the sufferings of the saints come to an end, and justice and righteousness will be able to prevail. Therefore Luther understands Psalm 10:18 eschatologically (W. V, 352, 20ff.). Another look at the lectures on Genesis shows that the thought about being foreigners is found not only in the younger Luther. We meet it in the Genesis lectures just as surely as the idea of the hidden God. For Luther the story of Abraham is the great, indeed the classic illustration of the thought of being aliens. And in this Abraham is the father of us all (W. XL, 102, 37ff.). We are all "exiles and sojourners"; the Pauline "possessing as though they did not possess" should be the leitmotiv of our practical behavior (W. XLII, 441, 40ff.; LW 2, 252f.).[143]

B. The Christian Life as Discipleship in Suffering

So far we have spoken of the hiddenness of the Christian life in purely formal terms. Now we must ask how this hiddenness expresses itself as to content. Let us recall the definition of faith in *The Bondage of the Will.* There we heard that all objects of faith must be hidden. "It cannot, however, be more deeply hidden than under an object, perception, or experience which is contrary to it" (W. XVIII, 633, 7ff.; LW 33, 62). The Christian estate must also be hidden "under an object which is contrary to it." That is to say, its glory must present itself in lowliness, its nobility in disgrace, its joy in grief, its hope in despair, its life in death. The hiddenness of the Christian life does not remain something formal, but expresses itself in practice in a very perceptible way. In concrete terms, the hiddenness of the Christian life is a following of Christ's suffering. Great earnestness dominates these thoughts of Luther. If it is ever asserted that Luther made lesser practical demands of men than medieval Catholicism, one glance at Luther's theology of the cross should be sufficient to convince one of the opposite. The most radical asceticism and the most sublime mysticism, stripped of their false tendencies, are here given their due in their rightful concerns and are even surpassed in the seriousness of thir approach. Unvaried in its emphasis, the melody sounds forth from Luther's theology of the cross: Whoever would follow me, let him deny himself and take up his cross, and follow me! Here the enormous claim of this theology becomes directly clear. A glance at Reformation history shows that Luther did not evade this claim.

The great mass of available material forces us to be brief, all the more since it always deals basically with the same idea.

1. Christians must become like their Master in all things. They must therefore take Christ's disgrace upon themselves. The Christian life is one of lowliness (W. XXXI, 2, 36, 38ff.; LW 16, 52; W. XLIII, 672, 27ff.; LW 5, 353ff.; W. XLIV, 109, 38ff.; LW 6, 147), just as surely as Christ lived here on earth in the state of humiliation (W. II, 600, 10ff.; LW 27, 385).[144] Christ has preceded us on the way that rejects all human greatness (W. XXX, 2, 412, 25ff.; LW 17, 194). Forsakenness, impotence, and despair become our lot in this discipleship (W. I, 198, 20ff.; LW 14, 181f.; W. V, 82, 31ff.; W. XL, 1, 191, 25f.; LW 26, 106). The Christian's glory consists exclusively in this weakness and lowliness (W. II, 613, 31ff.; LW 27, 404; W. V, 256, 9ff.). For in spite of everything faith knows of a "nevertheless" (W. V, 53, 31ff.; LW 14, 321).

2. The Christian life is a discipleship of suffering (W. V, 177, 15ff.). It demonstrates its lowliness in that it leads into suffering (W. V, 108, 38ff.). Christ's suffering is still repeated daily in our

lives (W. III, 167, 24ff.; LW 10, 139).[145] Therefore our sufferings
are a work of the Holy Spirit (W. V, 639, 20f.); God does not want
self-chosen sufferings (W. XVIII, 489, 15ff.; LW 14, 152). When
our will is not done, then God's will can be done (W. II, 106, 26ff.;
LW 42, 44f.). But our suffering is God's will. God does his alien
work when he leads us into suffering. But thereby he aims at his
proper work, even when we do not recognize it (cf. W. XLIV, 600,
25ff.; LW 8, 29). Through suffering we shall arrive at the sabbath
of the soul (W. VI, 248, 1ff.; LW 44, 77).

This has already brought us to the question concerning the sense
and purpose of these sufferings. It is none other than that of un-
folding faith and making it assert itself.[146] Luther certainly knows
of a suffering that is punishment for sin (W. I, 182, 16ff.), but the
fact that suffering and faith belong together is a characteristic of
the theology of the cross (W. V, 137, 36ff.; 382, 9ff.; VI, 208, 6ff.;
LW 44, 28). Suffering proves to be the surest way to God,[147] or
rather, in suffering God meets us (W. VI, 223, 15ff.; LW 44, 46; W.
XXXI, 2, 386, 32ff.; LW 17, 160f.). Hence suffering is to be regarded
as a sanctuary which hallows man, that is, sets him apart from his
natural works for service to God (W. VI, 248, 16ff.; LW 44, 78).
Sufferings are a sign of God's grace, proof that we are God's children.[148] For God's eyes are always directed toward the depth and
nothing lofty can stand before him. But when a man is hidden in
this depth he experiences God's wonderful, saving creative power.[149]
Of course, the suffering of the saints will come to an end only at
the last day (W. V, 352, 20ff.). But in contrast to the suffering of the
ungodly, its purpose is not punishment and destruction but grace
and cleansing (W. V, 367, 11ff.).

3. The discipleship in suffering, however, is nothing else but following the cross. Since the cross stands in the midst of Christ's life,
the Christian's life is a discipleship of suffering. The idea of suffering in the theology of the cross does not rest on cosmological and
metaphysical presuppositions, but is oriented to a concrete event.
It has nothing to do with the ascetically dualistic conception of the
body. It does not in any way proceed from the idea that the body
as a hindrance to the higher faculties of man must be killed. This
is already excluded on the basis of the central thought of justification. Suffering may never become a good work. But even the
theology of the cross has essentially nothing to do with this ascetic thought. In the theology of the cross suffering is understood
throughout theologically, not anthropologically, that is, not on the

basis of reflection on human nature, but on the basis of God's reve-
latory activity in history. And the fact that this revelation of God
in history is summed up in the cross explains the high significance
of the idea of suffering.

Christ's cross and the Christian's cross belong together (W. XXXI,
2, 165, 1ff.; LW 16, 229f.; W. XL 2, 171, 23ff.; LW 27, 133f.). Already for this reason every thought of man's merit that he might
acquire through suffering is excluded (W. XXXI, 2, 153, 29ff.; LW
16, 215f.). When we bear our cross we are doing nothing special,
but we are simply showing that we are linked together with Christ
(W. III, 646, 20ff.; X, 3, 119, 3ff.). And not every suffering may
claim to be discipleship of the cross (W. X, 3, 115, 15ff.).

What does it mean to bear Christ's cross? "The cross of Christ is
nothing else than forsaking everything and clinging with the heart's
faith to Christ alone, or forsaking everything and believing that
this is what it means to bear the cross of Christ" (W. I, 101, 19ff.).
Thus the cross becomes the sign of being God's children (W. LVI,
194, 9ff.; LW 25, 77). But beyond this, Luther can see in all of creation reference to the cross (W. III, 646, 39ff.).

Why, then, does man shun the cross and seek to extricate himself
from this general connection with it? It is because we do not press
on from the alien work to the proper work; for the alien work is,
at the start, the cross (W. I, 112, 24ff.; III, 62, 36ff.). The way of
the cross signifies an annihilation, but precisely in this it proves itself to be the "short way" (W. I, 123, 38ff.). The way of the cross
steps as a third new thing over against the active life and the
contemplative life, equally distant from mysticism and work piety.

> So we are taught here to believe in hope against hope. This
> wisdom of the cross is today exceedingly hidden in a deep
> mystery. Nor is there any other way to heaven than this cross
> of Christ. Therefore we must beware that the active life with
> its works and the contemplative life with its speculations do not
> lead us astray. Both are very attractive and peaceful, but for
> that reason also dangerous, until they are tempered by the cross
> and disturbed by adversaries. But the cross is the safest of
> all. Blessed is he who understands it (W. V, 84, 39ff.).

In a different way, but no less than the contemplative life, the cross
is a school of understanding (W. V, 216, 38ff.). "The cross puts
everything to the test" (W. V, 179, 31; cf. W. V, 188, 18ff.).

Thus the Christian's life according to the theology of the cross is nothing else than a "being crucified with Christ." [150] Orthodoxy has emphasized this thought in its practical piety. But it has removed it from its immediate connection with the doctrine of Christ's work and assigned it to the doctrine of sanctification. Orthodoxy was totally concerned with emphasizing the all-sufficiency of Christ's sacrifice. For that reason it isolated the doctrine concerning Christ's work. Luther knew that the true meaning of Christ's suffering can be discovered only in the act of experiencing, acting, and suffering. "The real and true work of Christ's passion is to make man conformable to Christ, so that man's conscience is tormented in like measure as Christ was pitiably tormented in body and soul by our sins" (W. II, 138, 19ff.; LW 42, 10). "For it is inevitable, whether in this life or in hell, that you will have to become conformable to Christ's image and suffering" (W. II, 138, 35ff.; LW 42, 10f.). "Christ's passion must be met not with words or forms, but with life and truth" (W. II, 141, 37f.; LW 42, 14). Luther said this in his *Meditation on Christ's Passion*, 1519, a writing in which for the first time he presented a basic rejection of the monastic romantic devotion to Jesus, for which the contemplation of Christ's passion was a spiritual treat. Consequently the charge of Catholicizing cannot be raised against Luther's demand of "being crucified together."

There exists on the Protestant side a false reliance on Jesus' wounds which Luther would have designated a genuine veneration of the cross as little as the eager cult of the relics of the cross on the part of medieval Catholicism.[151] What matters is not that we encase the splinters of the cross in gold and silver, but that we bear with joy the marks of Christ's suffering (W. II, 613, 37ff.; LW 27, 404) in our own body.[152] Only when we experience suffering is the treasure which Christ provided for us according to orthodox teaching, namely, forgiveness, imparted to us (W. XXXI, 2, 153, 8ff.; LW 16, 215).

Being crucified with Christ takes place in two ways: inwardly through mortification, and outwardly through enmity of the world.

a) "Those who belong to Christ have crucified their flesh" (Gal. 5:24). It will not be necessary to review in detail what light the theology of the cross sheds on this word of Paul. What was said about the critical delimitation of faith needs to be repeated here. Except that now all of this will have to be related to the practical function. What was true there is true also here: "It is necessary that we be destroyed and rendered formless, in order that Christ may be formed and be alone in us" (W. II, 548, 28f.; LW 27,

308).[153] Baptism [154] stands not only at the beginning of the Christian life, but in the act of baptism we have the symbol of the whole Christian life: a constant dying and rising with Christ (W. VI, 534, 31ff.; LW 36, 69).

The monastic life also rests on the idea of mortification. But we have already shown how Luther's understanding of the discipleship of suffering differs from every ascetic-dualistic one. And the monastic understanding is such a one. That Luther's understanding of mortification is in no sense monkish is shown by a sentence from his lectures on Genesis: "These are true mortifications. They do not happen in deserts, away from the society of human beings. No, they happen in the household itself and in the government" (W. XLIII, 214, 3ff.; LW 4, 109). But the sharp line of demarcation between monkish self-mortification and Luther's thought of the dying of the old man must be drawn already on the basis of the doctrine of justification. Mortification is no meritorious work. It is not the precondition for faith which obtains grace, but the other way around, mortification presupposes faith. Luther expressly affirmed this in opposition to the Enthusiasts (W. XVIII, 139, 13ff.; LW 40, 149). They, too, strongly emphasized the thought of the "cross." In this point they simply stand on Luther's shoulders. But they have bent this idea back into its medieval form. They have again subsumed the cross under the concept of "the work of man." [155] They seek the cross, Luther stands under the cross. They boast of their cross, Luther boasts of the grace of God (W. XVIII, 65, 24ff.; LW 40, 81). Luther's thought concerning the cross dare under no circumstances be understood legalistically. The theology of the cross stands in the sharpest contrast to every kind of moralism (W. II, 597, 12ff.; LW 27, 379f.).

b) Being crucified with Christ shows itself also in that, according to Luther, a true Christian must necessarily incur the enmity of the world (W. X, 1, I, 40, 19ff.). The world's enmity is a sign of the genuineness of discipleship (W. I, 214, 1ff.). The gospel itself is an offense to the world; it arouses strife and conflict everywhere (W. XVIII, 626, 22ff.; LW 33, 52). For that reason Christians, as champions of this gospel, are "accounted as sheep for the slaughter" (W. VI, 226, 3ff.; LW 44, 49f.). In all seriousness Luther considers martyrdom a concomitant of the Christian life that is not to be deemed strange any longer. In fact, he seems to find a significant difference between the Old and New Testaments in that in the Old Covenant God allowed his people to come only into mortal danger, while in the New Covenant he surrenders them to death itself (W. V, 276, 1ff.).[156] For Christians are deeply involved participants in the conflict between God and the devil; here it is hand to hand combat (W. XL, 2, 174, 24ff.; LW 27, 136). But since they know under whose banner they are fighting, they suffer according to the flesh but glory in the spirit (W. XL, 1, 680, 10ff.; LW 26, 453).

4. Into this context belongs the idea of conformity with Christ. Through suffering with Christ we are conformed to him. Like him we divest ourselves of the "form of God" and put on the "form of a servant" (W. LVI, 171, 16ff.; LW 25, 151). We renounce all pride, all glory and honor before the world and before ourselves, and let ourselves be drawn into Christ's suffering (W. I, 216, 28ff.; IV, 645, 15ff.). This says nothing about mysticism. At least it does not go beyond what we said earlier in connection with the question about faith and Christ. To be conformed to Christ means nothing else but experiencing the fact of the cross also in our lives. When the cross remains not simply a fact of history, but when it is erected in the midst of our life, then we are people who have been conformed to Christ (W. II, 138, 19ff.; LW 42, 10). We must all be conformed tc Christ, if not in this life, then in hell (W. II, 138, 35ff.; LW 42, 10f.). But, of course, it is not in our power to do this. Even with our best-intentioned exertions we cannot compel the "being conformed tc Christ"; it is God's gift, not our work.[157] However, we can and should pray for it (W. II, 138, 35ff.; LW 42, 11). For God himself wants us to be conformed in all things to the image of his Son (W. I, 571, 34ff.; LW 31, 153), and do this altogether voluntarily (W. IV, 645, 21ff.).

The life under the cross presents itself at its climax as "conformity with Christ." In this idea we have before us an exact parallel of what was said when the concept of faith was presented in connection with the question of faith and Christ. Just as the concept of faith in its negative and positive aspects finds its climax in relation to Christ, so the view of the Christian life in its negative and positive sides climaxes in the idea of conformity with Christ. In this idea both the hiddenness and lowliness as well as the supreme glory and greatest riches of the Christian life are comprehended.

C. The Cross and the Christian Life

It may be useful to demonstrate in individual concrete points the hiddenness and character of suffering of the Christian life, which we have presented in general.

1. The loveliest gift accompanying the Christian life is *peace*. Through faith we have peace (W. III, 567, 12ff.). But this happens through faith! The theology of the cross cannot dispense with that. If pietism demands more, it only shows that it has moved a considerable distance away from Luther. For that very reason it is so easily exposed to psychological distortions. Christian peace has nothing to do with such peace. The contrast "harmonious and inharmonious nature" lies beneath the peace which surpasses all understanding. But for that very reason this peace is an object of faith and therefore a hidden treasure (W. LVI, 246, 11ff.; LW 25, 232; W. Br. 1, 47, 27ff.). The world sees nothing of this peace, and feeling and experience go away empty-handed. Here, too, the cross proves itself to be a great sign of concealment (W. LVI, 424, 27ff.; LW 25, 415; W. LVI, 425, 8ff.; LW 25, 416f.).

The way of peace is the way of the cross; God himself is hidden under the cross, and therefore peace is to be found only under the cross and suffering (W. I, 90, 6ff.). One who seeks peace misses the true peace; one who shuns the cross will not find peace (W. V, 318, 34ff.). Peace is not to be sought by way of empirical experience, as pietism thinks. According to Luther, that would be tempting God. For in that way we would forsake the stance of faith and attempt to have peace in physical reality rather than in faith. But we also have Christ, who is our peace, only by faith (W. I, 541, 5ff.; LW 31, 100). But this peace brings with it discord in externals. The world's enmity is the dowry of the peace hidden in God (W. II, 456, 31ff.; LW 27, 170).

2. We may expect to find a similar line of thought as we ask about the nature of *joy* in the Christian life. Faith brings joy just as it brings peace (W. III, 57, 34ff.; LW 10, 70). God hates sadness (W. XLIII, 335, 1ff.; LW 4, 278). Sadness is an indication that God has forsaken us, at least for a time (W. XLII, 535, 39ff.). Why should we not rejoice when we look to God? (W. I, 173, 31ff.).

But this already touches the other side of the matter. It has to do with joy "in the Holy Spirit" (W. III, 57, 34f.; LW 10, 70). God's promises are the cause of joy; the certainty that God does not lie in his promises makes glad the heart (W. IV, 360, 6ff.). The Christian's joy is determined eschatologically through and through. There would be no joy without hope (W. IV, 380, 35ff.). Joy is based not on some earthly thing but in hope (W. LVI, 465, 1ff.; LW 25, 457). Hence it cannot be understood as an expression of our inner mood. On the contrary, the joy we are dealing with here rises up precisely above sadness. This joy arises only when we despair of ourselves and experience nothing but displeasure and sadness in ourselves (W. I, 173, 24ff.). One who finds the cause of his joy in himself surely does not have the support of the word of God (W. LVI, 423, 23ff.; LW 25, 415). But this joy can be understood just as little on the basis of our external situation, for the Christian lacks everything that gives the carnal man occasion for joy (W. V, 178, 21ff.). Also our joy partakes of the character of hiddenness in our Christian life. All of this is comprehended in the sentence: Our joy is a work of the Holy Spirit (W. VII, 548, 4f.; LW 21, 300).

3. Also the Christian's *happiness* is hidden. Luther expresses himself on this subject in detail in his already mentioned explanation of the first psalm in his *Operationes in psalmos.* Under Luther's hand the text reaches a far greater depth than it originally possessed.

All people, says Luther, are concerned with the question about happiness. But neither the answer of philosophy nor general opinion satisfies (W. V, 26, 30ff.; LW 14, 287). The answer of Scripture, however, is placed in opposition to all others (W. V, 27, 5ff.; LW 14, 287). If we strip the answer of its Old Testament form, we arrive at the sentence that only the life under the cross can bring true happiness. But then this happiness is a hidden one, perceptible only to faith and experience (W. V, 36, 15ff.; LW 14, 298f.). Consequently, what the psalmist says about the prosperity of the godly dare not be understood in a physical sense (W. V, 41, 27ff.; LW 14, 304).[158] The psalmist is here speaking "in spirit"; he wants to be heard "in faith" (W. V, 42, 27ff.; LW 14, 305). For we take the greatest of all miracles upon our lips when we speak of the happiness of the godly (W. V, 41, 31ff.; LW 14, 304). Also the psalmist defines happiness as being free of evil; the only difference is that the world takes this with reference to earthly things, while the psalmist refers it to faith. Precisely because it is not meant in a physical sense, one can speak about it only figuratively and allegorically (W. V, 36, 29ff.; LW 14, 299). With all of this we are again moving in lines of thought that are thoroughly eschatological in their orientation. It is thus the final mark of the blessed man that he lives in hope (W. V, 38, 6ff.; LW 14, 300).

4. However, the character of hiddenness in the Christian life can be demonstrated not only at concrete points in the life of every single Christian, but we recognize it again as we look at Luther's thoughts on Christ's kingdom and on the church from this point of

view. Let us turn, first, to Luther's statements about the kingdom of Christ (regnum Christi).

First of all, we hear again that Christ's kingdom is spiritual and therefore hidden (W. V, 58, 38ff.; LW 14, 328. W. XI, 182, 17ff.; XVIII, 514, 20f.; LW 14, 185), whose only weapons are the Word and faith (W. V, 377, 34ff.; IX, 184, 6ff.). Its subjects are poor, despised people (W. V, 286, 31ff.; XVIII, 513, 33ff.; LW 14, 184; W. XXXI, 2, 86, 15f.; LW 16, 120). The kingdom of grace is a kingdom of faith, and here we must recall what was said about the critical delimitation of the concept of faith (W. II, 457, 21ff.; LW 27, 171; W. V, 285, 29ff.). When we call to mind the contexts of faith, the hidden God, and the cross, we are not surprised to hear that the cross stands in the midst of this kingdom of faith (W. V, 129, 1ff.). But we share in Christ's cross only when we take the cross upon ourselves (W. V, 69, 5ff.; LW 14, 342). Thus the course of this kingdom is the exact opposite of that of all other kingdoms (W. V, 453, 32ff.). For that reason it is an insurmountable offense to the natural man; he cannot and will not acknowledge it (W. V, 68, 35ff.; LW 14, 342).

But as a hidden kingdom of faith the kingdom of Christ points beyond itself, just like the Christian life. The kingdom of glory will follow the kingdom of grace. Christmas is prelude to the parousia (W. X, I, 1, 44, 5ff.). Then Christ will rule in glory over his enemies also (W. IX, 183, 23ff.; W. XXXI, 2, 79, 8ff.; LW 16, 111).[159] Consequently, if the water sometimes reaches up to the neck of the subjects in Christ's kingdom, they may comfort themselves with the hope, "We suffer with him, that we may also be glorified together with him" (Rom. 8:17; W. I, 204, 20ff.).[160]

5. What is true of Christ's kingdom is true, self-evidently, also of the church. For the true church is nothing else than Christ's kingdom. Therefore in Luther's writings, from the earliest to the latest, we meet the idea of the hiddenness of the true church. We may dispense with a detailed review of the passages, since in substance they offer little that is new. In the Dictata super Psalterium the idea is expressed mainly in the familiar antitheses "carnal—spiritual, visible—invisible," which characterize this work in general.[161] Later on the visible—invisible model recedes, but the idea of the church's hiddenness remains (cf. W. V, 451, 1ff.; 456, 31ff.; VI, 293f.). "The church is hidden, the saints are unknown" (W. XVIII, 652, 23; LW 33, 89). Consequently, when Erasmus appealed against Luther to the unanimous tradition of the church, Luther replied that pre-

cisely therein lay the problem as to what the true church is. "The church of God is not as commonplace a thing, my dear Erasmus, as the phrase 'the church of God'; nor are the saints of God met with as universally as the phrase 'the saints of God.' They are a pearl and precious jewels, which the Spirit does not cast before swine but keeps hidden, as Scripture says, lest the ungodly should see the glory of God" (W. XVIII, 651, 24ff.; LW 33, 88).

Perhaps it is a basic error when we appeal to church history (W. XVIII, 650, 27ff.; LW 33, 86). The true church has always been a "forsaken city" (W. XXXI, 2, 407, 3ff.; LW 17, 186). Hence it is altogether consonant with the theology of the cross to say, "I believe in the church," because the church is hidden under the cross (W. XXXI, 2, 220, 32ff.; LW 16, 299; W. XXXI, 2, 506, 13ff.; LW 17, 318). It may be noted that these last citations are from Luther's lectures on Isaiah (1527-1530), hence from his later period. The idea of the church's hiddenness is not from the pre-Reformation period, but from the Reformation years. A few passages from the Genesis lectures will serve to document this fact (W. XLIV, 109, 25ff.; LW 6, 147; 110, 3ff.). The church, the world's most precious treasure, is regarded as nothing by the world (W. XLIII, 139, 37ff.; LW 4, 6).

The hiddenness of the church, however, is given expression in its form of suffering. It is a fault of Protestantism that at times it has taken this idea of Luther's so lightly. Luther regarded cross and suffering as the church's most precious treasure; but the church that bears Luther's name has often not taken this sufficiently to heart (W. I, 613, 23ff.; LW 31, 227). In Luther's eyes a church that is all too militant and vocal in its politics is suspect (W. V, 227, 7ff.). The true church, on the contrary, is a church of martyrs. The new humanity that Christ wanted is the suffering church (W. V, 307, 36ff.). Only that church has the full right to call itself the church of Christ which follows her Lord in all things. Hence Luther lists cross and suffering among the marks of the church. In his book *Of the Councils and the Church,* 1539, Luther counts seven marks by which the church can be recognized, and he would prefer to call them the seven sacraments of the church, if the term "sacrament" had not already taken on a different meaning (W. L, 643, 2ff.; LW 41, 166). As the seventh mark of the church Luther mentions "the holy possession of the sacred cross" (W. L, 641, 35ff.; LW 41, 164). Hence it is part of the church's essence to be in suffering; a church of which that cannot be said has become untrue to its destiny. Against this it may not be urged that we are dealing here with an isolated utterance of Luther which should not be pressed. For, in the first place, it is not isolated (cf. W. XLII, 188, 14ff.; LW 1, 253f.), and furthermore, it follows from the entire context of his theology of the cross. Luther therefore uses the idea of the church's suffering condition in a critical way against the papacy [162] and in his judgment of church history.[163]

We may finally close with the same thought as in our presentation of the kingdom of Christ. Even though the church here too exists in hiddenness, it is the only thing in the world that has permanence (W. XL, 3, 505, 14ff.; LW 13, 88) and will finally gain the victory (W. V, 533, 16ff.).

6. In this connection, finally, new light is shed on Luther's attitude toward *allegory*.[164] It is known that Luther rejected allegorical exegesis already at an early stage.[165] It is, of course, equally true that he did not free himself completely of it as long as he lived. But this is not our concern at this point. Here we are not asking about Luther's attitude toward allegorical *exegesis*, but about the way he evaluated the allegories that he found already in the text. Luther himself was fully clear on this difference (W. V, 51, 33ff.; LW 14, 318f.). In certain cases allegory contains the real meaning. But why does the writer employ figurative speech? Luther explains it on the basis of the confessional character of scriptural statements.[166] God himself reveals himself in concealment; and therefore Scripture, too, speaks in the cloak of a figure. The Word addresses itself to faith; and faith is directed to what is hidden (W. V, 36, 29ff.; LW 14, 299; W. V, 52, 9ff.; LW 14, 319).

Luther wants to understand allegory in this profound sense. To him it is not rhetorical trifling, but the verbal expression of God's allegorical activity. Luther takes the meaning of allegory back to the distinction between God's alien work and God's proper work (W. V, 63, 28ff.; LW 14, 335). With this formula Luther was able to give expression to the profoundest insights of his theology of the cross. The cross of Christ is itself an allegorical work of God (W. V, 245, 6). By means of his theology of the cross a unique understanding of allegory disclosed itself to Luther.

D. Humility, Trial, Prayer

We have presented the hiddenness of the Christian life and we have seen that according to its content it had to be described as a discipleship in suffering. We sought to understand both on the basis of Luther's view of God and of his concept of faith. In the third place, we demonstrated these basic elements in connection with various individual problems. Now, in conclusion, we want to discuss in a separate section three especially important marks of the life under the cross. They are humility, trial, prayer. In them the special nature of the ideas developed here will once more appear in adaptable form. In three concentric circles we will once again circumscribe the center of Luther's theology of the cross.

1. Humility

Humility [167] is an old monastic ideal. Luther takes up this familiar concept. He uses it as an expression of his new insights.

This concept plays a large role in the *Dictata super Psalterium*. Humility is the basic virtue of the life under the cross, just as pride is the real and greatest sin.[168] For Luther humility becomes most intimately connected with faith. Faith teaches humility (W. IV, 76, 37ff.). For faith is denial of ourselves, total rejection of self and reliance on God's grace. In this negation of all human claims, faith is one with humility (W. III, 462, 29ff.; LW 10, 404). It is no longer humility when it begins to boast. Humility is the conscious renunciation of all human qualities that we might bring to bear.[169] Humility is perfected self-knowledge in the presence of God (W. III, 290, 31ff.; LW 10, 239; W. III, 26, 28ff.; LW 10, 27; cf. LVI, 346, 18ff.; LW 25, 235). In that respect humility must precede faith and belongs to the critical substructure of faith. Only where this substructure has been laid, can justification by faith come into being (W. III, 345, 29f.; LW 10, 290). Luther emphasizes this aspect of faith so strongly that he can even say, "Humility alone saves" (W. IV, 473, 17). The righteousness of God consists in humiliation down to the lowest depths of the heart (W. III, 458, 3ff.; LW 10, 401f.; W. IV, 405, 23). Here humility and faith are used interchangeably. Like faith, humility is not one virtue among other virtues, but is, in the first instance, a renunciation of all virtuousness.

Humility is awareness of the fact that we cannot stand before God on the basis of our virtues (W. III, 301, 30ff.; LW 10, 250). But this is also the basic insight of faith. For that reason Luther can use humility and faith interchangeably with regard to justification (W. III, 462, 34ff.; LW 10, 404). With the idea of humility thus understood Luther has already left the sphere of Catholic work-righteousness behind. It is true, however, that this humility cannot completely deny its monkish coloring. Our relationship to our neighbor and to the world is to be regulated by humility. In this regard we may sometimes detect almost quietistic [170] notes in the *Dictata super Psalterium* (W. IV, 231, 7f.).[171] But we may not label everything specifically monkish that is often simply New Testament teaching. The demand to overcome evil with good and to suffer injury rather than do it is quite in line with the spirit of the Sermon on the Mount and is Pauline besides (W. III, 160, 7ff.; LW 10, 135; W. IV, 131, 33ff.). One who really takes justification by grace seriously can no longer wish to be dogmatic in his life.[172] The ethic of grace crowds out the ethic of the law. It makes no sense to brand this as a monkish stance.

Thus the view of humility in the Dictata is not entirely uniform. In it we can distinguish two lines that have not been fully harmonized. The concept of humility Luther derived from monastic tradition. From this perspective the first line is to be understood: humility as humble behavior. In the main it manifests itself in a very specific stance toward the world and toward the neighbor. Hence it is an ethical concept. But Luther has traced the monastic ideal of humility to its ultimate basis and has pursued it to its ultimate implications, thus gaining the upper hand over it. Even the most consummate act of humility is a work of man. He always has something left in his hands of which he can be proud. But humility must then be something that must be delimited against all pious human exertion. In this way it moves next to faith. This is the second line in the *Dictata*. Humility is nothing else than perfected self-knowledge, which includes justifying faith. When Luther speaks of justification through humility, this may not be understood in the Catholic-synergistic sense. On the contrary, it corresponds most exactly to the concept of faith in the theology of the cross, when Luther occasionally equates humility with faith (cf. also the expression "humility of faith," W. IV, 231, 7).

As expected, the further development of the concept moves in the direction of the second line. In the lectures on Romans we still find the "monastic elements" (e.g., W. LVI, 448, 20ff.; LW 25, 440f.; W. LVI, 449, 20ff.; LW 25, 441f.). But we also find again the characteristic coordination of faith and humility (W. LVI, 218, 7ff.; LW 25, 204). The lectures on Romans do represent a long step forward with regard to our question. Luther notes that the Latin word *humilitas* has a twofold meaning, depending upon whether it is the translation of *tapeinosis* or *tapeinophrosyne* (W. LVI, 471, 18ff.;

LW 25, 463). In the one case *humilitas* should be rendered lowliness and nothingness, in the other case humility. This distinction becomes important for Luther later on.

The Heidelberg Disputation offers us nothing new (W. I, 357, 17ff.; LW 31, 44; W. I, 358, 30ff.; LW 31, 46). Of interest here is only the fact that a clear parallel between the relationship of humility and grace and that of alien work and proper work is drawn (W. I, 361, 1ff.; LW 31, 50f.). However, this thought is implicitly present already in the *Dictata*.

On the contrary, the *Operationes in psalmos* provide an important advance,[173] and this in a twofold respect.

a) Here Luther arrives at the basic knowledge that in the Scriptures *humilitas* hardly ever means the virtue of humility, but rather must be taken to mean lowliness, nothingness, and being suppressed (W. V, 656, 24ff.).[174] Only in this way has the concept been completely divested of its monkish garb. Every form of synergism is excluded. But this passage shows all the more clearly what central significance this concept has in the theology of the cross. As delineated earlier, the entire Christian estate is nothing else than *humilitas* in this sense. The less the concept is understood in the Catholic sense, the better it fits into the theology of the cross. Hence, the idea of *humilitas* should not have been exploited as proof for the monkish character of the theology of the cross.

b) If in this way the second of the lines set forth in the *Dictata* is featured with all clarity and thereby the first is already pushed into the background, the validity of the latter, the real monkish line itself, receives a further strong limitation. The boundary of humility is love to the neighbor. There may be cases where the suffering of injustice is plainly a violation of the duty of love (W. V, 233, 33ff.). In the *Operationes* the monkish ideal of humility is therefore shattered from two directions. This clears the track to the wonderful expositions of Luther on *humilitas* in his explanation of the Magnificat. Luther has never depicted the essence of *humilitas* more beautifully. At the same time we come here to the high point of the development of the thoughts in the concept as already outlined.

Luther is concerned with the explanation of the words, "He has regarded the low estate of his handmaiden" (Luke 1:48). Here Luther harks back to the basic insight he had gained in the *Operationes*. *Humilitas* cannot be translated with "humility," but it is "nothing else than a disregarded, despised, and lowly estate, such as that of men who are poor, sick, hungry, thirsty, in prison, suffering and dying" (W. VII, 560, 16ff.; LW 21, 313),

> for how should such pride and vainglory be attributed to this pure and righteous Virgin, as though she boasted of her humility in the presence of God? For humility is the highest of all the virtues, and no one could boast of possessing it except the very proudest of mortals. It is God alone who knows humility; he alone judges it and brings it to light; so that no one knows less about humility than he who is truly humble (W. VII, 560, 7ff.; LW 21, 313).[175]

For that reason the monkish striving after humility makes no sense at all. The way of humility is not from outside in, but from inside out (W. VII, 562, 5ff.; LW 21, 315). Thus the monkish ideal of humility is overcome precisely by being taken seriously. True humility can only consist in nothingness.[176]

But now a last misunderstanding must be cleared away. Our nothingness does not in a positive way fill the gap created by the rejection of the ideal of humility. We cannot place our nothingness before God as a merit. No, it is really nothing but nothingness in the strict sense of the term. Not our nothingness but God's grace alone is to be glorified. "Hence the stress lies not on the word 'low estate,' but on the word 'regarded.' For not her humility but God's regard is to be praised. When a prince takes a poor beggar by the hand, it is not the beggar's lowliness but the prince's grace and goodness that is to be commended" (W. VII, 561, 16ff.; LW 21, 314). With these thoughts we have arrived at the point where the two lines, which had to be distinguished in the *Dictata*, converge. With them Luther has thought through the idea of humilitas in the evangelical sense to its logical conclusion.

Excursus on the Concept of Humilitas in St. Bernard

In the writings of Bernard of Clairvaux we find the most beautiful and profound things that have been said about humilitas before Luther. There can be no doubt that Luther has learned from Bernard also in this respect (cf. W. V, 656, 24ff.).[177] For that reason we shall briefly examine Bernard's view of humilitas.

Also for Bernard humilitas stands in the center of the Christian life, in this case the monastic life. The whole spiritual life is built on humilitas *(in cant.* 36, 5). The first sin was pride (cf. Luther), the arrogance of Lucifer *(De divers.* 66, 1). Correspondingly, hu-

militas must now be the first virtue, for humilitas is the opposite of
pride. For that reason humilitas must, first of all, be defined negatively as "contempt of one's own worth" *(de gradd. humil. et superb.*
4, 14). Exactly as with Luther humilitas is described as perfected
self-knowledge *(ibid.,* 1, 2). [178] Humilitas is the way to truth *(ibid.,*
1, 1; 2, 3). But everything depends on self-knowledge; and therefore
humilitas is to be preferred to all pious monastic works *(epistolae*
142). With these thoughts Bernard towers high above the average
level of monastic piety.

For the purpose of gauging the greatness of the difference, the
Rule of St. Benedict may be adduced here by way of comparison.[179] It does indeed stem from a much earlier period, but has
always remained normative for monastic piety. Bernard himself
cites it repeatedly in his *Tractatus de gradibus humilitatis et su-
perbiae.* Hence a comparison is no error in method at this point.
In chapter 7 of his rule, which bears the caption, *De humilitate,*
Benedict distinguishes 12 steps of humility. We should expect that
this sequence of steps would lead from an external view of humility to a completely internal one, and direct us from the works of
humility to the attitude of humility. The opposite is the case. Already the fact of basing the first step of humility on the fear of hell
seems inadequate to our evangelical sensibilities, but we are even
more astonished when we hear the description of the highest step
of humility:

> The twelfth step of humility is when the monk, not only in
> his heart but in his very body always shows humility to those
> who see him; that is, in the work of God, in the oratory, in
> the monastery, in the garden, on the road, in the field, or
> wherever he is sitting, walking, or standing, he is always with
> bowed head, his looks fixed on the ground, at every hour judg-
> ing himself guilty regarding his sins, so that he already regards
> himself as being placed in the tremendous judgment; always
> saying to himself in his heart what the tax collector in the
> Gospel said with eyes fixed to the ground: Lord, I, a sinner,
> am not worthy to lift up my eyes to heaven. And likewise with
> the prophet: I am bowed down, and I am humiliated in every
> way (Butler, ed., p. 37f.).

Thus the highest step is reached when the humble attitude is dis-
played in every gesture. It matters that one notices the humility.
Here the question does not come up at all, whether precisely in
this outward sign of humility the worst kind of pride again finds a

hiding place. On this point the analysis of the pious attitude is still on a very primitive level. With Bernard it is altogether different. He knows that it is the death of humility when it desires to manifest itself outwardly. Here, too, reality and appearance stand in an incompatible contrast *(in cant.* 16, 10).

With these thoughts Bernard comes close to Luther (cf. W. VII, 560, 7ff.; LW 21, 313). Luther's first line of humilitas, demonstrated above, goes back directly to Bernard. We could also establish the starting point of the second line (humilitas as perfected self-knowledge) in the case of Bernard. For that reason humilitas moves into relationship to justification also for him. It is the only merit man can claim before God *(De divers.* 26, 1; *in cant.* 54, 9). But it is also just at this point that the paths diverge. While Luther, on the basis of the thought that "humilitas justifies," is impelled onward to the understanding of humilitas as "nothingness," *humilitas* remains for Bernard the virtue of humility.[180] It remains a quality of man. If it is to be defined positively, it is described as obedience *(De divers.* 26, 2). By the element of voluntariness it differs from mere humiliation *(in cant.* 34, 3). Hence it is, after all, a thoroughly human act, inserted as such in the sequence of human acts. Humilitas leads only to the first step of truth; it constitutes the door only to the forecourt of the sanctuary *(in cant.* 42, 6; *de gradd. humil. et superb.* 6, 19). In this way humilitas is not the end of all works, but the chief work. Humility is a new state of mind; but this state of mind is understood as a "work." But when the idea of monkish humilitas is radically thought through to its conclusion, it must put an end to itself. In spite of promising starts, Bernard did not accomplish the decisive step beyond the monkish ideal of humility; that remained for one who was greater than he.

2. Trial

In humility it is above all the hiddenness of the Christian life that is given expression. It corresponds to the faith that sees nothing and feels nothing. To this the idea of trial *(tentatio)* contributes the content. If we were to undertake an abstract distinction, we could say: In the idea of humility we have the parallel to the purely formal definition of faith as the opposite of all objective experience, while in the idea of trial we become aware that this concept of faith is oriented in content to the view of the hidden God. Trial may also be brought into closer relationship to what was said in Section B of this chapter on the Christian life as discipleship in suffering, while humilitas corresponds to Section A. Only we dare not over-look the fact that Section B is simply a concrete explanation of Section A. In any case, what could be called the dramatic in the Christian life has its place here with trial. Here the general charac-ter of hiddenness and lowliness appears in a lively up and down. Humilitas is constantly put to the test in trial. But inasmuch as humilitas is most intimately associated with faith, the same may be said also of faith. In trial the existential aspect of faith achieves its highest demonstration. But we do not want to anticipate the detailed presentation.

Trials *(Anfechtungen)* run through Luther's entire life. They are practically a piece of his vocational consciousness.[181] Through trials Luther in the monastery gains his reformation insights (cf. the fa-mous self-confession in the *Explanations of the Ninety-five Theses,* W. I, 557, 33ff.; LW 31, 129). Through trials this insight has to stand the test again and again in later years. Any study of Luther's character will have to take especially this point very much into account. Here we have a different goal in mind. We do not want to present either a contribution to the analysis of Luther's personal-ity, or a complete doctrine concerning trial.[182] Our task consists simply in showing that the concept of trial is thoroughly appropriate in the context of the theology of the cross.[183]

This can be demonstrated from the most diverse angles. Let us think, first of all, of the general concept of the theology of the cross. The cross, we said, is the great no to every genuine religion. The cross is the great disturber of every quiescent knowledge of God that refuses to take its place in the movement of faith. At the cross offense arises. But to this the fact that also the godly life cannot be a quiescent, self-satisfied condition corresponds most exactly. Here, too, the offense must constantly be overcome by faith. Where this offense is excluded we are no longer dealing with a life in faith. When the offense assumes its most radical form, we speak of trial. We may say this to begin with in the most general way. If, then, the Christian life were to be without trial, it would not, in its ultimate dimensions, be a life of faith. A pious consciousness as a state of affairs could substitute for the conflict of faith. By accept-ing this quiescent pious consciousness we should already have adopted the theology of glory. According to the theology of the cross the worst kind of trial consists in not having any trial; for trial keeps faith in motion (W. XXXI, 1, 95, 10ff.; LW 14, 60; W. I, 128, 28ff.; II, 125, 32ff.; LW 42, 75; W. VI, 223, 33ff.). Life under the cross is a life of trial (W. II, 123, 1ff.; LW 42, 73; W. VII, 785, 3ff.; LW 42, 183f.). Theology of the cross is theology of trial (W. XLIII, 472, 13ff.; LW 5, 63).

The movement of faith, however, constantly pushes through from the hidden God to the revealed God, from the alien to the proper work. Trial arises when faith cannot execute this breakthrough. Thus a trial may arise as a result of the question concerning the meaning of suffering (W. XLIII, 202, 7ff.; LW 4, 92f.). It is the temptation of the "why" that drives us into such trials (W. XXXI, 2, 361, 19ff.; LW 17, 127). Sometimes it looks as if God were playing a game with the saints, but we do not see through this game (W. XLIV, 97, 16ff.; LW 6, 130f.; W. XLIV, 536, 8ff.; LW 7, 319; W. XLIII, 371, 24ff.; LW 4, 326). Yet in this game of God's we are dealing only with his alien work (W. XLIII, 203, 4ff.; LW 4, 94).[184] Another trial arises for faith from the fact that at times God appears to be contradicting himself. Luther demonstrates this by the example of Abraham. It is for this reason that Abraham has become the father of faith, because God subjected him to especially severe trials. Thus in connection with this man Luther develops not only his theology of faith, but also his theology of trial, another indication of how inseparably linked faith and trial are for Luther. In trial faith wrestles with the self-contradiction of God.[185]

The most severe trial comes upon a person when he believes he has been forsaken and rejected by God. Such a trial comes only to the "greatest of saints" (W. XLIV, 97, 25ff.; LW 6, 131). The trials of which Luther speaks in the passage cited from the Explanation of the Ninety-five Theses (W. I, 557, 33ff.; LW 31, 129) were of this sort. Luther can speak about them only because he himself has experienced them. In the language of monasticism it was called "suspension of grace" (W. XLII, 336, 10ff.; LW 2, 104).

In all these cases we are dealing with the hidden God. The significance of the trials points us back to the view of God in the theology of the cross, to the thought of the hidden God who arrives at this proper work only by way of his alien work.

But this means at once that in the doctrine of trials the concept of faith that is characteristic of the theology of the cross comes into view (W. XIX, 218, 13ff.). Faith alone is able, in trial, to hear "the deep, secret yea beneath and above the nay" (W. XVII, 2, 203, 32). This is then the highest degree of faith, to cling to the grace of God even in the trial of God-forsakenness (W. VI, 208, 34ff.; LW 44, 28). This faith is no trifle (W. V, 385, 17ff.); it is nothing less than a struggle with God against God (W. XLIV, 99, 3ff.; LW 6, 132f.; W. XL, 3, 519, 13ff.).

It is God himself who attacks man through trials. Luther also labeled the devil as the originator of trial.[186] In that case it is not difficult to overcome the trial, for the devil no longer has any power over the Christian. He has been defeated by Christ. But Luther can also trace the trial directly back to God. Only in this way it receives its severity because God himself is "assailing" man. Luther explicitly turns against the view as expressed in James 1:13 (W. XLIII, 201, 25ff.; LW 4, 92). The hidden God is a reality, not a mere pretense. The devil is only God's instrument, while God himself is the one at work (XL, 3, 519, 13ff.). In such moments Luther feels the full brunt of God's wrath over him.

What kind of advice can Luther give in such cases? None other than that one must cling to the Word.[187] And the Word, for Luther, is nothing else than Christ.[188] We are in trials when that Word has been torn out of our heart. The trial is overcome when Christ again speaks to us, when we again hear the Word (W. XXXI, 2, 22, 3ff.; LW 16, 30f.). Alongside the appeal to the Word is the insistence on the sacrament, especially baptism (W. XLIII, 203, 23ff.; LW 4, 94ff.).

But what if God should want to withdraw his word of grace, if he would want to cancel his promise to me? Even then, says Luther, we must hold fast to the word of promise. Luther dares to make the audacious statement: We must fight against God himself (W. XLIV, 97, 38ff.; LW 6, 131).[189] That is the faith that presses through from the alien work to the proper work, from the hidden to the revealed God in his highest form. For at the basis of the contrast of God's Word and God himself there is no other contrast than the one between the revealed God and the hidden God. Thus the turning point in the trial has clearly arrived when faith recognizes the trial as an alien work.

In conjunction with Holl, we have differentiated a double way of viewing trial on Luther's part; at one time he traces the trial back to the devil, at another time to God. We see now that this can only be a tentative distinction. Both views find their unity in the idea of the hidden God or the alien work, as the case may be. God conceals himself under the devil's mask. If faith succeeds in recognizing this as a mask, if it comes to the insight that in the alien work of trial God has become the devil,[190] then the trial is overcome.[191] On the basis of the idea of the hidden God we can understand it when Luther at times designates the devil and at times God as the author of the trial. It is no accident that precisely in the book where the hidden God plays a major role Luther wrote the sentence, "God . . . moves and acts also in Satan and ungodly man" (W. XVIII, 709, 21f.; LW 33, 176). Certainly also pastoral concerns are involved in the twofold way of viewing trials. Not everyone is strong enough to bear the thought that God is tempting him. Think only of Luther's explanation of the Sixth Petition in the *Small Catechism*. But calling attention to the pastoral character of Luther's theology does not seem to provide sufficient explanation for the fact that Luther could employ both ways of looking at trials. Only in the idea of the hidden God can we find the unity which is basic to the two disparate conceptions, but which does not always enter the consciousness. Thus the theology of the cross again proves itself to be a fruitful heuristic principle at a decisive point.

Hence in trial everything depends on our arriving at this decisive insight. Then we will know that the trial is only a test which God has sent us (W. XLIII, 203, 19ff.; LW 4, 94f.). Just when we have seen through the trial as an alien work, as a work of the devil, the gracious will of God is disclosed to us in the same trial. When we have seen the hidden God, we have recognized the revealed God. This insight brings great consolation to the harassed soul (W. XLIV, 201, 21ff.; LW 6, 271).[192]

In conclusion, we note that the question concerning the meaning and purpose of trial has already been made quite clear by what has been said. In a passage from the lectures on Genesis Luther mentions three reasons why trials are necessary: "The flesh is beset by sundry trials and scruples, in order that (a) its smugness may be removed and (b) occasion may not be lacking for occupying oneself with the Word and (c) prayer" (W. XLII, 673, 7ff.; LW 3, 174). In the course of our investigation we have already touched on all three of these reasons.

1. The trial destroys every presumption (W. V, 397, 30ff.), leads man to the knowledge of himself (W. II, 125, 8ff.; LW 42, 74; W. XLIII, 203, 26ff.; LW 4, 95), and prevents pride from rising in him (W. XLII, 491, 11ff.; LW 2, 320; XLII, 551, 37f.; LW 3, 5). At this point the inner connection between trial and humility is made strikingly plain.

2. The Word is grasped only by faith. But faith remains alive

only when it continues to overcome offense. It experiences God's
mercy only when it has felt God's wrath, and continues to feel it.
This happens in trial (W. XXXI, 2, 506, 30f.; LW 17, 319). If faith
is thus aroused in trial, it will be stronger when the trial is overcome (W. XLIII, 230, 37ff.; LW 4, 132).

3. In trial the existential aspect of faith comes to its full expression. The same must be said of prayer. Trial teaches prayer, prayer
overcomes trial (W. VI, 223, 15ff.; LW 44, 46f.; W. III, 62, 19ff.).

For that reason the Christian should gratefully receive the trial
as a gift from God's hand (W. VII, 785, 15ff.; LW 42, 183f.). He is
not to reflect on the trial but experience it (W. VII, 787, 1ff.; LW
42, 185). Then the experience of God's gracious guidance will not
fail to come in the end (W. XLII, 464, 14ff.; LW 2, 283).

All of this will have made clear that trial is a central concept of
the theology of the cross. It could be seriously considered whether
the entire theology of the cross might not best be developed on the
basis of this concept.[193] In any case, the three basic motifs of the
theology of the cross are crystalized in it: The view of the hidden
God, the thought of faith, and the message about life under the
cross.

3. Prayer

The last decision about the value of Luther's theology of the
cross must be made in connection with the question regarding
prayer. Just as every individual may consider his attitude toward
prayer as a test of the state of his faith—where there is no prayer,
there is in reality no faith—so it is also a vital question for a theology whether it has room for a doctrine of prayer. If the theology
of the cross fails at this point, it has not stood the test, and the
charge of "nihilism" can rightfully be raised against it.

There is no doubt that, viewed in the light of the theology of the
cross, the meaning and justification of prayer is by no means without its problems. Does not prayer aim at establishing that unbroken
communication between God and man, which must be labeled a
forbidden one according to the theology of the cross? Does it not
aim at leading beyond "believing" to "seeing"? Furthermore, is it
possible to speak of a certainty of being heard if God is a hidden
God? Dare we approach God with our petitions at all, knowing
that the Christian's way is the way of the cross, and that it is "directly contrary to our reason" when God wants to deal with us?

a) In all seriousness Luther raises such questions too. He has felt in its full weight the enormity of the process involved in a person's wanting to pray to God.[194] Prayer is either madness or marvel. When a person considers that with his prayer he wants to step into the presence of the living God, must not his courage fail? For prayer leads a person to know himself (W. II, 93, 20ff.; LW 42, 35). When man then sees his sin and senses God's holy wrath, how shall he then call on God, that God from whom he would prefer to flee? (W. XIX, 222, 25ff.).

But in this Luther sees the greatest temptation. As long as we stay with the question concerning our worthiness, we have not yet been liberated from the false stance of the person who thinks that he can offer God something in his prayer. Whoever thinks thus has not yet penetrated to a full knowledge of himself and does not yet know humility. True prayer is always a prayer with empty hands (W. III, 42, 21ff.; LW 10, 46). The true praying man has nothing but God, and him only by faith (W. XVIII, 484, 16ff.; LW 14, 146). A "secure" man cannot pray (W. I, 160, 21ff.). The validity of prayer consists in no way in our worthiness, or in anything that we might be able to contribute. Luther regards it as a prompting of the evil spirit when we constantly stare only at our unworthiness (W. VI, 235, 21ff.; LW 44, 62). There is a consciousness of sin which is disobedience to God. We must not look at our unworthiness but at God's command and promise (W. XLIII, 84, 1ff.; LW 3, 291). For it is God's word and promise alone that makes our prayer good and acceptable to God. The ardor and fervor of our devotion will not do it (W. II, 127, 36ff.; LW 42, 77; W. II, 175, 4ff.; LW 42, 87).

Thus Luther is anxiously concerned about not basing the validity of prayer on a subjective quality in the praying person. Such a quality may be present in a smaller or greater measure—but what constitutes the real essence of prayer is independent of that. This corresponds exactly to what we saw earlier in connection with the critical delimitation of faith. Just as faith had to be distinguished there from all given psychic functions, so here it has to be protected from being mistaken for a pious mood. Only because this critical substructure has been built can Luther encourage prayer (W. XLII, 663, 20ff.; LW 3, 161). Thus already in the question concerning prayer the special nature of the concept of faith in the theology of the cross becomes manifest.

b) But this is true in a far stronger degree when we consider Luther's thoughts on the answer to prayer. Here we find the thrust of his theology of the cross developed in all its cogency. All of its distinctive views are here repeated: the view of God, the concept of faith, the thought of suffering. The question concerning answer to prayer contains the whole theology of the cross in a nutshell.

In his lecture on Romans 8:26 (W. LVI, 375-381; LW 25, 364-370) Luther expounded his most original ideas on the answer to prayer.[195] At the head of his exposition Luther places the sentence: "It is not a bad sign, but a very good one, if things seem to turn out contrary to our requests. Just as it is not a good sign if everything turns out favorably for our requests" (W. LVI, 375, 1ff.; LW 25, 364f.). This harsh thesis follows with inexorable logic from Luther's theology of the cross. Behind it is clearly the view of the hidden God who can get to his proper work only by way of his alien work. The work of this God is hidden "under that which appears contrary to our conceptions and ideas" (W. LVI, 376, 32f.; LW 25, 366). Revelation is present only in concealment. Accordingly, apparent non-answer is the best answer.

But now, quite analogous to the presentation of the concept of the "rear parts," we can make the observation that this simultaneous relationship of answer and non-answer is joined by a successive one. "It is always the case that we understand our own work before it is done, but we do not understand the work of God until it has been done" (W. LVI, 377, 24ff.; LW 25, 367). God delays his answer, but in the end it will come. The further development can be linked predominantly with this thought. In this form the "under the contrary appearance" continues to remain in force for Luther.[196] Thus in his exposition of Psalm 130 (1517) Luther explains that we must wait for God's answer and not attach a "name" to God's help (W. I, 208, 30ff.). God proves himself to be the hidden God especially also in his answer to prayer, and hence we dare not prescribe measure or goal to his help (W. II, 177, 12ff.; LW 42, 89; W. VI, 233, 17ff.; LW 44, 59).[197] God often postpones granting our request in order to increase the zeal of our prayer (W. XLIII, 677, 23ff., 31ff.; LW 5, 360f.). To the praying person God becomes hidden, so that faith in prayer penetrates from the hidden God to the revealed God. (W. XLIV, 192, 27ff.; LW 6, 259).

c) With this we proceed to the third question which concerns the certainty of being heard. If the question concerning the answer to prayer corresponded more to the idea of the hidden God, we will now view the matter once again from the other side which corresponds to the idea about faith. In the last analysis, of course, the question concerning the certainty of being heard can be separated from the question concerning the answer to prayer as little as the concept of faith in the theology of the cross can be separated from the view of the hidden God. The full picture results only from both together.

We can be brief. A very definite concept of faith corresponds to the idea of the hidden God. What we have just said about the question concerning the answer to prayer determines what needs still to be said about the certainty of being heard. Here Luther gives equally strong emphasis to two things: [198]

1) The certainty of being heard is a certainty of *faith*. We now understand what that means. We remind ourselves here of the critical delimitation of the concept of faith (cf. W. II, 130, 14ff.; LW 42, 81; W. V, 87, 36f.; W. XVIII, 495, 36ff.; LW 14, 160).

2) The certainty of being heard is a *certainty* of faith. Precisely as certainty of faith it is more certain than empirical or rational certainty. Without this certainty prayer is fruitless; more than that, it is sacrilege, it is robbing God of his honor (W. II, 127, 6ff., but see also 127, 19ff.; LW 42, 76f.). To regard God as truthful under all circumstances is the highest form of worship, the highest religion (W. XLIII, 399, 28ff.; LW 4, 366).

Thus we see that in the question about prayer the whole complex of problems involved in the theology of the cross is summed up once again. Not only humility and trial have their place here (the former in the question concerning the validity of prayer, the latter in the question about the answer to prayer), but also the basic views of the theology of the cross (the ideas of God, of faith, and of suffering) can not for one moment be lost sight of. In the position which prayer occupies in Luther's theology [199] it becomes evident that the theology of the cross is no playing with terms. The existential element of faith, which we demonstrated already in connection with the concept of experience and again in connection with trial, is projected here with full clarity once again.[200] Prayer is the self-realization of faith.[201] Prayer and faith belong together in the most intimate way.[202] On this basis Luther engages in criticism of the Catholic practice of prayer, and on this basis he offers practical directives on how to pray properly. Unfortunately we cannot pursue these valuable ideas, since they do not belong into the framework of this investigation (cf. the tract addressed to Peter, the Master Barber: "A Simple Way to Pray for a Good Friend," 1535.

W. XXXVIII, 358-375; LW 43, 193-211). These thoughts prove to us again that the theology of the cross does not exclude the concreteness of the "godly life," but rather demands it. This does not make Luther unfaithful to the basic insights of his theology of the cross. For in prayer he does not, after all, seek an escape from all the hard paradoxes. Prayer is not a little garden of Paradise, where the one who is weary of the Word of the cross might take a little rest, but prayer is just the battleground where the sign of the cross has been raised.

PART THREE

THE

THEOLOGY OF THE CROSS

AND

MYSTICISM

Introduction

Thus far we have developed the ideas of Luther's theology of the cross without paying much attention to the question of its genesis. This corresponds also to the principal feature and goal of this work. We are here not concerned, in the first instance, with a historical investigation, but with introducing a point of view for the consideration of Luther's theology which we believe has wrongfully been neglected. Our chief task is to set forth what we understand to be Luther's theology of the cross according to its innermost coherence, and to clarify the inner unity of these ideas. We have largely forgotten how to grasp an intellectual phenomenon in its own logic—much to our loss. Think, for example, of a kind of New Testament exegesis that is less interested in the text itself than in what stands "behind the text." Since Denifle's attack also our Luther research has in part become a little overanxious in the endeavor to get "behind Luther," as important and necessary as this work still is. The justification of our presentation stands and falls with itself.

Even if it could be demonstrated beyond objection—something that can never succeed—, that Luther's theology of the cross is really only a shoot from the tree of medieval mysticism and monastic theology, it would still be worth while to trace this theology as an organic whole. Historical classification can never have the sense of being dispensed from a serious consideration of the object to be classified. On the contrary, we must say that the attempts to establish dependence will get away from a haphazard groping only when

147

the respective object of our investigation is clearly in view. It is this latter task, which must be the first one, that we have assumed here.

Nevertheless, we consider it our duty not simply to bypass the historical question. It impinges on us too closely to be ignored. Especially in the chapter on "Life under the Cross" we were reminded step by step of ideas from German mysticism. Humility, resignation, following the cross, conformity with Christ, all these are concepts familiar to late medieval mysticism. Did Luther simply take them over from there? Is his theology of the cross nothing more than "monk's theology," or was Luther able to put the stamp of his own spirit upon it? We have already touched on this question in our presentation, but to avoid repetition we did not want to unfold it at every individual point. We shall try to fill in the gaps as we now present in broad outline our position on the problem of the theology of the cross and mysticism. At the same time we stress that we must confine ourselves to a presentation of the main themes. A thorough investigation of all the details would go beyond the scope of our work. We would have to deal extensively with problems of Luther's biography (e.g., the questions concerning the contacts between Staupitz and Luther, the influence of the Brethren of the Common Life on Luther's development), but this is not the place for it. A study of the relevant sources, which are now available to us in critical editions, seemed more appropriate for our purpose.[203]

I.

Preliminary Systematic Considerations

For an investigation such as ours it is a perplexing circumstance that the views on what really constitutes mysticism do not at all agree.[204] Obviously the essence of mysticism is disclosed neither by way of etymology nor by way of psychology.[205] The psychological understanding has its limits in the forms in which mysticism appears in any age; but in these forms the essence of mysticism often enough appears blurred. We can grasp its essence only if we see in it an ultimate concern of man. But this is not possible by way of neutral observation. It is possible only when we on our part approach it with an ultimate stance. Concretely, only one who knows about faith by his own experience can have an open ear and a clear eye for the concerns of mysticism. Hence the question concerning the essence of mysticism can be answered only by means of the apparent detour through the other question, "faith and mysticism." But here, too, there is a wide divergence of views. At present three groups may be differentiated.

The first group (Barth, Gogarten, Brunner) insists vigorously on the incompatability of faith and mysticism. The second group (Otto, Heiler) is equally insistent on their belonging together. A third group (Schraeder, Deissmann) sees the solution in a distinction between valid and invalid mysticism. On the whole, we shall have to decide in favor of the first group.[206] What is here understood by mysticism bears the following marks:

1. Like faith, mysticism is a religion determined by its content. Both mysticism and faith ask for the ultimate meaning, both are

concerned about the question regarding God. Hence mysticism is not primarily a philosophy but religion.

2. All mysticism thinks ontologically. It can grasp God only under the concept of the "Supreme Being." [207] God and creature are bracketed together by the concept of being.

3. With that the inadequacy of mysticism has been established. Because of the fact that mysticism in its thinking does not get beyond the category of being, its genuine religious concern does not come to fruition either.[208] Metaphysics stands in opposition to religion. Once the category of being becomes the one that controls everything, then the difference between God and man coincides with the difference between infinite and finite. The idea of personality cannot be realized. Therefore the goal of the religious process is oneness, not fellowship. There can be fellowship only where there is personality. But oneness is to be understood in the sense of identity without any difference. This is the point at which the incompatibility of faith and mysticism becomes obvious. Faith knows of no absorption in God, but always only of a standing before God in the fellowship of I and Thou.

Most intimately connected with this is the following:

4. For mysticism sin is creatureliness, for faith it is disobedience toward God's will. The most serious lack in mysticism, strictly speaking, is that there is no place for the idea of guilt. For that reason it does not know what to do with forgiveness and atonement. Mysticism is unable to affirm anything like an activity or being addressed by its Supreme Being. Here the soul does not wait for the life-creating word of forgiveness, but is submerged in the bottomless abyss of the uncreated being. Faith and mysticism are two different ways to one and the same goal. But mysticism "cannot bear the paradoxical tension of faith and therefore dissolves it" (Heinzelmann, l.c., p. 63). Hence faith and mysticism are related to each other like fire and water. In any event, in agreement with Heinzelmann (pp. 110ff.) it must be asserted that faith can never pass over into mysticism without surrendering itself, and that, consequently, expressions like "mysticism of faith" or "mysticism of justification" can do nothing but evoke false conceptions.

The contrast between faith and mysticism should now be clear. We had to make these preliminary remarks in order to provide a clear basis for our detailed investigation.[209] Right from the beginning these remarks have been unable to create in us a favorable disposition toward the view that wants to draw the theology of the cross as close as possible to mysticism. If, as we have just demonstrated, faith and mysticism stand in such sharp antithesis to each other, then the theology of the cross would have to be in irreconcilable opposition to Luther's theology of faith, if it were really a child of mysticism. We saw that this is out of the question. The theology of the cross is theology of faith, as has been shown again and again.

Does this dispose of the question concerning the theology of the cross and mysticism? Not at all. What has nothing in common in principle can still enter into an historical relationship. And in our case this is all the more possible, since the mysticism with which Luther came into contact was a weakened mysticism, inhibited in a Christian way. This constitutes the second difficulty of our investigation: in the mysticism that concerns us here we are not dealing with a uniform structure. Only in this way can we understand two such opposite evaluations of this movement as those of Ullmann [210] and A. Ritschl. Hence we cannot in principle decide the question concerning the theology of the cross and mysticism, but must follow the path of observation in detail.

II.

Historical Investigation

Investigation has made it clear that mysticism did not help Luther make his decisive reformation discovery. We may simply accept this result. But this does not yet answer our specific question. For the theology of the cross is widely regarded as Luther's pre-Reformation theology. We have seen that this temporal limitation is not appropriate, but on the contrary, the theology of the cross is an abiding element of all of Luther's theology. But then one could still ask whether perhaps this abiding element were the mystical leaven in Luther's theology. We shall come closer to an answer only as we now enter upon a detailed, though admittedly sketchy, investigation.[211]

A. Tauler

We begin with Tauler.[212] Studying him will lead us most quickly to the goal, not only because he is the leading mystic of the late Middle Ages, but also because Luther's relationship to him can be established with the greatest certainty.[213] We have a number of Luther's remarks from his early period about Tauler, which show us how Luther himself understood his relation to Tauler.[214] Furthermore, thanks to the discovery of Buchwald, we are fortunate to possess a copy of Tauler's sermons that contains Luther's marginal glosses (see W. IX, 95ff.). These glosses are from the year 1516. Around this time Luther had learned to know Tauler. And at that time Tauler's name turns up also in the lectures on Romans (W. LVI, 378, 13f.; LW 25, 368). Already this historical datum shows that Luther's theology of the cross did not result from his study of Tauler; [215] he promoted it long before this. Rather, he sees in Tauler nothing more than one who holds the same views. Tauler's sermons corroborate for him the fact that his own Wittenberg theology is no absolute novelty.[216] Hence Luther's theology of the cross cannot be traced back to a direct influence on the part of Tauler.

But how about the inner relationship between the ideas of Luther and of Tauler regarding the theology of the cross, a relationship that was so keenly felt and so strongly accented by Luther? Are we in both cases really dealing with the same matter, or do Luther and Tauler mean something different when they say the same thing? We must dispense with an extended comparison and confine ourselves to featuring the most important points of view.

We proceed from Tauler's sermon on Peter's catch of fish: "Jesus entered the boat that was Simon's" (Vetter, No. 41, in Luther's edition, No. 45). It is not only Tauler's finest sermon, but it grants us the most comprehensive look into his world of thought. Self-evidently, as always with Tauler, the interpretation is allegorical: The boat is "man's inner mood," the sea is the world. The call of Jesus to "launch out into the deep" is interpreted as the demand for man to direct his love beyond all creatures to God. The whole is a remarkable and profound depiction of the mystical way of salvation. The lowest step is contemplation of the life and suffering of Jesus. Since Bernard this is common property of medieval mysticism. But in its journey to God the soul cannot stop here. It is impelled to move to the second step. There all that man's lower powers can comprehend drops away. Joy and sorrow lie behind him, and even the sympathy evoked by the contemplation of Jesus no longer affects him. But he has not yet achieved peace. It is at this point that the trials arise in full force and assail man. That is the critical point of the way of salvation.

What matters now is that man does not run away from himself, does not seek counsel and consolation with any creature, not even with his father confessor, but only with God. For now the soul stands immediately before birth. The trials are nothing else than birth pangs. What rids the soul of them is what is born of it: be it God or a creature. This third step of the birth of God in the soul can be reached only through complete resignation. For that reason Tauler thinks so highly of suffering and pure passivity, since it is the short way *(via compendii)* to the mystical birth. This is the goal of the entire way. For its sake alone the pious contemplation on the first step is demanded, for its sake the trials and sufferings of the second step are necessary. But this third step is still not the end. "Children, if a man comes properly into this ground and this being, you may be sure that this net must necessarily tear" (V., 176, 3f.). All of man's "individuality" is destroyed (V., 175, 26). With that the fourth step has been reached: Man is submerged in God. "There the created nothing submerges in the uncreated nothing" (V. 176, 4), "the created abyss into the uncreated abyss" (V. 186, 8), "there the spirit has lost itself in God's Spirit" (V. 176, 9f.).

What, we ask, is the theme of this sermon on Peter's catch of fish? Without doubt it is God's birth in the soul. Everything said here about suffering, trials, and resignation aims at that. This outcome is not accidental. It can be said that just as every sermon of Luther (apart from his early monastery sermons) treats of justification, so every sermon of Tauler treats of the birth of God in the soul.[217] Here are a few samples: V. No. 1 "Concerning three births": Here Mary is the symbol of the soul giving birth to God. The theme of V. No. 2: "How does the child Jesus find the way to Jerusalem, that is, how does the soul come to true peace, to birth?" The title of V. No. 4: "Where is he who was born King of the Jews?" and the theme: The star as guide to birth. According to the Pentecost sermon, V. No. 26, it is the highest gift of the Spirit when man loses himself in the divine abyss. The sermon on the lost coin, V. No. 37, has as its goal the idea that the soul "is brought beyond itself into God" (V. 146, 24), that it "may become God-conscious, godly, God-like" (V. 146, 21). "Blessed eyes" (Luke 10:23) are the eyes that see how the created abyss flows into the uncreated abyss (V. 201, 5). These examples could be multiplied. But enough! We see clearly what Tauler has in view.

Did Luther take up this chief concern of Tauler? One can point to the passage in the lectures on Romans (W. LVI, 379, 1ff.; LW 25, 368). Here Luther actually expresses himself in the language of mysticism. The passage can be interpreted only as referring to the mystical birth. The "endurance of God" (W. LVI, 378, 13; LW 25, 368) may not simply be referred to justification.[218] But a more thorough study of the passage shows that it stands in a completely different context.[219] In no case does the accent lie on this mystical section. On the contrary, it acts like a foreign element which is again rejected. Furthermore, it is to be noted that even this passage does not go nearly as far as Tauler. With Luther there is no thought of a submersion in God (in spite of the "annihilation").

Thus in this passage from the lectures on Romans Luther did not reject the mystical birth, although, as we saw, it no longer fits well in the total context of his thought. In another passage, however, we may observe that Luther is already suspicious of it (W. LVI, 299, 27ff.; LW 25, 287f.).[220] In the first place, he regards it as a great danger to listen to the "secret word," the uncreated Word in us, "that is spoken in a holy whisper to the innermost part of the soul" (V. 63, 18f.); for man cannot listen to the incarnate Word enough. Thus Luther cannot pass beyond that first step of the way of salvation as quickly as Tauler. In fact, in the second place, he considers it an exception, such as happened, for example, to the apostles, if there is a "rapture." And in practice the "access" (Rom. 5:1), in which we participate on the first step, is much more important for the Christian than that exceptional event of the rapture.

We note that just that which was the most important and the highest for Tauler is here set aside as unimportant, even dangerous. Luther expresses himself in a similar way in his marginal glosses on Tauler's first sermon on the three births. "Hence this sermon proceeds out of mystical theology, which is experimental, not doctrinal wisdom. For no one knows except one who accepts this hidden business. It speaks concerning the spiritual birth of the uncreated Word. But proper theology concerning the spiritual birth of the incarnate Word has the one thing needful and the best part" (W. IX, 98, 30ff.). Proper theology is placed in opposition to mystical theology.

Here the ways between Tauler's mysticism and Luther's theology of the cross clearly separate. Theology of the cross is theology of revelation, while for mysticism the historical revelation is only a preliminary step to a direct, unbroken, and unmediated intercourse between God and the soul. Even the word "intercourse" is still far too external to express what the mystic has in mind. God and the soul no longer face each other as two persons. On this last step one can no longer distinguish between God and the soul. In another passage, on the other hand, Luther cannot conceive of the "birth" in any other way than as an "acting" of God in us (W. IX, 102, 10), as the carrying out of a "plan" (W. IX, 102, 26) for us, as a "taking hold" of God on our part (W. IX, 101, 29). Here we are dealing with a clear confrontation, just as in the biblical picture of the clay and the potter, which Luther likes to use in this connection (cf. W. IX, 97, 15f.; 102, 17ff.; LVI, 376, 21ff.; LW 25, 366. W. LVI, 378, 2ff.; LW 25, 367). Since the God of the theology of the cross is the

God of historical revelation, he is always an acting God, he remains person, he never becomes an "abyss," a "nothing," in which the soul can be submerged.

To this different concept of God in Luther and Tauler corresponds their different anthropology. In short: Luther does not believe in the mystical "ground of the soul." [221] Also according to Tauler, man does not arrive at this "true ground" (V. 358, 23) without the grace of God. This must be remembered.[222] But the characteristic difference remains: With Tauler the approach to God consists in an entrance into the innermost core of the soul, while for Luther this approach is possible only through a creative Word of God to man. And connected with this is the last difference between Tauler and Luther: [223] Luther rejects the speculative elements of mysticism, which constitute the indispensable presupposition for Tauler's mysticism, even in its ecclesiastically mitigated form.

In summary we may say: The very core of Tauler's mystical theology must remain incomprehensible to the theology of the cross, for it is manifestly a theology of glory. Thus the theology of the cross is the sharpest protest imaginable against Tauler's mysticism, rightly understood. For that reason the thesis that the theology of the cross is of mystical-monastic origin is to be flatly rejected. Viewed from their center, mysticism and the theology of the cross form the harshest kind of antithesis.

The generally prevailing acceptance of this thesis would really be incomprehensible,[224] if the two phenomena did not exhibit some strong similarities in spite of this decisive difference. One need only recall the powerful emphasis on suffering (V. No. 3), on following the cross (V. 355, 21f.), on "annihilation" (V. No. 41), on trial (V. No. 41), on resignation, which can elevate itself to the point of "resignation to hell" (V. 108, 16). These we may observe step by step in both. Without a doubt we are dealing here with a common store of mysticism and theology of the cross. For that reason Luther was glad to hail Tauler as a kindred spirit. However, on the basis of the results we obtained above, we have been skeptical from the start about this broad agreement in details. It does exist, and it can hardly be decided in the case of each individual statement of Luther's whether we could not find the statements also in mysticism and vice versa.[225] But we ask: Can we seriously speak of an identity in detail when the contrariety of the basic ideas is known? [226] We make the claim: Even in details Luther associates a different meaning with the above-mentioned expressions than Tauler. We must briefly demonstrate this.[227]

Tauler speaks most extensively of suffering in his sermon on the three myrrhs.[228] Here we do in fact find much that is also a part of Luther's favorite ideas. For one, the statement that all self-chosen sufferings are no merit before God, because God accepts only his own work.[229] Furthermore, the view that the severest and bitterest suffering is "the inner stress and the inner darkness" (V. 19, 5), "when God comes with horrifying trials" (V. 19, 8). "The third myrrh is the suspension of grace [230] and the spirit," Luther notes on the margin (W. IX, 90, 29). We are again reminded most forcefully of Luther when we read: "Man must always have a cross" (V. 355, 22).

But what purpose does this cross serve? In the sermon "If I have been lifted up" (V. No. 65), from which this remark is taken, Tauler distinguishes three parts of man: the sensual, the rational and the highest, man conformed to God (V. 357, 16ff.).[231] The cross causes man to elevate himself with all his strength to the highest man (V. 357, 34f.), to get "into the true ground" (V. 358, 23), into the inner man and so into the uncreated Spirit. We must take the yoke of the cross upon ourselves; for by it we arrive at the "bottomless resignation" (V. 293, 6), and if we stand in it, "then he will surely come, he will be born" (V. 397, 6f.). The trials about which Tauler can speak ultimately have no other meaning; they are birth pangs (V. 171, 35ff.). But when the birth has taken place, the trials are finished. The man conformed to God will no longer be touched by any trials, for with his ego he has been submerged in the sea of the Godhead.

In this description of the purpose of sufferings and trials lies the first difference from Luther. With Tauler they are clearly inserted in the mystical way of salvation. Another look at his sermon on Peter's catch of fish (V. No. 41) should make that clear. With Tauler the question is: "How do I get to birth? Answer: Only by way of suffering. Luther, however, asks: How can God carry out his "plan" concerning me? Answer: Only when my plans are brought to nought. Tauler says: Birth in the soul only after birth pangs. Luther: God can complete his proper work only by way of his alien work. This is the difference: With Tauler, suffering and trial are the mark of our spiritual process of becoming; with Luther, the mark of divine activity. Tauler's view is oriented toward a state of affairs on the part of man; Luther's toward an act on the part of

God. This also explains the fact that with Tauler, suffering and trial
is something that man will finally transcend, that will eventually
have no further significance for him, that is, when the birth has
taken place. For Luther, on the contrary, suffering and trial remain
enduring concomitants especially of the mature Christian condition. They are, so to speak, only the obverse of his view of God,
his doctrine of the hidden God who has nothing to do with the mystical "abyss" in which the soul can be submerged.[232] Luther's trials
were not "mystical exercises," [233] but he saw in them the hand of
God at work, who always wants to deal with us "under the contrary
appearance."

But we must demonstrate a second basic difference between
Tauler and Luther in their understanding of suffering. In the case
of both Tauler and Luther, suffering serves to produce "annihilation." So far there is agreement. But what is the meaninng of annihilation for Tauler and for Luther? Here the speculative elements
already mentioned come into view in Tauler's case. Sin is creatureliness, the detachment of the finite being from the infinite. "Individuality" as such is sin. Hence the way to birth is an "un-becoming" *(Entwerden)*, and for that purpose suffering is useful. The highest goal is for the individuality to be submerged in the abyss of
God (V. 145, 23ff.). Accordingly, the first work of the Holy Spirit is
to make man empty; for "if God is to come in, the creature must
necessarily go out" (V. 305, 29f.). Luther also speaks again and
again about being annihilated, and he, too, combats self will.[234]

But while Tauler sees the cancer in the will as such, Luther
thinks of the term "self will" as of a will that is specifically qualified as to content, namely the evil will. For him sin lies in the
evil quality, not in the creatureliness. Compare Tauler's sermon,
"Blessed Eyes" (V. No. 64) and Luther's marginal glosses (W. IX,
103, 31ff.). "Children, in the will, that is where the damage lies"
(V. 348, 14); "All true blessedness lies in proper resignation and
being without a will" (V. 348, 30f.). Luther, on the other hand, does
not speak of the will as such, but—and this makes his gloss extremely interesting—he leaps at once to the concrete, the content, and
warns against self-will, first, because it violates love of the neighbor
(W. IX, 103, 34f.) and second, insofar as it is a boasting of one's
own wisdom and righteousness (103, 36).

This differing judgment regarding the will leads to the difference
in the understanding of suffering. For Tauler, suffering is the most
excellent means of un-becoming. Luther could also use this expres-

sion, but what Tauler intended metaphysically, Luther turned with almost instinctive certainty into the purely ethical-religious. "That God would break and hinder every *evil* counsel and will," that was basically Luther's concern already in his mystical sounding explanation of the Lord's Prayer in 1519. And the marginal glosses of Tauler's sermons nowhere betray any indication that Luther might have adopted the metaphysical interpretation of suffering.

Let us briefly summarize what has been said about Tauler and Luther:

1. The theme of Tauler's message is the birth of God in the soul, and the goal is to bring out the hidden identity between God and man. In its central point the mysticism of Tauler is a theology of glory.

2. Tauler's idea of suffering and cross must be seen in this larger framework. Two things result:

a) Suffering is for Tauler an important but passing station on the mystical way of salvation. For Luther, suffering is primarily an activity of God who keeps coming to his proper work by way of his alien work.

b) In Tauler's idea of suffering, the speculative, Neoplatonic [235] basis of his mysticism is revealed. In Luther's use of expressions that sound alike, these are never meant in a metaphysical sense, but always in an ethical sense.

We have demonstrated: For chronological as well as substantive reasons it is impossible to derive Luther's theology of the cross from Tauler's mysticism.

B. German Theology (*Theologia Deutsch*)

In connection with our investigation of Tauler a word needs to be said about the German Theology.[236] In many respects we could simply repeat our judgment regarding the relationship of Luther and Tauler. Here, too, the chronological question leads us to the same result. In his first preface to the German Theology, 1516, where Luther surmised that Tauler was the author (W. I, 153) Luther was not only guilty of a historical error, but he also overlooked substantive differences. Since the German Theology is, in fact, not simply an "epitome" drawn from Tauler, it needs to be given special treatment in our context, all the more so since this work generally does not receive special treatment in comprehensive works on Luther.

If Tauler already represents a process of making Eckehart's mysticism more churchly, then this process, which is characteristic for late medieval mysticism as a whole, appears to me to be even more advanced in the case of the "Franckfort man." [237] Karl Mueller is surely correct, in opposition to Mandel and others in designating as "the chief concern of the booklet" to determine and defend "the churchly and historical bases of all true mysticism" over against the false mysticism of the "brethren of the free spirit." The settlement of that issue is a decisive step toward answering the general question of "Luther's reformation discovery and mysticism." The more mysticism itself rests on churchly bases,[238] the more independent is Luther's discovery. But this makes the situation more complicated for our specific question. For our proof for the difference in principle between Tauler's mysticism and Luther's theology of the cross led to the conclusion that the central concern of mysticism was incompatible with the theology of the cross, and that the harmonious echoes on the periphery must be judged in the light of the central concern. But the more mysticism becomes churchly, the more its consciousness of this central concern disappears and the practical-edifying tendencies, to which Luther is much closer, move into the center. The less sharply a view is defined, the more easily it can exert an influence also on those who stand at a distance theologically. For that reason the evaluation of the German Theology has fluctuated widely in history (Cf. the articles in RGG[2] and RE[3]).

In order to come closer to an independent judgment, we look once more at the statement of Karl Mueller cited above. He has undoubtedly characterized the tenor of the writing correctly. But this tenor itself suffers from lack of clarity.[239] Does it really exist, this "churchly and historical basis of all mysticism"? Does not this join together things that simply do not fit? Is what appeals to churchly and historical bases still genuine mysticism, and, vice versa, can one still arrive at a genuine mysticism by way of the churchly bases? If by churchly bases we mean the gospel, the message of the New Testament, then we must answer with a flat no, on the basis of our systematic considerations at the beginning of this discussion. But if by it we mean the medieval view of salvation modified by Catholicism then at least one problem remains, namely the problem of all medieval mysticism, only now in a more pointed form. We can, in fact, demonstrate a certain ambiguity in the German Theology.[240]

Let us clarify this by means of the view of sin. What is sin? We get the clear answer, "Disobedience is itself sin" (21,12).[241] That is definitely biblical.[242] Sin does not consist in man's creatureliness but in the wrong direction of his will: "Sin is nothing else than that the creature wants something different from God and in opposition to God" (39, 24f.) "and the contrary will over against God is called and is disobedience" (39, 38). Sin is man's "self-will" (50,6; 56,2), that withholds from God the honor due him [243] by "assuming for himself"—as the German theology characteristically expresses it [244] —what belongs to God alone (10, 5). But precisely in this formula of "assuming for oneself" there is already an ambiguity. Man is not to assume anything for himself; this may be understood on the basis of the thought of creation. Everything comes from God, and man may not ascribe anything to himself. Hence the "assuming for one-self" would be disobedience, and therefore sin, because it would not give God what belongs to him. Thus from the perspective of creation the concept fits quite well into the framework of the above sketched biblical view of sin, which does not judge sin metaphysically but ethically. Yet certain overtones are unmistakable. We are not to "assume" anything for ourselves, because the creaturely in itself draws away from God (63, 2). And that leads us back to the ground of Neoplatonically colored speculation. In the German Theology the idea of emanation stands beside the idea of creation,[245] leading to this twofold result:

1. All things have emanated from God and are therefore good.[246] "Therefore all things are good in essence" (54, 26f.), "everything that exists is good and pleasant" (55, 29). In the creatures the eternal Good, God himself "shines and beams and works" (11, 23).

2. But as effluence from God, the creature is to God what the incomplete is to the complete, the fragmented to the whole.[247] "What is fragmented or incomplete has sprung or will spring as a gleam or a ray that flows out of the sun or a light. And it shines so or so. And that is called a creature, and of all these fragmented parts none is complete" (7, 21ff.).

The fragmented has no real essence, but has its essence in that which is perfect (8, 26ff.). Accordingly, the more we get rid of the creature, the more receptive for God we become (8, 5ff.). For one who has once taken the "leap" (11, 33) into the perfect, the imperfect the creature, becomes "unappetizing" (11, 38). Hence sin is defined, after all, in the style of speculative mysticism as a turning away from the unchangeable and a turning to the changeable (8, 33ff.). Here it is no longer a matter of disobedience, guilt, violating God's honor, but sin is a surrender to multiplicity. But "salvation does not rest on many or on variety, but it rests on one and on unity" (14, 39). We have arrived again at the formula of Eckehart [248] in his *Book of Divine Consolation:* "The one, that is what saves us" (Strauch, p. 26).

Thus, in the German Theology the biblical view of sin, which is oriented in a purely ethical-religious way, and the Neoplatonic-speculative view are juxtaposed without being reconciled. But more needs to be said. It is not only a matter of not reconciling two views, but the proper purpose of the first view is completely destroyed by the second view.

We heard above that sin is nothing but disobedience, the evil (self) will. That sets the bounds against the speculative misinterpretation of sin. The creature in itself is not evil, the essence of all things is good. There is nothing evil but the evil will. But the German Theology is not strong enough to maintain this biblical thesis in combat with the basic speculative thought. On the contrary, this theology goes from the frying pan into the fire in the following manner (C. 47, p. 54).

The evil will is not good.

The essence of things is good, because God is the essence of things.

Ergo: The evil will does not belong to the essence of things, and hence is "not good or not anything at all" (54, 30f.). It is a non-being.

This conclusion, at least in the first premise, still betrays the biblical, ethical-religious view of sin as its starting point. But this first consideration is invaded, even overlaid by a second one that is purely metaphysical. All "essence" is good, also "the evil spirit is good insofar as it is" (54, 21f.). But "willing is not essence,[249] and therefore (note: therefore!) it is not good either" (54, 23f.). Consequently the ethical categories are brought back to the categories of being. This can not be more clearly expressed than it is here. And then the last step from here is to explain sin as a non-being. Speculation has won out over the ethical-practical tendencies of the German Theology.[250]

What may be gained from this investigation concerning the character of the German Theology for our question regarding the relationship between Luther's theology of the cross and the little book of the "Franckfort Man?"

It has become clear how much weight the speculative elements have in the German Theology despite the "churchly and historical basis" of its mysticism. But then the same thing must be said here as above in the section on Tauler: Luther did not adopt these speculative elements On the contrary, Luther's theology of the cross stands in sharpest antithesis to these elements. Hence the distinctiveness of Luther's theology of the cross can be derived from the German Theology as little as from the theology of Tauler.[251]

C. The New Piety *(Devotio moderna)*

By means of two examples we have demonstrated the difference in principle between mysticism and the theology of the cross. But this does not yet fully dispose of our task. For at the close of the Middle Ages there is, alongside mysticism proper, another great movement that is to a large extent sustained by the ideas of mysticism, namely the new piety *(devotio moderna)*. This movement should be regarded as a reaction of living piety against the externalized church. It is clear that each such reaction had to see in mysticism a natural ally. So, for example, the influence of the mysticism of the Netherlands on the Brethren of the Common Life,[252] who must be considered the chief representatives of the new piety, can be demonstrated. From its spirit has come forth also the classic of this piety, the *Imitation of Christ* by Thomas a Kempis.

But the new piety was not confined to the circles of the Brethren of the Common Life.[253] It must be assumed from the start that their influence also reached Luther. We know that in Magdeburg Luther attended the school of the Brethren of the Common Life. But we cannot determine with certainty what effect this contact had on him.[254] In general, the historical bases for the problem of Luther and the new piety are still quite unsettled.[255] It would take us too far afield to pursue this historical question. In this way we could gather nothing regarding the relationships that might exist between the new piety and the theology of the cross. We shall therefore take the other course open to us and reflect briefly on the kinship and the difference in the ideas in both areas. For this purpose we will single out Thomas a Kempis and Staupitz as representatives of the new piety.

1. The little book of Thomas a Kempis, *Imitation of Christ*,[256] is perhaps the most beautiful product of monastic piety. We need not discuss it at length. The highest virtue is humility [257] (cf. I, 2; I, 4,

17; II, 20; III, 56, 36, et al.). It manifests itself, first of all, in monkish obedience (I, 9; II, 2; III, 13) and in the specifically monkish
virtues of contempt for the world (I, 1; III, 4, 55ff.) and of silence
(I, 20). In the interests of humility knowledge is warned against
(I, 3, 52ff.; III, 43; III, 58): Humility is better than knowledge.
Jesus himself is the model of humility (III, 13, 24). We must go
the way of Jesus *(imitatio)*, for Jesus is the way of life ("Thy life is
our way"; III, 18, 30).

This way leads to cross and suffering. Therefore one must surrender self-love (II, 11, 46; III, 2), in willing readiness to suffer
(III, 19) deny oneself (III, 32; III, 37, 14; III, 39, 16; III, 56) and,
animated by love of the cross (II, 11, 115; III, 56, 40, 63), follow
Jesus on the "royal road of the holy cross" (III 12). One who even
in the severest trials (compunction, I, 21, 50ff., withdrawal of grace,
II, 9, 86, temptation, I, 63, 2, tribulation, I, 13, 2) does not seek consolation and help from creatures (III, 26, 15; III, 30, 5), but arrives,
by way of annihilation (III, 42, 21), at resignation (III, 26), will then
also experience the blessing of suffering and of trial (I, 12; I, 13, 12;
II, 12, 144). For he knows that through suffering he becomes more
like *(conformior,* II, 12, 77) Christ and all the saints. But he experiences the highest blessedness when, in the departure of the
mind (III, 31, 15; 22) he elevates himself to the contemplation of
God (III, 31; 15; 18; 37).

These are the main thoughts of the *Imitation.* At no point do they
go beyond the bounds of medieval Catholicism. Even Ullmann (II,
p. 141) must concede that Thomas was a strict Catholic. We look in
vain for reformatory ideas in him. But may we not speak about a
theology of the cross also in his case? Without doubt we find many
thoughts here that are related to the theology of the cross. We might
express it thus: A study of the Imitation shows clearly that Luther
could never have arrived at his theology of the cross if he had not
been a monk. But just as powerful is the other impression, namely,
how different the two views are nevertheless. Since we must here
repeat in part what has already been said, we shall summarize at
once:

a) With Thomas as with Tauler, the thought of the cross is
oriented to man's way of salvation. The cross is not seen, in the first
instance, as God's way to man but as man's way to God.

b) Thomas does not achieve a "theology" of the cross, but at most
an ethic of the cross. The cross is not understood as the prefigure-

ment of all knowledge of God, but is utilized only as the symbol of the pious monastic life.

c) While Luther's theology of the cross, as "a new signification of things," challenges the reigning theology of glory, the cross ethics of the *Imitation* is not even conceivable without the church's theology of glory.

Hence our conclusion must be: the distinctiveness of Luther's theology of the cross cannot be derived from the ideas of the *Imitation*.

2. On the relationship between Staupitz and Luther we have the benefit of a recent and thorough investigation.[258] It cannot be our task to wish to supplement the insights of that work. We only want to attach a few observations with regard to our specific theme:

a) Wolf has called attention to the fact that in comparison with Thomas a Kempis the so-called ascetic technique with regard to the imitation of Christ recedes noticeably in the case of Staupitz, and the idea of imitation is referred much more strongly to the idea of conformity (p. 97, note). It is clear, that as a result we are moving much more closely to Luther's theology of the cross in the case of Staupitz than in the case of Thomas. For it was precisely the technical significance of cross and suffering that permitted us to distinguish sharply between the two views. Accordingly, also the concept of resignation to hell has a different coloring in the case of Staupitz than in mysticism.[259] While, for example, in the German Theology (chapt. XI) the resignation to hell is unmistakably described as the surest way to heaven, and hence is basically a spiritual exercise, in the case of Staupitz this idea follows, on the one hand, from the idea of conformity, but, on the other hand, also from the demand of pure love to God (Knaake, p. 94). Only once (Knaake, p. 80f.) does it appear also with Staupitz as a pious exercise in confirmation of resignation.

b) Attention must be called to the pattern of self-accusation in Staupitz, which is characteristic also for Luther's theology of the cross (see Wolf, pp. 95ff. and pp. 253ff.).

c) But above and beyond what they have in common, the differences must not be overlooked. The essential difference is that Staupitz did not basically break from the thought of merit. He does reject reliance on good works (Knaake, p. 86, 12) and he knows that our love to God flows from God's love to us (Knaake, 103, 3), but ultimately he can think of the relationship between God and man only in terms of the order of law.[260] Therefore the whole pious life is under the perspective of merit. This is true for self-accusation just as much as for suffering and trial (Knaake, 110, 4). Here the gulf that exists between Luther and Staupitz opens up despite all kinship. Wolf (l.c., p. 164) correctly formulates the difference with regard to the estimate of trial when he says that for Luther "the trials, though some of his statements may be similar to those of Staupitz, are not of value because they make meritorious achievements possible, but because there takes place an excellent confrontation with the reality of God, who precisely in this way seeks the person under trial."

d) Thus the thought of the cross did not prove strong enough with Staupitz to shatter the model of medieval theology. So, in the end, we must say the same about Staupitz as about Thomas a Kempis. The thought of the cross is recognized only in its practical significance for the pious life, and a theology of the cross cannot be gained from it.

By way of summarizing the results of our investigation of theology of the cross and mysticism we may say:

1. In principle, faith and mysticism stand in an irreconcilable antithesis. However, the theology of the cross is a theology of faith, a theology of revelation.

2. In medieval mysticism we are dealing with a mysticism that has been changed by the church. Only for that reason may the proposition, theology of the cross and mysticism, be posed at all.

3. Theology of the cross and mysticism agree extensively in emphasizing the cross for the practical pious life. The theology of the cross is inconceivable without monasticism.

4. But the practical demands in both instances receive a different meaning when we go back to the basic concepts behind them.

5. Neither the mystical doctrine of salvation nor the monkish ideal of humility provides an explanation for the distinctiveness of Luther's theology of the cross. Though it may have been affected by them, it stands as his own structure in direct antithesis to both sides.

6. The result of this investigation is for us an indirect proof that the theology of the cross does not constitute the pre-Reformation first stage of Luther's real theology, but that, on the contrary, it must be reckoned as a mark of Luther's total theological thought.[261]

CONCLUSION

We have finished our task. Luther's theology of the cross has been unfolded in its essential points of view and delimited over against mysticism. Two more remarks in closing:

1. We have designated the theology of the cross as something that impinges on Luther's total theology. Hence there would remain for us the task of testing this in detail in connection with the individual doctrines in Luther's theology. We would have to investigate whether for example, the stamp of the theology of the cross could also be demonstrated in connection with Luther's Christology or his doctrine of the Lord's Supper. But to do that we would have to enlarge our study into a comprehensive presentation of Luther's theology. We undertook the more modest task of working out the basic elements of a theology of the cross.

2. In our investigation we have dealt with the fact of the theology of the cross, not with the question of its validity. If we wanted to pursue the latter, our study would be enlarged in two directions. First, we would have to undertake a thorough investigation of the New Testament [262] (for example, also with regard to the relationship of Paul to Jesus), and second, we would have to undertake a comprehensive systematic consideration that would mean nothing less than the setting up of dogmatic prolegomena. Neither of these has here been our aim. Only one remark to the point: As important as such an investigation would be, it would in no case free us from having to take a stand on this question ourselves. More than a purely scientific question is at stake here. "The cross puts everything to the test. Blessed is he who understands." [263]

Notes

1. Cf. Holl, *Unchristentum und Religionsgeschichte*, 1925 (now *Gesammelte Aufsätze*, Vol. II, pp. 1-32).

2. Here is a brief overview in chronological order on the definitions of the concept "theology of the cross" in the past literature (for the complete references see the Bibliography).

   Theodosius Harnack, *Luthers Theologie*, 1862, makes only casual reference to the concept theology of the cross by calling attention to the Heidelberg Disputation (Vol. I, p. 41, in the new edition, 1927). But he saw correctly that it involved the question of theological method, not just a practical-ethical question. For him the concept is a proof for the Christocentric, antispeculative stance of Luther's theology ("upward from below!"). Harnack does not place the concept in a special relationship to Luther's early period. Noteworthy is also the motto *(Operationes in psalmos, 6:11)* which Harnack put at the head of his book, even though it cannot be understood in quite the same sense as in our work. By placing the doctrine of atonement into the center of Luther's theology Harnack also gives strong emphasis to the concern of the theology of the cross. This observation suggests an investigation of the relationship between the theology of the cross and the doctrine of atonement (specifically the orthodox teaching).

   Hermann Hering, *Die Mystik Luthers*, 1879, devotes a separate section to "cross and theology of the cross" (pp. 86-90). But for him the "cross" has only ascetic significance. The Heidelberg Disputation is not cited. "Cross" means "annihilation," and is dissolved in "mortification." This agrees with Hering's idea that the theology

169

of the cross is simply an inheritance of mysticism, specifically "Germanic" mysticism (Tauler). Hering observes a difference between Luther and mysticism (p. 89), but he does not make critical use of it. (Concerning Hering, see Part Three, "The Theology of the Cross and Mysticism"). Hering has nothing on a methodical significance of the idea of the cross.

Siegfried Lommatzsch, *Luthers Lehre,* 1879, pp. 631ff. The cross and suffering occupy a prominent, decisive place in Luther's *ethic.* "Thus the Reformer's ethic is the theology of the cross, which he opposes to the Roman teaching" (p. 105). Luther values the cross, first, in the ethical-pedagogical sense, secondly as martyrdom. Hope is most intimately connected with the cross. The negative trend of ethics, which is criticized as inadequate, is traced back to the influence of quietistic mysticism. A relationship between the doctrine of the hidden God (likewise "mysticism," according to Lommatzsch) and the doctrine of the cross is touched on, p. 105.

August Wilhelm Dieckhoff, *Luthers Lehre in ihrer ersten Gestalt,* 1887, indeed makes the statement that "the doctrine of the cross in its connection with the doctrine of contrition takes its place, beside the doctrine of faith, in the center of Luther's doctrinal thought" (p. 142). But it is treated only in the chapter on sanctification, hence quite on the margin of Luther's doctrinal ideas. In this connection Dieckhoff cites ample documentation, but all of it features only the ascetic-practical significance of the cross.

Julius Köstlin, *Luthers Theologie,* 1901, offers no information whatever on the theology of the cross; he does not even mention it in his (short) discussion of the Heidelberg Disputation (Vol. I, p. 184).

Karl Bauer, *Die Heidelberger Disputation Luthers,* 1901, presents an investigation of the historical relationships of the Heidelberg Theses rather than a connected presentation of their doctrinal content. (Regarding his judgment of the connection between the theology of the cross and mysticism, see Part Three, "The Theology of the Cross and Mysticism"). His judgment on the theology of the cross, p. 323: "The elaborations concerning the theology of the cross, despite its most evangelical core, still correspond much more to the Catholic mood of escaping from the world than to the active participation in the course of affairs corresponding to Protestant Christianity."

Köstlin-Kawerau, *Martin Luther,* 1903, mentions the theology of the cross (p. 174), but offers no positive definition of terms.

Friedrich Loofs, *Leitfaden,* 1906, pp. 723ff., understands the concept of theology of the cross on the basis of the Heidelberg Disputation. In the theology of the cross he sees Luther's renunciation of the speculative mysticism of Dionysius, but of Augustine as well, since in that program the exclusive relationship to the historical Christ is emphasized. The entire knowledge of God is enclosed in the Incarnate One. The humility of the historical Christ is the center of revelation. Thereby Luther goes beyond all mysticism, including Bernard, and without any knowledge of the history of dogma of the ancient religious modalism returns to its circle of ideas. Theology of the cross versus theology of glory means history-of-salvation theology versus speculative theology. We are especially interested in Loofs' calling attention to the antithesis between the theology of the cross and mysticism. At issue, of course, is Roman mysticism. For the influence of German mysticism on Luther, see pp. 709f. (There the concept of the theology of the cross is not used).

Wilhelm Braun, *Die Bedeutung der Concupiszenz in Luthers Leben und Lehre*, 1908, designates as the first of the "three great inner experiences that constitute Luther's life in the monastery" (p. 65), "the old monkish ideal of humility" (p. 50). However, he does not use the theology of the cross concept that might have suggested itself in this connection.

Otto Ritschl, *Dogmengeschichte des Protestantismus*, II, 1, 1912, devotes a separate chapter to the theology of the cross under the distinctive heading, "Luther's pre-Reformation views as theology of the cross" (pp. 40-84). By theology of the cross Ritschl understands Luther's monastic theology. Augustine and Bernard, Tauler and the German Theology are listed as Luther's signposts to this theology (p. 83). Nevertheless, the "peculiar stamp" of Luther's theology of the cross is conceded. As to content it is determined by the ideal of humility, which is again led back to the above-mentioned origins (p. 48). It is in this respect that the monkish character of the theology of the cross shows itself. Ritschl was the first to give the theology of the cross a more detailed treatment. It is richly documented. But we regard it as a fault that this presentation is not introduced by a more accurate definition of terms. It is true that the Heidelberg Disputation, which must be the starting point for this treatment, is cited but not adequately exploited. What is offered is a cross section of Luther's beginning theology, but the perspective into which it is placed by the heading is not worked out clearly enough. This results from the fact that Ritschl uses the theology of the cross concept in the first instance not as a characteristic of a specific theological stance, but in a purely historical way to designate a specific period in Luther's development. Luther became the reformer precisely by overcoming the theology of the cross. "Raised to its zenith, this highest form of monkishness which Luther practiced (theology of the cross) had to turn into its very opposite" (p. 84). According to this statement it seems to have been Ritschl's view that Luther's Reformation theology not only super-seded his theology of the cross in point of time, but was also anti-thetical to it in content. Yet this is opposed by other statements in which the theology of the cross is pictured as the "positive dowry" of the monk Luther to Protestant theology and church, as the "tal-ent with which he traded unceasingly in his best years and which was never fully exhausted" (p. 84). Also the later "interests and directives for life" "in no way deny their descent from the theology of the cross." However, not only is the assertion of a substantive antithesis between Luther's Reformation theology and his theology of the cross modified, but also the basic thesis, "theology of the cross equals Luther's pre-reformation monks' theology," is at least strongly hedged in by the statement: "Like the theology of the cross, so also the prize of humility reaches far into Luther's refor-matory period" (p. 50). These observations show clearly the neces-sity of reflection on the concept of theology of the cross. And then it will no longer be possible to restrict the concept to pre-Reforma-tion theology, a restriction that Ritschl himself did not maintain.

Reinhold Seeberg, *Die Lehre Luthers,* 1917 *(Dogmengeschichte* IV, 1; trans. Charles E. Hay, Baker, 1954, Vol. II, Book III, Part I, Chap. 1) offers a separate chapter (par. 66) on Luther's early doc-trinal views, but makes no mention of the concept of theology of the cross (but see pp. 101, 130).

Emanuel Hirsch, *Initium theologiae Lutheri,* 1920 *(Festgabe für Kaftan,* pp. 150ff.), points to Luther's explanation of Ps. 4:3 (W. III, 62f. and LVI, 377; LW 25, 367) and believes that this verse became "the key to the theology of the cross" for Luther (p. 162, n. 1). But he does not develop this thought any further. (The essay is reprinted in Hirsch, *Lutherstudien* II, 1954, pp. 9ff. The quota-tion is on p. 24, n. 2).

Karl Holl, *Luther,* 1923, does not offer the concept of theology of the cross, but shows clearly (pp. 91f.), if only in broad outline, the inner connection of cross, trial, faith, and view of God (hidden God, God against God).

Heinrich Boehmer, *Der junge Luther,* 1925, p. 142 (trans. John W. Doberstein and Theodore G. Tappert, *Road to Reformation,* Muhl-enberg, 1946, p. 147), points out that in the years around 1517 Luther preferred to call his whole teaching the theology of the cross. Mysticism is said to have "helped to lead Luther directly" to the primitive Christian idea of the grace of unmerited suffering on the cross, but it soon assumed a form for Luther different from that of the mystics. Boehmer does not speak of the significance of the cross for knowledge, criticism, and theology.

Georg Merz, *Der vorreformatorische Luther,* 1926, emphasizes the antispeculative character of the theology of the cross and places it in sharp antithesis to the anthroposophic formula of the "knowledge of higher worlds" (pp. 25ff.); see the reprint of this work in: G. Merz, *Um Glauben und Leben nach Luthers Lehre (Theologische Bücherei,* 15), Munich, 1961, pp. 26ff.

Ernst Wolf, *Staupitz und Luther,* 1927, only grazes the concept of theology of the cross. As marks of this theology he mentions tribulation (against H. Thomas, p. 166) and self-accusation (p. 249).

3. Cf. the programmatic essay by P. Althaus, *"Die Bedeutung des Kreuzes in Luthers Denken"* (*Vierteljahrsschrift der Luthergesellschaft,* 1926, No. 4), but already Th. Harnack as well.

4. a. Already at this point we want to repudiate the opinion that we too did not know that Luther's theology of the cross appears most sharply delineated in his early years. It may also be conceded that here and there we find monkish elements in it. Concerning the possible medieval sources of the theology of the cross, see Part Three, "The Theology of the Cross and Mysticism." In most cases the text itself calls attention to characteristic changes within Luther's views. But it is not correct to try to restrict the theology of the cross to Luther's early period (see note 3).

   b. Our evidence for the views of the old Luther is very frequently taken from the Lectures on Genesis (W. XLII-XLIV; LW 1-8). Unfortunately, the printed version is not by Luther himself. Nevertheless, the following considerations justify its use: 1. We may in general trust the reliability of the copies (see also Bornkamm's verdict in *Vierteljahrsschrift der Luthergesellschaft,* 1927, No. 3, p. 60, n. 1); 2. Over against the misgivings there are also great advantages. Nowhere but in the Genesis lectures do we have such a wealth of the dogmatic and ethical views of the old Luther at our disposal. 3. The ideas of the theology of the cross are a decisive characteristic for the difference between Luther and his epigones. The fact that these ideas are especially prominent again precisely in the Genesis lectures indicates that in this trend, according to all the rules of logic, we are not dealing with the work of editors, but are confronted with the "authentic" Luther at this very place. And we shall not fail to raise critical questions at times in specific cases.

    c. That we have preferred to rely on Luther's lectures and commentaries rather than on his sermons should require no special justification (see also Otto Ritschl, Vol. II, p. vi).

5. Th. Harnack has made this convincingly clear.

6. W. I, 350-374; DW 31, 39-70. Stange, *Die ältesten ethischen Disputationen Luthers, Quellenschriften zur Geschichte des Protestantismus,* No. 1, Leipzig, 1904. Karl Bauer, *Die Heidelberger Disputation Luthers,* 1901.

7. See Hirsch, "Randglossen zu Luthertexten" (*Studien und Kritiken* 91, 1918, pp. 135ff.).

8. See Althaus, "Die Bedeutung des Kreuzes im Denken Luthers," and Th. Harnack, Vol. I, p. 58.

9. Cf. the joint rejection of wisdom and righteousness of the flesh in many passages in the lectures on Romans, e.g., W. LVI, 157ff.; LW 25, 136f.; W. LVI, 171, 14ff.; LW 25, 150f. Also W. II, 613, 37f.; LW 31, 225; W. V, 293, 24ff.

10. Cf. W. III, 463, 15ff.; LW 10, 405: "For this reason it is called the judgment of God, because it is contrary to the judgment of men. It condemns what men choose and chooses what men condemn. *And this judgment has been shown us in the cross of Christ.*"

11. See P. Althaus, "Theologie des Glaubens" (*Zeitschrift für systematische Theologie,* 2, 1924, No. 2, pp. 281-322).

12. "The Gospel destroys those things which exist, it confounds the strong, it confuses the wise and reduces them to nothingness, to weakness, to foolishness, because it teaches humility and a cross. . . . Let all those whose pleasure is in earthly things and in their own doing shrink back before this rule of the cross, complaining, 'This is a hard saying.' Therefore it is not surprising that this saying of Christ is most odious to those who desire to be something, who want to be wise and mighty in their own eyes and before men, and who consider themselves to be 'the first' " (W. I, 617, 7ff.; LW 31, 232; cf. W. V, 70, 5ff.; LW 14, 343, and W. II, 613, 37ff.; LW 27, 404).

13. C. Stange, *Die ältesten ethischen Disputationen Luthers,* p. 68, n. 1, objects to the statement that metaphysics is rejected in Thesis 20 of the Heidelberg Disputation. It must be granted Stange that Thesis 20 does not contain a "scientific theory," but must not "the matured experience of the pious man" reject metaphysics as the way to the knowledge of God, as soon as that experience becomes clear as it reflects on itself?

14. Cf. W. LVI, 174, 18ff.; LW 25, 154; W. LVI, 177, 25ff.; LW 25, 158.

15. ". . . to God who is hidden under the cross and is not found anywhere else" (W. V, 418, 34ff.).

16. This is true not only of "natural man," as Kattenbusch thinks, *Deus absconditus bei Luther*, p. 204, n. 29.

17. On the use of the concept the hidden God in the lectures on Romans, see F. W. Schmidt, *Der Gottesgedanke in Luthers Römerbriefvorlesung, Drittes Lutherheft der Theologischen Studien und Kritiken*, 1920/21, pp. 185-190. We can only voice our agreement with the theological judgment expressed there.

18. "But do we not preach the world over that God's power, wisdom, goodness, righteousness, and mercy are great and marvelous without understanding them? For we understand things metaphysically, that is, according to the way we understand them, namely, as things that are apparent and not hidden, although he has hidden his power under nothing but weakness, his wisdom under foolishness, his goodness under severity, his righteousness under sins, and his mercy under wrath. Hence they do not understand the power of God when they see infirmity, etc." (W. LVI, 380, 31ff.; LW 25, 370).

19. The oldest passage in Luther is in W. III, 124, 29ff.; LW 10, 119f. The reference to Dionysius appears to speak in favor of the thesis of Lommatzsch that Luther's teaching on the hidden God was inherited from mysticism. But the immediately following reference to the hiddenness of God in humanity cannot be called mystical. But the hiddenness of God is always brought especially into relationship to the incarnation. Cf. W. IV, 648, 27ff.

20. The incarnation as such is concealment. Cf.: "Wisdom was made incarnate *and is thus hidden*" (W. LVI, 237, 21; LW 25, 223).

21. For the familiar teaching about the alien work see the definition, W. I, 112, 10ff.

22. He who speculates about God deals with God no differently than a cobbler judges his leather (W. LVI, 185, 26ff.; LW 25, 167).

23. Cf. the analysis of this writing by Zickendraht, *Der Streit zwischen Erasmus und Luther über die Willensfreiheit*, Leipzig, 1909. The following quotations are all from W. XVIII; LW 33, unless otherwise indicated.

24. This is the reason Harnack identifies the hidden God with the Creator God; similarly R. Seeberg.

25. See E. Hirsch, *Luthers Gottesanschauung,* 1918, p. 3.

26. On the difference between "concealing" and "hiding" see Kattenbusch, p. 183, n. 14.

27. Hence the full knowledge of God is possible only in the light of glory. "Do you not think that the light of glory will then with the greatest of ease be able to solve the problem that is insoluble in the light of the Word or of grace, seeing that the light of grace has so easily solved the problem that was insoluble in the light of nature? Let us take it that there are three lights—the light of nature, the light of grace, and the light of glory, to use the common and valid distinction. According to the light of nature it is an insoluble problem why a good man should suffer and a bad man prosper; but this problem is solved by the light of grace. According to the light of grace it is an insoluble problem how God can damn one who is unable by any power of his own to do anything but sin and be guilty. Here both the light of nature and the light of grace tell us that it is not the fault of the unhappy man, but of an unjust God; for they cannot judge otherwise of a God who crowns one ungodly man freely and apart from merits, yet damns another who may well be less, or at least not more, ungodly. But the light of glory tells us differently, and it will show us hereafter that the God whose judgment here is one of incomprehensible righteousness is a God of most perfect and manifest righteousness. In the meantime, we can only *believe* this, being admonished and confirmed by the example of the light of grace, which performs a similar miracle in relation to the light of nature" (W. XVIII, 785, 23ff.; LW 33, 292).
From this we see how strongly eschatological Luther's concept of faith is. The same eschatological stance is given expression in the doctrine of the hidden God. This doctrine belongs to eschatology, not to metaphysics! But the eschatological stance is a characteristic of the theology of the cross.

28. "But since he is the *one true* God, he is wholly incomprehensible and inaccessible to human reason" (W. XVIII, 784, 11f.; LW 33, 290).

29. Cf. W. XVIII, 719, 4ff.; LW 33, 190.

30. See W. XLII to XLIV; LW 1-8. On the question of authenticity see note 4, b.

31. "The well-known God is in Scripture called 'God,' or 'Object of

Worship,' as in 2 Thess. 2:4; that is, he is not visible to us, nor does he converse with us in an absolute way, but he is clothed in some form" (W. XXXI, 2, 77, 21ff.; LW 16, 109).

32. "When God works, he turns his face away at first and seems to be the devil, not God. Thus in the present account his face was turned toward the harlot and the tyrant; he disregards Joseph and cherishes these alone. Thus Jeremiah also complains, 'Thou art near in their mouth' (12:2). Therefore they boast that God is at their side, is well-disposed toward them, and cherishes them. 'God dwells here,' they cry out. But Joseph, Jacob, and Abraham do not have this face turned toward them. This means that the devil is dwelling here. 'You cannot see my face' (Ex. 33:20). For God is accustomed to lead and govern his own in this way" (W. XLIV, 376, 1ff.; LW 7, 103; see also 104).

33. "Why he (God) hides himself in this way we shall see on that day, when all enemies will have been put under his feet (1 Cor. 15:25). Meanwhile we should believe and hope. For if one could see it now before one's eyes, there would be no need of faith. . . . For it is the wisdom of the saints to believe in the truth in opposition to the lie, in the hidden truth in opposition to the manifest truth, and in hope in opposition to hope" (W. XLIII, 393, 9ff.; LW 4, 357).

34. See already W. LVI, 377, 24ff.; LW 25, 366f.

35. " 'For God leads down to hell and brings back' (cf. 1 Sam. 2:6). Now you see his back parts, and God seems to be shunning you, but sometime later you will see his front parts and his face. This is what it means for him to love those whom he chastises. This love must be learned from experience, nor should chastisement be avoided and shunned" (W. XLIV, 113, 20ff.; LW 6, 151f.).

36. Here the question about genuineness should be raised.

37. "I have often advised and still advise younger theologians today that they must so study the Holy Scriptures that they refrain from investigating the Divine Majesty and his terrible works. God does not want us to learn to know him in this way. You cannot nakedly associate with his naked Godhead. But Christ is our way to God. Those who speculate about the majesty are crushed and led to despair by Satan" (W. XXXI, 2, 38, 21ff.; cf. especially lines 33ff.; LW 16, 54f.).

38. "Therefore the well-known hermit was right when he gave the advice: If you see a monk ascending to heaven and, so to speak, putting one foot in heaven, pull him back at once; for if he puts both feet there, he will see that he is not in heaven but in hell' " (W.

XLII, 647, 11ff.; LW 3, 139. The same passage, W. XLIII, 72, 4; cf. 72, 9ff.; LW 3, 275f.).

39. Kattenbusch, *Deus absconditus bei Luther*. It is a shortcoming of this excellent investigation that it is confined almost exclusively to the writing against Erasmus. In my view this leads to a twofold defect:

1. The presentation would have gained much in cogency if it had been shown that what we have called the first line in *The Bondage of the Will* is a direct continuation of Luther's ideas in his early years, and hence belongs to the insights of the theology of the cross.

2. He would then have seen more clearly that in *The Bondage of the Will* a second line in fact runs alongside the first line. Luther's exposition of the Ezekiel passage cannot be disposed of quite so simply as is done here, p. 205, n. 31. Because the existing difficulty at this place is not taken seriously enough, the otherwise very valuable reference to the Heidelberg Theses, p. 204, n. 29, does not make the point. On p. 203 Kattenbusch gives the sense of the hidden God: "God is so great, so exalted in his majesty, that he cannot become fully manifest to man, certainly not on earth," and right after that, p. 204, n. 29, points out that in the Heidelberg Disputation the incarnate God as such is characterized by the adjective "hidden." This shows that he does not make clear that the two are not the same. The statement that ultimate secrets remain also in the revealed God is not identical with the statement that revelation is in principle possible only in concealment. We believe that by our distinction of the two lines we are doing better justice to the criticism of *The Bondage of the Will* by Th. Harnack and A. Ritschl—which undoubtedly must be taken seriously—than Kattenbusch is able to do without having to surrender what is correct in his presentation.
We need not here go into Kattenbusch's first work, *Luthers Lehre vom unfreien Willen und von der Prädestination nach ihren Entstehungsgründen untersucht*, Göttingen, 1875, since Kattenbusch himself no longer agrees with it. See p. 178, note 11.

40. "Geschichtliche Studien zur christlichen Lehre von Gott," *Jahrbücher für deutsche Theologie* XIII, 1868, 2nd Art., pp. 67ff.; reprinted in: *Gesammelte Aufsätze*, New Series, 1896, pp. 65ff.

41. Likewise according to A. Harnack, *Dogmengeschichte*, Vol. III, 4th ed., p. 148

Also Kattenbusch originally (1875) supported this view (see pp. 17, 93, 95).

42. Karl Heim, *Das Gewissheitsproblem in der systematischen Theologie bis zu Schleiermacher*, Leipzig, 1911, Chapt. 11.

43. Also Stange's interpretation of the hidden God is on the wrong track in saying that it is an abstract concept for the pretemporal cause of the world. *Theologische Aufsätze*, 1905, p. 46.

44. Th. Harnack, *Luthers Theologie*, 1927, Vol. 1, Chaps. 2 and 3.

45. Vol. IV, 1, par. 77.

46. Pohlmann, *Die Grenze für die Bedeutung des religiösen Erlebnisses bei Luther*, Gütersloh, 1918, sides with Th. Harnack. Hence, what is to be said against the latter applies also to Pohlmann. But because of his "genetically psychological method" he goes beyond Harnack and arrives at the conclusion that the hidden God is the pre-Reformation God and that Luther's inner development is mirrored in the juxtaposition of *God hidden* and *revealed* (p. 48). But this was said without a genetically psychological method even before Pohlmann by A. Ritschl, whom Pohlmann had just disposed of a few lines earlier. The confusion becomes still greater when the natural knowledge of God, that is to say, the knowledge of the hidden God, is designated as the theological fruit of Luther's conflicts in the monastery. If one has not already become suspicious of this "genetically psychological method" (cf. especially p. 11), then one must surely become so in view of such statements.

47. Cf. F. W. Schmidt, op. cit., p. 187, n. 2, with whose verdict on Harnack we agree.

48. On this cf. Hirsch, *Die Gottesanschauung Luthers*, n. 15.

49. On page 147 Seeberg names three reasons why Luther did not drop the hidden God altogether:

1. Every scientific discussion needs the metaphysical frame of transcendence and absoluteness for the theoretical knowledge of God as love.

2. In view of the irrational in the world a volition "that does not exhaust itself nor appears to exhaust itself in the formula of love" must be placed in the "primordial basis" (sic!).

3. The introduction of the metaphysical will of God offered Luther a "purely rational argument" against Erasmus for the enslavement of the will. Would Ritschl have let himself be moved by these reasons to a revision of his verdict, according to which a

mere remnant of scholastic philosophy was to be seen in the doctrine of the *hidden God?* Cf. Seeberg, op. cit., p. 147, n. 3.

50. Julius Köstlin, *Luthers Theologie,* 2nd ed., 1901, offers the doctrine of the hidden God, Vol. I, p. 359 and Vol. II, pp. 71ff. But at this point his presentation does not rise above that of a mere report; he did not succeed in setting forth the problematics of the idea. Cf. also the verdict of Kattenbusch, *Deus absconditus,* p. 172, n. 1.

Johannes Gottschick, "Luthers Theologie," *Zeitschrift für Theologie und Kirche,* 24, 1914; I. Ergänzungsheft, is right in emphasizing that Luther continued to have an immediate religious interest in the doctrine of the hidden God (p. 44). The doctrine is an expression of reverence before God. Gottschick does not see the relationship to the idea of revelation. This may be also because in connection with the hidden God he thinks immediately of the determining, predestinating God. Our presentation has intentionally bypassed the question concerning predestination. The doctrine of the hidden God may not be reduced to it.

51. Cf. F. Nitzsch, "Über die Entstehung der scholastischen Lehre von der Synteresis," *Jahrbuch für protestantische Theologie,* 5, 1879, pp. 492ff.; M. Kähler, Article on "Gewisssen," RE, 3rd ed., 6, pp. 646-654; Wetzer and Welte, *Kirchenlexicon,* 2nd ed., Vol. V, p. 564. The word *synteresis* is common in late Greek and means the same as conservation, observation. As a technical term it only goes back to a passage in Jerome, Commentary on Ezekiel, Book I, Chap. 1 (for the text see Nitzsch, p. 499). Jerome interprets the inaugural vision of Ezekiel allegorically in detail. Here we are dealing specifically with the four living beings, each one of which has four faces. Three of them, the face of a man, a lion, and an ox, are interpreted, "according to Plato," as the three powers of the soul, namely as the *logikon,* the *thymikon* and the *epithymetikon.*

There remains the fourth face. It is like that of an eagle. The fourth power of the soul is called *synteresis* by the Greeks according to Jerome. How Jerome arrives at this assertion which contradicts the facts, we do not know. Nitzsch believes we are dealing with a corrupted text. Originally it read *syneidesis.* In his view this is not contradicted by the fact that *synteresis* is circumscribed by the words "spark of conscience." According to him, spark of conscience means nothing else than conscience itself. Accordingly, the scholastic doctrine of the synteresis would have to be traced back to a copyist's mistake.

Notes 181

52. In addition to the cited passages, cf. also W. III, 535, 36; 603, 33; IV, 253, 24.

53. On this sermon see Dieckhoff, op. cit., pp. 41ff.; Hering, op. cit., pp. 75ff.; Köstlin, op. cit., Vol. I, 51ff. and F. Kropatscheck, *Die natürlichen Kräfte des Menschen in Luthers vorreformatorischer Theologie*, 1898, pp. 34ff.

54. This reminds us of Luther's position over against indulgences; cf. Thesis 49, W. I, 235, 34f.; LW 31, 29f.

55. This thought Luther could also have found in Tauler (Vetter edition, p. 350, 28f.). Tauler develops it in the sermon "Blessed Eyes," which, demonstrably, Luther read (see W. IX, 103, 31ff.). Luther's marginal notes on Tauler are from the year 1516, while the sermon is dated by the Weimar edition at 1514. The obvious echo of the passage in Tauler does not compel a redating. The idea, once expressed, need not have reached Luther by a direct literary route.

With regard to the concept of synteresis in Luther, Hering (op. cit., p. 67f.) opposes the assumption of a connection with ideas of mysticism. But his proof fails, on the one hand, with his opinion, since rejected by recent research, that mysticism and scholasticism are clear-cut opposites. The mystical "spark" and the scholastic synteresis have a common origin. Cf. Siedel, *Die Mystik Taulers*, 1911, p. 61, who offers quotations from Thomas in which synteresis and spark are explicitly equated, and M. Grabmann, *Thomas von Aquin*, 1926, p. 134. Luther translates Tauler's "pure and bare substance of the soul" (Vetter, p. 21, 11) with "the mind or apex of the mind, or synteresis" and expressly refers to Gerson's "*Mystica theologia*" (W. IX, 99, 40).

On the other hand, in our opinion Hering misinterprets the sentence in W. I, 32, 4f. in understanding the synteresis as a part of corrupted nature. The accent rests rather on "survival," and "nature" does not refer to corrupted nature but to original nature, as the antithesis "corrupted nature" and "to be restored nature" clearly shows. Finally, the (scholastic) expression used here fits very well with the picture of the "spark." Consequently, it cannot be the case that Luther surrenders the concept of synteresis under the influence of mysticism. On the contrary, this step of Luther's means the renunciation of a view that was held in common by mysticism and scholasticism. Regarding the conjectured reasons why Luther rebukes the Pelagian use of synteresis in scholasticism but not in mysticism, see Braun, op. cit., p. 300.

56. "Thus nature can be revived, unless an obstacle is placed and grace is resisted. This is what the ungodly do who rely on their own synteresis, and because of their own will and wisdom do not want to be restored, but consider themselves whole. Therefore this portion of the will, as to its root, is still present, so that even in the damned it is almost the only cause of their total hell that they do not want him, and with an immeasurable intensity want a contrary salvation. Thus says St. Augustine that grief is the disagreement of the spirit with those things that happen to the unwilling, and that, on the contrary, pleasure and joy is the agreement of the spirit with those things that happen to the willing, and because of this the ungodly seek forever to escape damnation and will move away from it, and yet constantly run toward it" (W. I, 32, 14ff.).

57. In mysticism we do indeed have the demand for the "resignation to hell." Cf. "Tauler" (Vetter, pp. 108, 16), "Staupitz" (Knaake, p. 81), "German Theology," Chap. 11 (Uhl, p. 16). For the difference that exists nevertheless between Luther and mysticism, see Part Three, "The Theology of the Cross and Mysticism."

58. In the *Dictata super Psalterium* there are frequent quotations from Book 8 of the Confessions which relates Augustine's conversion.

59. Cf. also W. LVI, 275, 19ff.; 355, 28ff.; LW 25, 262, 349; W. II, 184, 12ff.; I, 356, 5ff.; LW 31, 43; W. V, 119, 12.

60. Hunzinger, A. W., *Lutherstudien*, No. 1, *Luthers Neuplatonismus und die Psalmenvorlesung von 1513 bis 1516*, Leipzig, 1906. But cf. by the same author, "Luther und die deutsche Mystik," N.K.Z. 19, 1908, pp. 972ff. On the *Dictata super Psalterium* in general, see Heinrich Boehmer, *Luthers erste Vorlesung*, Leipzig, 1924.

61. Gerson also calls the higher ability of knowledge "intelligence" in distinction from "reason" and "sense perception." See H. Hermelink, *Die theologische Fakultät in Tübingen vor der Reformation, 1477-1534*, Tübingen, 1906, p. 125, n. 1.

62. "But this discernment is not according to human wisdom, but according to the spirit and mind of Christ, about which the apostle argues beautifully that only the spiritual and believing have this understanding. And briefly it means: "Understanding none but heavenly, eternal, spiritual and invisible things, which takes place through faith alone, namely the things that the eye has not seen nor ear heard, nor have entered into the heart of man, which no philosopher and no man, none of the princes of this world knew. For this is the wisdom hidden in a mystery and concealed in the veil of faith" (W. III, 171, 32ff.). The "philosophy" is Occamism.

63. Luther can indeed also speak in such terms (W. IV, 268, 18).

64. Hearing is a voluntary capacity of the soul. Luther can even assert that in the beginning faith is directed against understanding (W. IV, 356, 17ff.).

65. Cf. W. III, 173, 11; 176, 1, 12; LW 10, 147f.; W. III, 204, 36; 229, 1; 230, 22. LW 10, 190; W. III, 321, 22; IV. 109, 3; 300, 20; 304, 8.

66. Cf. W. III, 150, 28; LW 10, 125; W. III, 185, 35f.; 231, 28. LW 10, 191; W. III, 400, 5f. LW 10, 336.; W. IV, 276, 13. The fact that Luther also knows "being out of one's mind," the rapture and ecstasy (e.g., W. IV, 265, 30; 273, 14ff.) is not relevant to our question. For this ecstasy does not lead beyond faith (W. IV, 267, 16ff.). A mystical rapture that elevates itself above faith is out of the question (cf. W. III, 185, 35ff.). Also, Otto Scheel, "Die Entwicklung Luthers," p. 171, and E. Wolf, pp. 150f., n. 1.

67. I cannot understand how Ficker (p. lxxxii) can make the claim that "understanding" is no longer found in the mystical sense.

68. The fact that Luther sees no difficulty here should make us cautious about Hunzinger's thesis.

69. Cf. W. LVI, 237, 23ff.; 239, 5ff.; 238, 17ff.; LW 25, 223f. This passage gives the authentic interpretation of the unclear "consider only their own opinion" (W. LVI, 239, 7).

70. We have seen above that the inclination precedes understanding, and hearing precedes seeing. Certain passages in the lectures on Romans appear to contradict this (W. LVI, 238, 15ff.; LW 25, 224). Here the understanding is presupposition for the seeking, for the inclination, and knowing is presupposition for willing and doing. But this is only an apparent contrast. In reality we are dealing with two entirely different questions: There we are dealing with the question of how understanding comes to be; here with the question of how understanding is active. It is certainly not Luther's view here either that understanding, which is equated with faith, is produced in a purely theological way. But, of course, without the constant movement of the inclination, of willing and loving, the understanding created by the "drawing of the Father to the Son" would be just as dead as faith without works. A knowledge of God that could be maintained in a purely theoretical way would not, in Luther's view, deserve this name at all (W. LVI, 238 and 239; LW 25, 224-225).

71. "Luther und die deutsche Mystik," N. K. Z. 19, 1908, 972ff.

72. Also Loofs, op. cit., pp. 292f., embraced it.

73. Heim (op. cit., p. 233) asserts this over against Hunzinger. On this point he agrees with Hermelink. According to Hermelink (op. cit., p. 124), the source of Luther's "Neoplatonism" is to be sought in the Occamistic theology, especially in the *Collectorium* of Biel. (Cf. the well-known remark of Melanchthon: "He could from memory recite Gabriel and Peter d'Ailly almost verbatim" (C.R. VI, p. 159). Hermelink distinguishes three disparate basic views in Occamism: 1. the Scotist-indeterministic concept of God; 2. the Platonic-Augustinian concept of the world; 3. the Aristotelian-"modern" doctrine of freedom. The three elements are held together by the concept of faith (faith in antithesis to rational proof, dependent on positive revelation).

    Accordingly, Luther took over the Augustinian-Platonic doctrine of God and of ideas from Occamism. Moreover, the Occamistic-Lutheran separation between the world of appearance and the world of genuine being is something completely different from the Platonic doctrine of the scales of being. For between these two worlds there is no compromise. Only faith grasps the invisible.

    Yet Hermelink concedes that in the *Dictata super Psalterium* Luther follows the terminology of the mystical literature (Areopagite!) and of the Bible; thus he explicitly delimits his concept of understanding against the Occamistic concept. Cf. the article on Bonaventure (RE, 3rd ed., Vol. III, pp. 284, 38 and 286, 35). Hermelink thus acknowledged the validity of Hunzinger's posing of the questions (which, however, to a considerable degree leads to "distortion and exaggeration," p. 123, note 2). In fact, much of what Hunzinger regards as Neoplatonism is good Occamism. Hence the assertion of Scheel ("Die Entwicklung Luthers," p. 172), "there is no trace of Neoplatonism anywhere," an assertion taken up again by Schubert (*Luthers Frühentwicklung*, p. 31), goes too far.

74. Stange, *Theologische Aufsätze*, No. 8, and Hunzinger, *Lutherstudien*, No. I.

75. Cf. the detailed picture of the pursuit of studies at Erfurt in Scheel, *Luther*, Vol. I, 2, pp. 121-234.

76. See Boehmer, *Der junge Luther*, p. 136; *Road to Reformation*, p. 140.

77. See Heim, *Gewissheitsproblem*, pp. 220ff. On this whole section see also Clemens Baeumker, *Philosophie des Mittelalters*, 3rd ed., Leipzig-Berlin, 1923.

78. Cf. Kropatscheck, *Occam und Luther*, pp. 43ff.

79. Cf. W. VI, 195, 17; LVI, 371; LW 25, 361. Furthermore, the sermon of December 25, 1514, W. I, 20ff., especially 29, 27ff. On this see Hans Preuss, *Die Entwicklung des Schriftprinzips bei Luther bis zur Leipziger Disputation,* p. 17. In opposition to Heim, cf. Seeberg, *Dogmengeschichte,* IV, 1, p. 241, n. 1.

80. That in such cases Luther made no special attempt to be generous in his understanding is shown in LVI, 383, 11ff.; LW 25, 372; W. XVIII, 617ff.; LW 33, 39ff.

81. Cf. F. Nitzsch, *Luther und Aristoteles;* there you will also find a grouping of the material.

82. *Ibid.*

83. Occasionally he refers to the "sacrifice of the intellect," e.g., W. VI, 511, 18ff.

84. H. Preuss, "Was bedeutet die Formel 'Convictus testimoniis scripturarum aut ratione evidente' in Luthers ungehörnter Antwort zu Worms?" pp. 62ff.

85. On this see also L. Ihmels, *Die christliche Wahrheitsgewissheit.*

86. Cf. Heim's essay, "Zur Geschichte des Satzes von der doppelten Wahrheit."

87. On this term see Torsten Bohlin, "Luther, Kierkegaard und die dialektische Theologie."

88. Cf. the judgment on paganism, W. LVI, 176f.; LW 25, 156f.

89. On the usage of *sapientia* (wisdom): Frequently sapientia means the same as *ratio* (reason). It is then simply a general term for the human capacity for knowing. There is no religious connotation in the word (W. LVI, 212, 30ff.; LW 25, 198). Yet the memory of the old *sapere* (savor) has not entirely disappeared (cf. W. LVI, 361, 5ff.; LW 25, 350). Luther makes a similar distinction, by likewise appealing to tradition, between *sapientia* (wisdom) and *scientia* (knowledge) (W. LVI, 440, 10ff.; LW 25, 432). In both cases the ontological sound of *sapientia* is still in evidence.

90. Cf. furthermore W. I, 32, 36; 34, 4ff.; 36, 37ff.; 138, 13ff.; XXXI, 2, 412, 27; LW 17, 194; W. LVI, 217, 8ff. 28ff.; LW 25, 202f. The "wisdom of the flesh" is defined in the "Sermon on one's own wisdom and will" and "sensuality" (W. I, 34, 1ff.). That this is not meant to transfer the victory of sin to the realm of sensuality ("Neoplatonically") in opposition to the intellect is shown by the further explanation: "that is, when reason is wise and states what

seems right and good to it." Also reason aims at seeing and in this sense belongs to sensuality, which is therefore not to be understood in a sexual sense.

91. In view of the unalterable fact of death, which was a word of God for Luther, reason either travels the way of contempt or the way of blasphemy (W. XL, 3, 537, 18; LW 13, 107). Or it comes with its unbelieving question about the causes and does not see how foolish its undertaking is (W. VI, 291, 8ff.). But if the temptation to inquire about the "why" also assails the believing Christian, he must not admit these "temptations" (W. XXXI, 2, 361, 19ff.; LW 17, 128).

92. An interesting parallel is offered by a comparison of Luther's Scripture principle with that of Occam. See Kropatscheck, *Occam und Luther,* and Preuss, *Die Entwicklung des Schriftprinzips bei Luther.* For Occam Scripture has a formal authority, apart from its content. What is new in Luther, for whom Scripture is, of course, *also* a formal authority, is precisely the discovery of the content. Because of the emphasis of the epistomological question, Occam demands the formal authority of the Bible, while for Luther it is again the "majesty of the material" upon which, in the last analysis, his "biblicism" rests. This difference is the reason why for Luther the authority of Scripture does not in practice coincide with the church, as it does for Occam.

93. See Brunstäd, *Idee der Religion,* p. 157.

94. Cf. W. I, 357, 9f.; LW 31, 44; W. LVI, 423, 23; LW 25, 415; W. X, 3, 180, 1.

95. Scheel, "Die Entwicklung Luthers," p. 193.

96. Cf. Part Three, "The Theology of the Cross and Mysticism."

97. See the letter to Scheuerl, W. Br. 1, 93f.

98. See Part Three, "The Theology of the Cross and Mysticism."

99. See also O. Ritschl, pp. 105f. "The seventh fruit is 'faith,' which St. Jerome understands to be what is described by the apostle in Heb. 11:1 as 'the substance of things hoped for.' For Jerome explains 'substance' as being 'possession.' He says: 'Because we hope that what we possess by faith will come.' For a long time I, too, was of this opinion, because I had observed that in Holy Writ 'substance' is used almost everywhere for goods and possession, especially since for this I had the support of what Jerome says about this passage. For why should one recount what the sententiaries have compiled regarding 'substance'? But after my dear

Philip Melanchthon—who, though young in body, is a venerable old graybeard in intellect and whom I avail myself of as my instructor in Greek—did not allow me to understand it this way and showed that when 'substance' means 'goods,' it is called in Greek not *hypostasis* (the word the apostle uses in Heb. 11:1) but *ousia*, *brōton* or *hyparchis*, I have changed my opinion and concede that according to my understanding *hypostasis* or 'substance,' properly means 'existence' and the 'essence' of which anything subsists in itself, as Chrysostom understands it. Or it also means a promise, an agreement—but there is no time now to discuss this more extensively—or an expectation—meanings that the force and the peculiar nature of the word from which *hypostasis* comes permit. But it is possible in this passage for 'faith' to be taken, not without reason, as 'truthfulness,' 'faithfulness,' or 'honesty,' which deceives no one" (W. II, 595, 12ff.; LW 27, 377).

100. Cf. Rudolf Otto, *Die Anschauung vom Heiligen Geist bei Luther*, pp. 31ff.

101. Cf. Tauler, Vetter Edition, Sermon 65.

102. Cf. W. XLII, 385, 27ff.; 39f.; LW 2, 175f.; also W. XLIV, 751, 36ff.; LW 8, 236: "So great and wonderful an art it is to believe and hope!. And faith is very aptly defined by the author of the Epistle to the Hebrews when he says: 'Faith is the assurance of things hoped for, the conviction of things not seen' (11:1). He recounts many examples of this. Thus Noah believed that he would be preserved in the Flood when he saw with his own eyes that the whole world was being submerged and perishing. *And he who does not know this art is not a Christian* and will not be the heir of the things that are offered to those who believe in the Word."

103. The same thought also appears already in W. LVI, 377, 24ff.; LW 25, 366f.

104. Cf. H. Preuss, *Luthers Frömmigkeit*, p. 71: "The eschatological belongs to the iron substance of his piety."

105. On the difference between a general human hope and Christian hope see the important passage in W. LVI, 295, 14ff.; LW 25, 283.

106. It would be an attractive task to compare the portrait of Abraham in the lectures on Romans with that of the lectures on Genesis, to which perhaps also the portrait given by Kierkegaard should be added.

107. Cf. W. V, 419, 2f.; and XL, 3, 542, 31f.; LW 13, 110f.

108. Cf. W. III, 543, 10ff.; LVI, 411, 1ff.; LW 25, 401; W. II, 690,

34ff.; V, 377, 34ff.; VII, 554, 6ff.; LW 21, 306f.; W. XVIII, 652, 7; LW 33, 88; W. XIX, 219, 2ff.; XLIII, 219, 28ff.; LW 4, 117.

109. Cf. Brunstäd, p. 157. He also distinguished the "Ego" from the empirically given "self."

110. "Faith . . . is the head, life, and strength of all other works and most truly that universal reality which is one in all, so that no work is good unless faith has produced it, yea, unless it was thoroughly imbued with and permeated by faith as by a new ferment." This passage is especially interesting because of the two terms "universal" and "real." Faith as the point of unity ("one in all") is the "universal real." For Nominalists the universal is an abstraction, for terminists it is the concept in judgment. Through the concept the individual thing is elevated into the thinking. Thus in the concept it is inserted into a higher unity. But this universal, through which knowledge first comes about, is here designated as the real in distinction from Nominalism. Is it saying too much if we see in this a starting point, though not carried through, for a new epistemology? Or does Luther, consciously or unconsciously, perhaps playfully, reach back to the old ontological arguments? Is not faith precisely in its nonsubstantivity the presupposition for all that is substantive? In any case, every attempt to place faith on the same level with the powers and works is to be rejected. On the contrary, faith in the strict sense must be placed over them as the whole over the parts.

111. Cf. Ihmels, *Wahrheitsgewissheit*, p. 20: "Faith and Word are inseparable correlates."

112. A few more supportive references: W. XVII, 2, 202, 2ff. We find the thought of the exclusiveness of the Word over against all external objects expressed with the same clarity in the lectures on Genesis, e.g., W. XLIII, 395, 13ff.; LW 4, 360. The return to the Word means nothing less than "being reduced to nothing" (W. XLIV, 270, 10ff.; LW 6, 361). And how much faith in the word of promise coincides with what we call hope is again demonstrated by Abraham, the model of faith (W. XLII, 463, 12ff.; LW 2, 281).

113. Cf. Ihmels, *Das Dogma in der Predigt Luthers*, p. 57, and *Das Christentum Luthers in seiner Eigenart*, pp. 32f.

114. "Through whom we have obtained access by faith. In a most useful manner the apostle joins together these two expressions, 'through Christ' and 'by faith', as he did also above in the expression 'since we are justified by faith . . . through our Lord, etc.' In the first place, the statement is directed against those who are

so presumptuous as to believe that they can approach God without Christ, as if it were sufficient for them to have believed, as if thus *by faith alone,* but not through Christ, but beside Christ, as if beyond Christ they no longer needed him after accepting the grace of justification" (W. LVI, 298, 21ff.; LW 25, 286).

"So at sunset the rays of the sun and the light of the sun go down together. But he who is wise does not set such high value on the light that he no longer needs the sun, rather he wants to have both the sun and the light at the same time. Therefore those who approach God through faith and not at the same time through Christ actually depart from him" (W. LVI, 299, 13ff.; LW 25, 287).

"Second, the apostle is speaking against those who rely too heavily on Christ and not enough on faith, as if they were to be saved through Christ in such a way that they themselves had to do nothing and show no evidence of faith. These people have too much faith, or actually none at all. For this reason it is necessary to emphasize both points: 'through faith' and 'through Christ'" (W. LVI, 299, 17ff.; LW 25, 287).

115. But see Seeberg, *Dogmengeschichte* IV, 1, p. 241, n. 1, and n. 79 above.

116. Also the relationship of causality is felt to be inadequate (see W. I, 219, 30ff.).

117. " 'I,' as a person distinct from Christ, belongs to death and hell. This is why he says: 'Not I, but Christ lives in me.' Christ is my 'form,' which adorns my faith as color or light adorns a wall. (This fact has to be expounded in this crude way, for there is no spiritual way for us to grasp the idea that Christ clings and dwells in us as closely and intimately as light or whiteness clings to a wall.) 'Christ,' he says, 'is fixed and cemented to me and abides in me. The life that I now live, He lives in me. Indeed, Christ himself is the life that I now live. In this way, therefore, Christ and I are one" (W. XL, 1, 283, 24ff.; LW 26, 167).

118. See Holl, p. 81, n. 1. On the fact that Luther's teaching on union is oriented quite differently from that of High Orthodoxy, see Koepp, "Wurzel und Ursprung der orthodoxen Lehre von der unio mystica," p. 70, n. 2; pp. 157 and 164ff.

119. This equation of the Christ, who is fused mystically with the Ego, with the Lord of Scripture, with the substantive content of the trans-logically given Word of Scripture, is precisely what is new in Luther's understanding, according to Heim (op. cit., p. 240).

But see also Seeberg, *Dogmengeschichte* IV, 1, p. 234, note 3, in opposition to Heim.

120. Cf. Gottschick, *Luthers Theologie*, p. 82, b. Also W. I, 28, 36ff.: "For the Word did not become flesh in such a way that it forsook itself and was changed into flesh, but that it assumed the flesh and united it to itself, by which union he is said not only to have flesh, but also to be flesh. So we, too, who are flesh, do not become the Word in such a way that we are in substance changed into the Word, but that we assume it and unite it to ourselves by faith, by which union we are said not only to have the Word, but also to be the Word."

121. For that reason the passage caused Denifle considerable difficulty. See Heim, p. 247.

122. For the sake of better style, the passage was cited from the 1535 edition. Compare the 1531 manuscript. As to content there is no essential difference between the two.

123. "Hard on this faith there follows, of itself, a most sweet stirring of the heart, whereby the spirit of man is enlarged and enriched (that is love, given by the Holy Spirit through faith in Christ), so that he is drawn to Christ, that gracious and bounteous testator, and made a thoroughly new and different man. Who would not shed tears of gladness, indeed, almost faint for joy in Christ, if he believed with unshaken faith that this inestimable promise of Christ belonged to him?" (W. VI, 515, 29ff.; LW 36, 40f.). "To this faith (that God desires to help me) all things are possible, as Christ says (Mark 9:23); it alone abides; it also comes to experience the works of God and thus attains to the love of God and thence to songs and praise of God, so that man esteems him highly and truly magnifies him" (W. VII, 554, 6ff.; LW 21, 307).

124. Cf. Ihmels, *Wahrheitsgewissheit*, pp. 17ff. "Of course, Luther cares far too little about all terminology than that he would himself have indicated or even observed in fact this difference between feeling and feeling, experience and experience" (p. 19).

125. Cf. Walther, *Das Erbe der Reformation*, No. II, p. 91: "When Luther speaks of 'certainty of faith,' he wants to isolate this certainty from every other known perception. Hence, in the concept 'certainty of faith' the accent is to be placed on faith, not on certainty.

126. This is true also against Seeberg, who otherwise has spent more effort than many others on the problem of experience in the case of Luther. Cf. p. 217 for the passages on the use of "experience" and the valuable section on faith and experience as a whole, pp.

217ff. Seeberg emphasizes the difference between religious experience and all natural empiricism. Religious experience is "supernatural empiricism" (p. 222). But he does not enter more fully into the problem contained in this paradoxical formula. This does not enter his consciousness because he does not attach sufficient importance to the critical delimitation of the concept of faith. By introducing the idea of the Holy Spirit, we believe that we are moving beyond Seeberg's presentation.

127. "And he can make himself known only through those works of his which he reveals in us, and which we feel and experience within ourselves. But when there is this experience, namely, that he is a God who looks into the depths and helps only the poor, despised, afflicted, miserable, forsaken, and those who are nothing, there a hearty love for him is born. The heart overflows with gladness and goes leaping and dancing for the great pleasure it has found in God. There the Holy Spirit is present and has taught us in a moment such exceeding great knowledge and gladness through this experience" (W. VII, 548, 4ff.; LW 21, 300).

128. See Rudolf Otto, *Die Anschauung vom heiligen Geist bei Luther*, pp. 25ff.

129. Robert Winkler, *Das Geistproblem*, 1926, appears to proceed from a posing of the problem similar to the one before us when he designates the Holy Spirit as the "synthesis." But this appearance cannot survive a more careful investigation. There, too, the issue is the question concerning the experience of faith. But the inner dialectic of this concept is not sufficiently sensed. It should not, as is done there (cf. p. 32) be confused with the dilemma between historicism and psychologism. But we cannot accept the formula that the Spirit is the synthesis between the divine and the human (p. 7). In the first place, it blurs the character of event in the impartation of the Spirit. Basically the Spirit is nothing else than the religious consciousness. It is not stated (pp. 9f.) that it cannot be a matter of an inert synthesis with Luther. Secondly, synthesis is taken to mean the higher unity of two contrary entities. Accordingly, the Spirit would be the higher unity between God and man. But that is in no case the meaning of the statement from the Large Catechism which Winkler quotes frequently, "these two belong together, faith and God." Between God and man it is not a matter of a synthesis by means of which a Paul, for example, could "hitch together" the divine and the human (p. 7). On the contrary, God addresses man and thereby creates fellowship. That man hears this address is the work of the Holy Spirit. But in that case the Holy Spirit is something essentially other

than the "clamp" between the divine and the human (p. 7). "The mystical flood-tide of recent days" is precisely not related to "an overemphasis on the doctrine of the Spirit," as Winkler claims, but rather to its misunderstanding. The fact that Winkler did not see this gives us the best directive for a critique of his position.

130. In my opinion T. Bohlin did not sufficiently observe this in pitting the paradox-line against the experience-line, even though this formulation proves to be very fruitful for an understanding of Luther and Kierkegaard.

131. Cf. R. Otto, *Die Anschauung vom heiligen Geist bei Luther.* This writing proposes to show that with regard to Luther's view of the Holy Spirit, alongside the traditionalistic line (Spirit as a trans-empirical factor joining in the process of salvation), there is another line according to which the process of salvation presents itself as an unbroken chain of causation and motivation (instead of Spirit: Faith and Word), and that this second line offers Luther's real contribution to the problem of the Spirit. Two things are correct in this assertion:

1. Certainly the Holy Spirit as trans-empirical cause cannot simply be integrated into the causal connection, as this was done, for example, in the teaching about the "witness of the Holy Spirit" in the doctrine concerning Scripture on the part of Orthodoxy. But this also is not the original sense of the traditionalistic line.

2. The conception of the Holy Spirit is heavily encumbered with mythological traits. In fact, Luther is not interested in trinitarian speculations.

Yet we must have misgivings about Otto's presentation. Certainly the antithesis "supernatural and natural," "other-worldly and this-worldly" is ultimately untenable. But it is not a bad habit of thought when we refuse to be satisfied with the causal relationship, whose parts, according to Otto, substitute for the Holy Spirit, "and fully occupy the space," and exclude him as trans-psychological cause of the new life (p. 95). The delimitation of this event over against all other events does not receive its due. Certainly all that happens is an act of God; event and miracle are not mutually exclusive. But revelation dare not become a special case of predestination. We are painfully reminded of Schleier-macher by Otto's remark (p. 40) that the effects of the Spirit, which are equated with the effects of faith, are "only experiences and conditions of the believing heart." It is against just this psychologizing that the doctrine of the Holy Spirit aims to be a safeguard. In its perhaps inadequate form it does nail down the problem that arises in connection with the question "Faith and Word." How does "address" take place? This question cannot be answered psychologically. It is the sense of the doctrine concerning the Holy Spirit to emphasize this in a most urgent way. It is, of course, not a logical solution; logically it must always appear as an untenable compromise between the empirical and the "religious" view (in the sense of Otto and of Schleiermacher). But does it not lie in the essence of the matter that something is not "undone" here? Precisely the questionable form of the doctrine of the Holy Spirit can point to this. At the very least, it seems to me that Otto has not escaped the danger of psychologizing into which one falls if one wants to dispute the form of this doctrine, a form which is indeed moot.

132. "But because this is the wisdom of the cross, God alone knows the way of the righteous. It is hidden even to the righteous; for his right hand leads them in such a wonderful way that it is not the way of the senses or of reason but of faith alone, which is able to see even in darkness and behold the invisible" (W. V, 45, 30ff.; LW 14, 309).

133. "The treasure is hidden in this outward life. Externally the Christian life is a sack and a skin, and the internal treasure must not be evaluated on that basis. Our outward life is like a wretched sack which has beautiful gold in it" (W. XXXI, 2, 562, 21ff.; LW 17, 387f.).

134. Cf. XLIV, 378, 3ff.; LW 7, 106 (notice the word "must"); W. XLIII, 392, 16ff.; LW 4, 355f.; W. XLII, 147, 22ff.; LW 1, 197. Only hope can penetrate the darkness of the hiddenness of our life.

135. In this fact Luther finds the meaning of the limitation in Gal. 2:9. W. II, 482, 31ff.; LW 27, 209f.

136. Cf. W. XL, 1, 440, 31ff.; 445, 19ff.; 445, 32ff.; LW 26, 281f.; 285-286; 350; W. XL, 2, 20, 12f.; LW 27, 17.

137. The Christian freedom which the new life brings with it is "a completely spiritual matter. The unspiritual man does not understand it" (W. XL, 1, 688, 27; LW 26, 461).

138. Cf. W. IV, 295, 14f.; 412, 11ff.; I, 208, 17ff.

139. Cf. W. LVI, 476, 1-26; LW 25, 468f.; W. XLIV, 265, 33ff.; LW 6, 355.

140. Cf. W. I, 61, 17ff.; III, 617, 34ff.

141. See the section on faith and Christ; also XL, 1, 48, 1ff.; LW 26, 9.

142. Cf. W. III, 37, 31ff.; 47, 2ff.; LW 10, 53; W. III, 27, 14ff.; LW 10, 28; W. IV, 238, 12ff. It is true that the doctrine of justification is here still Augustinian, as especially Dieckhoff has emphasized, but the eschatological idea that concerns us here persists also with the later Luther.

143. It would be worthwhile to examine Luther's vocational ethics once more from this point of view. In any case it is not quite so modern-middle-class as this is sometimes pictured. Also A. Harnack, *Dogmengeschichte*, Vol. III, p. 831, in opposition to the understanding of A. Ritschl, emphasizes the eschatological thrust of Luther's "social ethics."

144. Since monasticism was, shortly before the Reformation, the most despised condition, Luther could commend it to his students who heard his lectures on Romans (W. LVI, 497, 27ff.; LW 25, 491).

145. Whether this idea should be traced back to the ongoing effect of the Catholic concept of the Mass (as Kattenbusch, p. 190, n. 17, does) seems doubtful to me.

146. "Because he who has faith also has all of these things, but they are hidden; yet through tribulation they are exercised until they excel" (LVI, 50, 16ff.; LW 25, 44).

    " 'Vexation alone (Isa. 28:19) shall make you understand what you hear,' that is, the Word of God becomes intelligible to the unfeeling, if they have been thoroughly vexed by sufferings. The cross of Christ is the unique instruction in the words of God, the most genuine theology" (W. V, 216, 38ff.); see also W. V, 531, 27ff.

147. For only after we have been utterly annihilated can God use us. Cf. W. I, 183, 39ff.; II, 92, 37ff.; III, 38, 51ff.; VII, 546, 32ff.; LW 21, 299; W. VII, 548, 12ff.; LW 21, 302; W. XLII, 254, 5ff.; LW 1, 345; W. XLII, 437, 7ff.; LW 2, 246.

148. Cf. XLIV, 265, 18ff.; LW 6, 355; W. XLIV, 397, 9ff.; LW 7, 133. Who knows whether with the removal of suffering God's grace may also be taken from us? (W. II, 106, 36ff.; LW 42, 50f.). In the *Dictata super Psalterium* Luther can still list suffering among the causes of merit. See W. III, 126, 21ff.; LW 10, 122. But see also W. VI, 208, 23ff.; LW 44, 28.

149. Cf. W. X, 1, 69, 15f.; VII, 547, 8ff.; LW 21, 300; W. VII, 548, 4ff., 12ff.; LW 21, 301; W. XXXI, 1, 74, 12ff.; LW 14, 58; W. XXXI, 2, 34, 25ff.; LW 17, 48f.

150. Cf. W. I, 338, 12ff.; IV, 476, 26ff.; V, 445, 37ff.

151. W. XLIII, 617, 16ff.; 33f.; LW 5, 274f.

152. "What good will it do you if you carry even in gold and precious stone, not only the distinctive tokens but also the very nails, yes, the very wounds and blood of Christ, and never express the living image in your body?" (W. II, 615, 35ff.; LW 27, 407); Cf. W. LVI, 301, 11ff.; LW 25, 288f.; W. Br. I, 37, 15ff.; W. L, 642, 22ff.; LW 41, 164f.; see also the Sermon for the day of the discovery of the cross (May 3, 1522) W. X, 3, 113ff.

153. Cf. W. III, 437, 29ff.; LW 10, 379f.; W. V, 507, 7ff.; 211, 36ff.; XLIV, 265, 33ff.; LW 6, 355.

154. On this meaning of baptism for Luther, see Carl Stange, "Der Todesgedanke in Luthers Tauflehre."

155. Apart from Münzer; see Holl, pp. 433 and 435.

156. Note on the significance of death with Luther. Without wanting to present here a complete theology of death, let the following be said about the significance of death for Luther. So far as I can see, Luther's views may be summed up in four ideas.

1. Death makes inexorably plain to man that life is an existential decision (W. X, 3, 1, 1ff.). Eschatology impels to ethics.

2. Death is a sign of God's wrath. Luther is not content with a biological evaluation of death, but moves on to a theological one. True, all creatures must die, but this happens "while God nods approval and laughs" (W. XL, 3, 536, 15; LW 13, 106). Man's death, on the contrary, is the wages of sin. Hence death is not overcome by contempt (W. XL, 3, 485, 22; LW 13, 76f.). For in our battle with death we are battling with an incensed God himself (W. XL, 3, 544, 29f.; LW 13, 112). The Christian knows about God's wrath, and therefore dying is more difficult for him than for other people.

3. Christ has overcome death (W. XL, 1, 48, 23ff.; 65, 11ff.; LW 26, 9.21). For that reason the Christian may die calmly (W. V, 122, 27ff.; cf. also the "Sermon on Preparing to Die," W. II, 680ff.; LW 42, 99ff.). For the Christian, death is the entrance into life (alien work!). However, this is not an inert truth (as it is for Fechner), but it is always true only as deed of faith which risks the leap into the darkness (W. XIX, 217, 12ff.). The statement that death is a new birth does not follow for Luther from the self-certainty of the spirit. The angry God stands too powerfully before him. Only in Christ is this statement true, only faith can pronounce it. For only the reality of Christ's act of reconcilia-

tion can cancel the reality of God's wrath (W. XLIII, 218, 40ff.; LW 4, 116.).

4. Insofar as death signifies a new birth, it is the end of the old man. Therewith death brings to completion a process which goes on in the Christian life daily. Death seals mortality (W. I, 188, 14ff.). Blessed is he, therefore, who experiences death already in this life (W. I, 160, 10ff.).

Hence we meet with decisive ideas of the theology of the cross (blind faith, alien work, element of the existential, mortification, relationship to Christ) in this view of death. For its sake we briefly dealt with it here.

157. For that reason Luther is quite reserved in his attitude toward the cherished idea of the imitation of Christ. He does not entirely reject it but assigns it only a secondary significance. In the first instance, Christ, according to the familiar formula, is not example but gift (W. XL, 1, 389, 20; LW 26, 247). Christ is an example also for Luther (W. II, 543, 6ff.; LW 27, 300), but what is decisive in our relationship to Christ cannot be described by means of this category (W. XL, 1, 540, 17ff.; LW 26, 352). In any case, we must make a clear distinction between the idea of conformity and the idea of imitation. The concept of *imitatio* remains throughout in the confines of the moral; it has to do with an activity of man. The concept of conformity bursts through these confines; it stands in connection with suffering, not one that is self-chosen, but one sent by God. In the case of conformity it is not primarily a matter of an activity of man, but an activity of God. In a word: The concept of conformity cannot be separated from that of the cross in a pregnant sense, but this cannot be said of the imitation.

158. Cf. the passage in the lectures on Genesis, W. XLII, 399, 37ff.; LW 2, 195).

159. At present we do not yet see any of it (W. V, 288, 4ff.).

160. God's kingdom is also a hidden kingdom. It is still engaged in battle with the realm of the devil (W. II, 96, 26ff.). We ourselves are to blame for this (W. II, 95, 25ff.).

161. Cf. W. III, 150, 27ff.; LW 10, 125; W. IV, 81, 12ff.; 137, 1ff.; 287, 22ff.

162. Cf. W. V, 42, 1ff., 8ff.; LW 14, 304; W. V, 46, 1ff.; LW 14, 309; W. V, 610, 4ff.; 649, 37ff.

163. Cf. W. V, 313, 22ff.; XLII, 187, 21ff.; LW 1, 253.

164. Cf. Karl Holl: *Luthers Bedeutung für den Fortschritt der Ausle-gekunst,* and K. A. Meissinger: *Luthers Exegese in der Frühzeit.* The whole question should be subjected once more to a thorough investigation. As far as I can see, Holl has contributed nothing to our specific problem.

165. Cf. W. V, 75, 3ff.; 111, 23ff.; 643, 32ff.; VI, 562, 24ff.; LW 36, 110; W. XLII, 367, 6ff.; LW 2, 150.

166. Thus not merely from poetic emotion or the pedagogical concern, as Holl thinks, p. 554.

167. See also RGG.² I, col. 1829-1832, and Braun, pp. 50ff. Thieme's book, *Die christliche Demut,* has appeared only in the first half (*Wortgeschichte und die Demut bei Jesus,* 1906), which is hardly relevant to our purpose.

168. Cf. W. III, 292, 11ff.; LW 10, 241; W. III, 355, 1ff.; LW 10, 298f.; also W. XXXI, 2, 34, 25ff.; LW 16, 49; W. I, 138, 17f. Christ himself proclaimed the need for humility (W. III, 561, 10f.).

169. In this respect presumption is the attitude that is the opposite of humility (cf. W. I, 359, 18ff.; LW 31, 48; W. II, 458, 36ff.; LW 27, 172; W. XXXI, 2, 49, 11ff.; LW 16, 70f.). Pride *(superbia)* is arrogance in general, or *hubris;* presumption is reckoning with factors that do not exist. "To hope for anything without merits cannot be called hope but presumption" Alexander of Hales, III, q 75 ml, Resp. (See Heim, p. 242).

170. We hear these echoes also in other writings of Luther. The inclination toward quietism is a heritage Lutheranism has received from its father (cf. W. XXXI, 2, 63, 27ff.; LW 16, 90f.). Luther was no friend of activism. It is, however, much to be questioned whether this may be explained as a monkish stance. It is equally certain that Luther's attitude also betrays a strong eschatological orientation (cf. XL, 1, 97, 13ff.; LW 26, 41f.). One can indeed explain the original monasticism as an attempt to keep alive in Christendom the eschatological radicalism of primitive Christianity. In this way both explanations could be traced back to one. But it cannot be denied that Luther, at least in his earlier writings, supports a strongly monkish (stoically influenced) ethic with his insistence on resignation (cf. the passage from the year 1521, W. VII, 582, 14ff.; LW 21, 335f.; also W. VI, 15, 11f.) and contempt of the world (W. LVI, 476, 1ff.; LW 25, 468; W. I, 198, 17ff.; III, 543, 15ff.). But even Luther's Reformation ethics might be far more monkish-eschatological than has often been assumed. Unfortunately we cannot investigate this matter in detail (see note 143).

171. Also the idea that Christ wept frequently belongs here (W. III, 70, 30f.).

172. Cf. the passage from the year 1523, W. XI, 249, something that no one would still regard as monkish.

173. By this time we also have familiar explanations, e.g., W. V, 71, 5ff.; LW 14, 344; W. V, 252, 40ff.; 661, 10ff.

174. It is true, Bernard understands the relationship of the two concepts exactly as the opposite of what Luther thinks (in Cant. 34, 3). O. Ritschl, p. 53, overlooked this.

175. Cf. Tauler (V., No. 45, p. 200, 26): "Even though man would have something of humility in him, it would be false."

176. Humility is the inner terror of the heart (W. X, 3, 87, 14ff.).

177. Cf. W. Koehler, *Luther und die Kirchengeschichte*, pp. 301-333; Dieckhoff, *Justin, Augustin, Bernhard und Luther;* G. L. Plitt, "Des heiligen Bernhard von Clairvaux Anschauungen von christlichem Leben"; E. Wolf, p. 105. The quotations from Bernard are from Migne, S. L., Vols. 182 and 183.

178. Seeberg, *Dogmengeschichte* III, p. 130, n. 1, ignored this entire aspect of humility.

179. The Rule of St. Benedict, ed. Butler.

180. See also Dieckhoff, pp. 62ff., for Bernard's thoughts on the origin of love.

181. Cf. Holl, pp. 383, 394, 408.

182. On this section see Th. Harnack, *Luthers Theologie*, Vol. I, par. 24; Holl, pp. 67ff.; O. Ritschl, pp. 17-39; Braun, p. 33; E. Wolf, pp. 150ff.; see also the biographies.

183. The individual terms for trial *(tentatio, tribulatio, compunctio)* cannot always be clearly distinguished conceptually; cf. E. Wolf, p. 139, n. 1. On the difference between *tribulatio* and *compunctio*, see O. Ritschl, pp. 19-21.

184. This is not intended to deny the reality of the wrath of God during trials. Cf. Th. Harnack, Vol. I, pp. 318ff.

185. "This trial cannot be overcome and is far too great to be understood by us. For there is a contradiction with which God contradicts himself. It is impossible for the flesh to understand this; for it inevitably concludes either that God is lying—and this is blasphemy—or that God hates me—and this leads to despair. Accord-

ingly, this passage cannot be explained in a manner commensurate with the importance of the subject matter" (W. XLIII, 202, 16ff.; LW 4, 93).

186. On this see Holl, p. 68; in addition to the references given there, see also W. XLIII, 64, 31ff.; LW 3, 265.

187. Thus most beautifully in his sermon on the Syrophoenician woman, W. XVII, 2, 200ff. (Cf. the analysis by E. Hirsch, *Zeitschrift für systematische Theologie*, Vol. 4, 1927, pp. 632ff.), also Luther's "Comfort When Facing Grave Temptations, 1521 (W. VII, 785, 3f.; LW 42, 183f.).

188. As is known, there is currently a controversy on the significance of Christ for trial. H. M. Mueller has most severely attacked Holl's presentation, pp. 67ff. "Der christliche Glaube und das 1. Gebot" (*Theologische Blätter*, Vol. 6, October, 1927). In opposition to him, see Bornkamm, "Christus und das erste Gebot in der Anfechtung bei Luther" (*Zeitschrift für systematische Theologie*, Vol. 5, 1927, No. 3, pp. 453ff.) and, in turn, Mueller's reply, "Der Glaube an Gott den Schöpfer als Glaube an Christus bei Luther" (*Theol. Blätter*, Vol. 7, 1928, February, col. 37ff.). We do not want to enter this debate because it is of no immediate concern to our theme.

189. "There is sufficiently abundant protection in the promise of God not only against the devil, the flesh, and the world but also against this lofty temptation. For if God sent an angel to say: 'Do not believe these promises!' I would reject him, saying: 'Depart from me, Satan, etc.' Or, if *God himself* appeared to me in his majesty and said: 'You are not worthy of my grace; I will change my plan and not keep my promise to you,' I would not have to yield to him, but it would be necessary to fight most vehemently against God himself" (W. XLIV, 97, 38ff.; LW 6, 131).

190. "God's faithfulness and truth always must first become a great lie before it becomes truth. The world calls this truth heresy. And we, too, are constantly tempted to believe that God would abandon us and not keep his word; and in our hearts he begins to become a liar. In short, God cannot be God unless he first becomes a devil" (W. XXXI, 1, 249, 21ff.; LW 14, 31). "To summarize, the devil does not become and is not a devil without first having been God. . . . I must grant the devil his hour of godliness and ascribe devilhood to our God. But this is not the whole story. The last word is: 'His faithfulness and truth endure forever' " (W. XXXI, 1, 250, 24. 35ff.; LW 14, 32).

191. " 'How long will my enemy be exalted over me?' Earlier he attributed this to God who forgets and turns away, and does not hear. Now he attributes it to the enemy. And here the victory already begins to lean toward the tempted one, and the temptation begins to have an end. It is a part of victory in this temptation to be aware of the enemy and now become superior to him. For although by God's design the enemy is exalted, yet in the midst of the temptation the enemy is not in view, but God alone appears to be doing everything. And the enemy is busy with this very thing, so that the tempted person does not attribute it to him but only to God, as was shown in Christ crucified, whom they attacked with blasphemies in such a way that he would seem to be hateful to God. . . . But he does not mention the enemy by name but speaks in general. However he has the devil and his schemes in mind. For he is the one who really rules in this temptation" (W. V, 386, 14ff.; 387, 5ff.).

192. Luther has much to say about comfort in trial especially in his lectures on Genesis; cf. W. XLII, 345, 35ff.; LW 2, 118; W. XLII, 494, 9ff.; 13ff.; LW 2, 325; W. XLII, 553, 8ff.; 32ff.; LW 3, 7f.; W. XLIII, 466, 34ff.; LW 5, 55.

193. Luther's theology of the cross may also be explained genetically on the basis of his trials in the monastery.

194. For that reason the old monastic saying that prayer is the hardest work receives a far greater earnestness with Luther. Cf. W. LVI, 446, 4ff.; LW 25, 437; W. XLII, 662, 32ff.; LW 3, 160.

195. Cf. my analysis of the passage, "Luther," *Viertaljahrschrift der Luthergesellschaft*, 1927, No. I/II, pp. 3-12.

196. One who knows about this "under the opposite appearance" will not want to be dispensed from suffering before God takes the cross away from him. Indeed, he even prays for cross and suffering so that his own will might be broken and God's will might be done (W. II, 105, 12ff.; LW 42, 48f.). Suffering, in turn, drives to prayer and thus strengthens faith. Cf. the remarkable presentation of this relationship in the "Treatise on Good Works" (W. VI, 249, 11ff.; LW 44, 79f.). Of course, where suffering drives to prayer, there it has basically already been overcome (W. V, 494, 14ff.; XIX, 222, 8ff.).

197. "With a condition" one may also pray to God for help at a specific time (W. XLIII, 326, 17ff.; LW 4, 266).

198. Luther places both points of view side by side (W. VI, 233, 27ff.; LW 44, 64ff.).

199. Cf. the value given to prayer as a mark of the church (W. L, 641, 20ff.; LW 41, 164).

200. For that reason no self-observation is possible during prayer. There is prayer only in the act itself (W. II, 85, 36ff.; LW 42, 26).

201. Luther developed this point of view most consistently in the explanation of the Third Commandment in the *Treatise on Good Works* (W. VI, 229ff.; LW 44, 54ff.). Without faith, prayer is dead (W. VI, 233, 10ff.; LW 44, 59). Conversely, it is prayer that reveals the weakness of faith (W. VI, 234, 16ff.; LW 44, 60). But the weaker the faith, the more necessary is prayer (W. VI, 237, 8ff.; LW 44, 64), for faith grows through prayer (W. VI, 234, 4ff.; LW 44, 60). All in all, prayer proves itself to be a "special exercise of faith" (W. VI, 232, 22ff.; LW 44, 58).

202. This correct thought is probably also the basis of R. Hermann's essay, "Das Verhältnis von Rechtfertigung und Gebet nach Luthers Auslegung von Röm. 3 in der Römerbriefvorlesung." For Luther, faith is justifying faith. There can be living with God—and that is what prayer is—only on the basis of justification. Prayer confronts us with our guilt and lives by the mercy of God. But the details of Hermann's interpretation often have something forced about them, so that they almost obscure the profound basic idea more than they illuminate it.

203. *Thomas a Kempis,* ed. Hirsche; *Tauler,* ed. Vetter; *German Theology,* ed. Uhl; *Staupitz,* ed. Knaake, ed. Buchwald-Wolf.

204. In what follows we are, to a considerable extent, following the little book by Heinzelmann, *Glaube und Mystik,* to which we owe much. But the work by Beth, *Frömmigkeit der Mystik und des Glaubens,* which also appeared in 1927, in my opinion lacks the clarity of definitions which Heinzelmann has provided. See also Brunner, *Die Mystik und das Wort.*

205. The latter way is followed in a masterful way by R. Otto in *West-östliche Mystik.*

206. Basically Heinzelmann does this, too, in spite of his protest against dialectical theology.

207. Precisely because of this concept of God, which it shares with scholasticism, speculative mysticism could establish itself in Catholicism. The fight of the medieval church against mysticism is a fight against one of its original elements. Cf. Heim, *Gewissheitsproblem.*

208. This is the point from which Brunstäd proceeds to criticize mysticism. See especially op. cit., p. 38.

209. Such a basis, in my opinion, seems to be missing for the presentation of Luther in Otto's *West-östliche Mystik,* pp. 277ff. Otto has no eye for the difference in principle between faith and mysticism. Note also the statement, p. 274, "Whoever says 'spirit' is somehow also saying 'mysticism'. " On this see the opposite thesis of Heinzelmann, p. 116.

210. Ullmann's thesis about the "reformers before the Reformation" could probably count on no more than slight approval, at least on the part of theologians. Among secular historians, on the contrary, it still appears to be getting a better assessment. On this see also Scheel, *Luther und Tauler,* pp. 299f. On A. Ritschl, see *Rechtfertigung und Versöhnung,* 2nd ed., Vol. I, pp. 117ff.

211. Hering, *Die Mystik Luthers,* is an attempt to demonstrate how highly the help of mysticism should be regarded in Luther's liberation from scholasticism. In individual details there are many valuable references here. Furthermore, the boundary between Luther's own view and the ideas of mysticism is not blurred. Yet, in the first place, every linguistic echo is too uncritically taken (often without any explicit documentation!) as influencing content. In the second place, the whole does not rest on a clear definition of the essence of mysticism. This, in the third place, explains the false antithesis: scholasticism-mysticism, upon which the whole structure is erected, but this antithesis is untenable. All in all, one can only agree with A. Ritschl's judgment concerning this book *(Rechtfertigung und Versöhnung,* 2nd ed., Vol. I, p. 129, n. 1).

212. For Bernard we direct you to our excursus on humility. There what Luther and Bernard have in common and where they differ has become clearly evident.

213. On this section see Koehler, *Luther und die Kirchengeschichte,* I, pp. 236ff.; Scheel, *Taulers Mystik und Luthers reformatorische Entdeckung;* Köstlin-Kawerau, Vol. I, pp. 110-115; Boehmer, *Der junge Luther,* pp. 139ff.; *Road to Reformation,* pp. 143ff.; Köstlin, *Luthers Theologie,* 2nd ed. Vol. I, pp. 105ff., where especially the differences between Luther and Tauler are clearly evident; Wilhelm Preger, *Geschichte der deutschen Mystik im Mittelalter,* Vol. III, Book I; Gottlob Siedel, *Die Mystik Taulers;* RE [3], Vol. 19, pp. 451-459 (Cohrs); RGG [1], Vol. V, col. 1112f. (Reichel).

214. For the sake of an overview we give the most important references: W. Br. I, 65, 14ff.; 79, 58ff.; 96, 8ff.; 160, 8ff.; W. LVI,

378, 13f.; LW 25, 368; W. I, 137, 14f.; 298, 29f. (cf. I, 586, 18f.); 557, 25ff.; LW 31, 128f.; W. I, 674, 34ff.; V, 203, 15f.; 305, 19f.; 353, 40; 459, 7; 564, 3.

215. As little as his reformatory discovery. In opposition to A. V. Mueller, *Luther und Tauler;* cf. Scheel, *Taulers Mystik und Luthers reformatorische Entdeckung.*

216. Cf. W. Br. I, 79, 58ff. As is known, Luther regarded the "Frankfort Man" as an "epitome" of Tauler's sermons.

217. That Luther's theme is richer in tension may, among other things, be demonstrated by the fact that one tires of Tauler's sermons in spite of (or perhaps just because of?) their beauty much more quickly than of Luther's sermons.

218. In my opinion, Scheel, *Tauler und Luther* (p. 317, n. 5), rightly makes this point over against Boehmer, *Luther im Lichte der neueren Forschung,* 5th ed., p. 65. But in his *Der junge Luther,* p. 140 (*Road to Reformation,* p. 145), Boehmer again included this controverted statement.

219. See my analysis.

220. "This also applies to those who follow the mystical theology and struggle in inner darkness, omitting all pictures of Christ's suffering, wishing to hear and contemplate only the uncreated Word himself, but not having first been justified and purged in the eyes of their heart through the incarnate Word. For the incarnate Word is first necessary for the purity of the heart, and only when one has this purity, can he through this Word be taken up spiritually into the uncreated Word. But who is there who thinks that he is so pure that he dares aspire to this level unless he is called and led into the rapture by God, as was the case with the apostle Paul, or unless he is 'taken up with Peter, James, and John, his brother'? In brief, this rapture is not called an 'access.' " (LVI, 299, 27ff.; LW 25, 287f.).

221. See the section on synteresis. On the term itself see Siedel, op. cit., pp. 51-65, who has especially investigated the relationships to the scholastic terms. Very correctly Luther translates Tauler's "ground" with "mind" or "synteresis" (W. IX, 99, 36ff.).

222. But see Holl, p. 10, n. 2.

223. This is now generally recognized and needs no further elucidation.

224. Luther's approving judgment of Tauler need not detain us here.

It is generally known that Luther read his own view into Tauler. Köhler, p. 284, correctly observes that the central thought, around which all of Luther's remarks about Tauler can be grouped, is "Man is nothing—God is everything." But this formula does not catch the distinctive nature of Tauler's theology.

225. This is of course to be understood with regard to substance, not language.

226. Frequently this question is not posed pointedly enough. For that reason, for example, an investigation like that of Bauer on the Heidelberg Disputation teeters a little unclearly back and forth in its verdict on the influence of mysticism; cf. pp. 306 with 308 and 316.

227. As is known, Holl did this on the concept of "readiness to go to hell." We simply call attention to his presentation, pp. 150ff.

228. Vetter, No. 3, cf. W. IX, 99, 1ff. Men like to call attention to this sermon particularly because of its similarity to Luther's thoughts. E.g., Bauer, p. 303.

229. Accordingly, one may not speak in general about "the mystics' high regard for self-imposed suffering," as Boehmer does, *Der junge Luther*, p. 142; *Road to Reformation*, p. 148.

230. On this see W. XLII, 336, 10ff.; LW 2, 104.

231. Cf. W. VII, 551, 19ff.; LW 21, 304.

232. Against Lommatzsch, p. 141.

233. Against Braun, p. 295.

234. Cf. his explanation of the Third Petition of the Lord's Prayer, 1519 (W. II, 106, 26ff.; LW 42, 42ff.). See also Steinlein, "Wandlungen in Luthers Auslegung der dritten Bitte."

235. Proclus is repeatedly adduced, e.g., W. V, 300, 27; 332, 21; 347, 21; 350, 20; 358, 15.

236. Cf. Karl Mueller, *Zur deutschen Theologie;* G. L. Plitt, "Einige Bemerkungen über die deutsche Theologie"; B. M. Mauff, *Der religionsphilosophische Standpunkt der sogenannten deutschen Theologie;* Hermelink, "Text und Gedankengang der Theologia Deutsch"; Herman Mandel, *Theologie Deutsch;* F. Reifenrath, *Die deutsche Theologie des Frankfurter Gottesfreundes,* RGG [2], Vol. I, col. 1866f. (Doerries); RE [3], Vol. XIX, 626-631 (Cohrs); also Braun, pp. 287ff.

237. On this see the section, "Die Besonnenheit der Theologia Deutsch," Mauff, pp. 46ff.

238. It is used in this sense, for example, by Scheel, *Luther und Tauler,* pp. 301ff.

239. This is not given its due on the part of Mueller who sharply rebuffs the view of the German Theology as spiritualistic mysticism, a view introduced by the Baptists and still at work to the present day (Hegler, Mandel).

240. Cf. Plitt, p. 54, who also speaks of a double line of statements, though in a sense different from the one here. According to him, the speculative statements are opposed by others which have come forth from the author's "experience of the heart." Here we prefer to speak of "biblical statements." Mauff, pp. 20 and 28f. also notes something of the discordant character of the German Theology, but makes no use of this observation, just as he seldom penetrates into the depths of the problems referred to.

     On the text-critical question see Hermelink and Mueller. Mueller's solution seems to be generally accepted now (cf. RGG ²). The matter is not decisive for our problem, inasmuch as both Text B (Luther's edition of 1518) and Text U (manuscript from 1497) clearly show the Neoplatonic elements.

241. The citations follow the edition of Uhl as to page and line.

242. This aspect is ignored by Braun, pp. 287ff. Disobedience and "self-seeking" are not, without further ado, identical.

243. The German Theology is greatly concerned about "the glory of God." Cf. 9, 38; 10, 5; 16, 5; 17, 5; 20, 19; 63, 12; 64, 4. The concept presupposes a strong personal view of God and thus bursts through the limits of a consistent mysticism. This is proof of the discordant character of the German Theology.

244. Cf. 8, 37; 9, 1; 9, 35; 9, 40; 10, 5; 10, 8; 10, 28; 10, 24; 10, 39; 11, 3; 11, 8; 22, 30f.; 57, 36; 58, 1; 62, 5, 12, 41; 63, 3. The term is also used by Tauler. Cf. V, 306, 26; 307, 11, 15, 18, 23, 29.

245. Cf. 55, 35: "The creatures are a pointer and a way to God."

246. It must be asked to what extent this is to be traced back to the idea of creation.

247. This Perfect God, Being, is in a genuine Neoplatonic way the *nihil,* the nothing (7, 28).

248. It is a principal concern of Mauff to demonstrate the relationship between the German Theology and Eckehart.

249. In the framework of an ontological mysticism (think of Augustine), this idea has something quite artificial in it. Elsewhere the German Theology knows very well (chapter II, pp. 56ff.) that reason and will belong inseparably together, and thus together constitute the "essence." Accordingly, it is there forced to seek a new explanation of the evil will. The discussion of this matter is one of the most interesting sections of the whole book which, however, need not be treated in our context. In spite of being closer to the biblical view of sin, it ultimately does not get beyond the speculative design.

250. In detail both are often difficult to disentangle. For that reason a twilight falls upon the concept of "one's own will," for example. Cf. the many passages in which the "being one's own" *(Eigenheit)* is attacked, e.g., 8, 14; 9, 30; 4, 40; 19, 24; 25, 38; 28, 1ff.; 33, 1; 37, 39; 49, 40; 52, 35; 56, 2.

251. This is not meant to deny that there are many points of contact. One such point, for example, would be the demand for resignation. Cf. 10:34; 13, 10; 15, 40ff.; 22, 25ff. (the limit of resignation); 26, 34ff.; 37, 1; 53, 35. Or one could think of the demand to imitate Christ and to follow the cross (27, 13; 59, 20), also annihilation as well as mortification (8, 15; 20, 24). Allusions on both sides can easily be demonstrated. But a far more important task is to ask whether on both sides the same word means the same thing. But this task can be aided only by a reflection on the basic differences.

Bauer, *Heidelberger Disputation,* p. 304, has pointed out that the antithetical position of the theology of glory and the theology of the cross has its model in chapter LI of the German Theology (56, 17-30). That may be correct; but then it should be likewise observed that in the very next sentence (56, 30) the German Theology itself goes over to the questions of the theology of glory.

It should still be emphasized that here the view concerning the "birth of God in the soul" recedes considerably in comparison with Tauler. But this is explained by the polemical thrust of the little book. In addition, it should be said that this idea is here also the secret point of direction. Cf. the outline in RE [3] following Reifenrath, which, however, is rejected by Hermelink (p. 16) as too artificial. Mandel offers a different division (p. xii). The birth of God in the soul (for nothing else is meant by "union" 61, 20, cf. 61, 11) is achieved in the condition of vision and ecstasy ("in one look or in one rapture," 61, 15f.). The "inner man" (11, 33) takes "a big leap" into the Perfect, into God. One who achieves that—and this is possible again and again (11, 35)—has "eternal life on earth" (13, 39f.). These ideas, which lead into the vicinity of Tauler and Eckehart, only serve to strengthen our stated thesis.

On the concept of "readiness to go to hell" see Holl, pp. 150ff.

252. See RGG ^{2}, I, 1275f. (Barnikol); RE ^{3}, III, 472-507 (L. Schulze); Scheel, *Luther*, I, 70ff., 275ff.

253. This is conceded also by E. Wolf, p. 96, footnote, with certain qualifications.

254. Scheel, p. 93, says that the boy Luther in the company of the Brethren in Magdeburg experienced a deepening and intensifica- tion of his Catholic piety. Boehmer, *Der junge Luther*, p. 33 (Road to Reformation, p. 17) does not think Luther was greatly influenced.

255. See also the thesis of Keller (Bibliography) concerning the "Old German Theology" and the Waldensian movement. This theory is today generally rejected, although there is also partial acceptance by O. Clemen, RE ^{3}, XVIII, 781.

256. See RE ^{3}, XIX, 719-733 (Schulze).

257. Cf. the "love not to know" from the "Little Alphabet of the Monk in the School of God" (ed. Pohl III, 317).

258. See E. Wolf. There (n. 1, pp. 1ff.) also is an overview of the lit- erature to date. This work is especially valuable because here, apart from N. Paulus, the Tübingen sermons of Staupitz are ex- tensively utilized for the first time. Cf. The edition of Buchwald and Wolf and the preface by Scheel. In addition, on Staupitz, see RGG ^{1}, V. 898 (Koehler) and RE ^{3}, XVIII, 781-786 (Clemen).

259. It seems to me that Wolf (cf. p. 122) has not, after all, refuted the general opinion that wants to classify Staupitz under mysti- cism. According to Dieckhoff, *Die Theologie des Johann von Staup- itz* (p. 170), the theology of Staupitz is completely free of the influ- ence of the "Neoplatonic-falseness" of German mysticism.

260. See Wolf, pp. 120ff.

261. A comparison of Münzer's mysticism of the cross with Luther's theology of the cross would be an attractive undertaking. We would indeed have to ask whether it was Münzer's mysticism of the cross that constituted the point of attack for Luther's polemics. In any case, Luther was more perceptive here than with regard to medieval mysticism, and he could well distinguish his own theol- ogy of the cross from the theology of Münzer. But since Münzer

is not involved in the genesis of Luther's theology of the cross, we may here waive presentation of his mysticism of the cross.

262. On a criticism of Luther on the basis of the New Testament, see Schlatter, *Luthers Deutung des Römerbriefs.*

263. W. V, 179, 31; 85, 5.

Bibliography

Althaus, Paul: "Die Bedeutung des Kreuzes im Denken Luthers," *Vierteljahrsschrift der Luthergesellschaft*, 1926, No. 4.

Althaus, Paul: "Theologie des Glaubens," *Zeitschrift für systematische Theologie* 2. 1924. no. 2, 281-322.

Baeumker, Clemens: *Philosophie des Mittelalters.* (Kultur der Gegenwart, Part I, Section 5; Allgemeine Geschichte der Philosophie, 338-431), 2. Ed., Berlin-Leipzig, 1903.

Barnikol, E.: "Brüder vom gemeinsamen Leben." RGG ³, Vol. 1, Col. 1438f.

Bauer, Karl: "Die Heidelberger Disputation Luthers," *Zeitschrift für Kirchengeschichte*, vol. 21, 1901, no. II, 233ff.

S. *Benedicti Regula Monachorum;* Ed. Butler, Freiburg, 1912.

S. *Bernardi Opera Omnia;* Ed. Migne, *Patrologia,* Series Latina, vol. 182-185.

Beth, Karl: *Frömmigkeit der Mystik und des Glaubens.* Leipzig-Berlin, 1927.

Biel, Gabriel: *Collectorium in quattuor libros Sententiarum.* Tübingen, 1499.

Boehmer, Heinrich: *Luther im Lichte der neueren Forschung.* 5. Ed., Leipzig-Berlin, 1918.

Boehmer, Heinrich: *Der junge Luther.* Gotha, 1925. 4. Ed., Stuttgart, 1951; trans. John W. Doberstein and Theodore G. Tappert, *Road to Reformation.* Philadelphia: Muhlenberg Press, 1946.

Boehmer, Heinrich: *Luthers erste Vorlesung. Berichte über die Verhandlungen der sächsischen Akademie der Wissenschaften zu Leipzig,* Phil.-hist. Klasse. Vol. 75, 1923, no. 1, Leipzig, 1924.

Bohlin, Torsten: "Luther, Kierkegaard und die dialektische Theologie," *Zeitschrift für Theologie und Kirche*, 1926, nos. 3 and 4.

Bornkamm, Heinrich: "Christus und das 1. Gebot in der Anfechtung bei Luther," *Zeitschrift für systematische Theologie*, 5, 1927. No. 3, 453ff.
Braun, Wilhelm: *Die Bedeutung der Concupiszenz in Luthers Leben und Lehre*. Berlin, 1908.
Brunner, Emil: *Die Mystik und das Wort*. Tübingen, 1924.
Brunstäd, Friedrich: *Die Idee der Religion*. Halle, 1922.

Clemens, O.: "Staupitz," RE ³, Vol. 18, 781-786.
Cohrs, Ferdinand: "Tauler," RE ³, Vol. XIX, 451-459.
Cohrs, Ferdinand: "Theologia Deutsch," RE ³, Vol. XIX, 626-631.

"Demut": RGG ³, Vol. II, col. 76-82. I. "Religionsgeschichtlich" (Mensching); IV. "Systematisch" (Mehl).
Dieckhoff, Aug. Wilh.: *Luthers Lehre in ihrer ersten Gestalt*. Rektoratsprogramm für 1887/88. Rostock, 1887.
Dieckhoff, Aug. Wilh.: "Die Theologie des Johann von Staupitz," *Zeitschrift für kirchliche Wissenschaft und kirchliches Leben*. VIII, 169ff.; 232ff. Leipzig, 1887.
Dieckhoff, A. W.: *Justin, Augustin, Bernhard und Luther*. 5 Vorträge, Leipzig, 1882.
Doerries: "Deutsche Theologie," RGG ², Vol. I, col. 1866f.; M. A. Schmidt, RGG ³, Vol. II, col. 107f.
Drews, P.: *Disputationen Dr. Martin Luthers in den Jahren 1535-1545 an der Universität Wittenberg*. Göttingen, 1895.

Eckehart: *Das Buch der göttlichen Tröstung*. Ed. Ph. Strauch, 2. ed. Bonn, 1922 *(Kleine Texte*, ed. H. Lietzmann, 55).

Der Franckforter: ("Eyn Deutsch Theologia"), ed. Willo Uhl, Bonn, 1912. *(Kleine Texte*, ed. H. Lietzmann, 96).

Gottschick, Johannes: "Luthers Theologie," 1. Ergänzungsheft, *Zeitschrift für Theologie und Kirche*, 1914.
Grabmann, Martin: *Thomas von Aquin*. München, 1926.

v. Harnack, Adolf: *Lehrbuch der Dogmengeschichte*. 4. Ed. Vol. III. Tübingen, 1910.
Harnack, Theodosius: *Luthers Theologie*, Vol. I and II. New ed., München, 1927.
Heiler, Friedrich: *Das Gebet*. München, 1921.
Heim, Karl: *Das Gewissheitsproblem in der systematischen Theologie bis zu Schleiermacher*, Leipzig, 1911.
Heim, Karl: "Zur Geschichte des Satzes von der doppelten Wahrheit,"

Studien zur systematischen Theologie (Festgabe für Häring), pp. 1-16. Tübingen, 1918.

Heim, Karl: "Das Gebet als philosophisches Problem." 1925. From *Glaube und Leben*, 484ff. Berlin, 1926.

Heinzelmann, Gerhard: *Glaube und Mystik*. Tübingen, 1927.

Hering, Herman: *Die Mystik Luthers im Zusammenhang seiner Theologie und in ihrem Verhältnis zur älteren Mystik*. Leipzig, 1879.

Hermann, Rudolf: "Das Verhältnis von Rechtfertigung und Gebet nach Luthers Auslegung von Röm. III in der Römerbriefvorlesung," *Zeitschrift für systematische Theologie*, 3, 1925/26, no. 4, 603-647 (reprinted in: R. Hermann, *Gesammelte Studien zur Theologie Luthers und der Reformation*, Göttingen, 1960, 11-43).

Hermelink, Heinrich: *Die Theologische Fakultät in Tübingen vor der Reformation*. 1477-1534. Tübingen, 1906.

Hermelink, Heinrich: "Text und Gedankengang der Theologia Deutsch," in *Aus Deutschlands kirchlicher Vergangenheit* (Festschrift zum 70. Geburtstag von Th. Brieger). Leipzig, 1912.

Hirsch, Emanuel: *Luthers Gottesanschauung*. Göttingen, 1918.

Hirsch, Emanuel: "Randglossen zu Luthertexten," *Theologische Studien und Kritiken*, 91, 1918, 122ff.

Hirsch, Emanuel: *Initium theologiae Lutheri. Festgabe für Jul. Kaftan*, 150ff. Tübingen, 1920. (Reprinted in: E. Hirsch, *Lutherstudien II*, Gütersloh, 1954, 9-35).

Hirsch, Emanuel: *Der Sinn des Gebets*. Göttingen, 1921.

Hirsch, Emanuel: "Antwort an Rudolf Bultmann," *Zeitschrift für systematische Theologie*, IV, 1926/27, no. 4, 631ff. (Contains, pp. 632ff. an analysis of Luther's sermon on the Syrophoenician Woman, W. XVII, 2, 200-204).

Holl, Karl: *Gesammelte Aufsätze zur Kirchengeschichte*, I. Luther, 2. and 3. Ed., Tübingen, 1923.

Holl, Karl: *Gesammelte Aufsätze zur Kirchengeschichte*, II, 1: Der Osten. Tübingen, 1927.

Hunzinger, A. W.: *Lutherstudien*. no. 1. *Luthers Neuplatonismus in der Psalmenvorlesung von 1513-1516*. Leipzig, 1906.

Hunzinger, A. W.: "Luther und die deutsche Mystik," *Neue Kirchliche Zeitschrift* 19, 1908, 972ff.

Ihmels, Ludwig: *Die christliche Wahrheitsgewissheit. Ihr letzter Grund und ihre Entstehung*. Leipzig, 1901.

Ihmels, Ludwig: *Das Dogma in der Predigt Luthers*. Leipzig, 1912.

Ihmels, Ludwig: *Das Christentum Luthers in seiner Eigenart*. Leipzig, 1917.

Kähler, Martin: "Gewissen," RE ³, VI, 646-654.

Kattenbusch, Ferdinand: *Luthers Lehre vom unfreien Willen und von der Prädestination. Nach ihren Entstehungsgründen untersucht.* Dissertation, Göttingen, 1875.

Kattenbusch, Ferdinand: *Deus absconditus bei Luther. Festgabe für Julius Kaftan,* 170ff. Tübingen, 1920.

Kawerau, G.: "25 Jahre Lutherforschung (1883-1908)". *Theologische Studien und Kritiken,* 81, 1908. No. 3, 334ff.; no. 4, 576ff.

Keller, Ludwig: *Die Reformation und die älteren Reformparteien.* Leipzig, 1885.

Keller, Ludwig: *Johann von Staupitz und die Anfänge der Reformation.* Leipzig, 1888.

Knaake, J. K. F.: *Johannis Staupitii Opera quae reperiri potuerunt omnia,* Vol. I, Deutsche Schriften. Potsdam, 1867.

Koepp, Wilhelm: "Wurzel und Ursprung der orthodoxen Lehre von der unio mystica." *Zeitschrift für Theologie und Kirche,* 1921, 46ff.; 139ff.

Koehler, W.: "Staupitz," RGG ¹, V, 898.

Koehler, W.: *Luther und die Kirchengeschichte nach seinen Schriften zunächst bis 1521.* I, 1. Erlangen, 1900.

Köstlin, Jul.: *Luthers Theologie.* 2 Vols. 2 ed., Stuttgart, 1901.

Köstlin-Kawerau: *Martin Luther.* 2 Vols. 5. ed., Berlin, 1903.

Kropatscheck, Friedrich: *Die natuerlichen Kräfte des Menschen in Luthers vorreformatorischer Theologie.* Dissertation, Greifswald, 1898.

Kropatscheck, Friedrich: *Occam und Luther. Bemerkungen zur Geschichte des Autoritätsprinzips.* Beiträge zur Förderung christlicher Theologie, ed. Schlatter-Cremer. Vol. 4, no. 1, 1900, 49ff.

Lommatzsch, Siegfried: *Luthers Lehre vom ethisch-religiösen Standpunkt aus und mit besonderer Berücksichtigung seiner Theorie vom Gesetz.* Berlin, 1879.

Loofs, Friedrich: *Leitfaden zum Studium der Dogmengeschichte,* 4. ed. Halle, 1906.

Mandel, Herman: *Theologia Deutsch. Quellenschriften zur Geschichte des Protestantismus.* No. 7, Leipzig, 1908.

Mauff, Bernhard/Max: *Der religionsphilosophische Standpunkt der sogenannten deutschen Theologie.* Dissertation, Jena, 1890.

Meissinger, Karl-Aug.: *Luthers Exegese in der Frühzeit.* Leipzig, 1911.

Merz, Georg: *Der vorreformatorische Luther.* München, 1926. (Reprinted in: G. Merz, *Um Glauben und Leben nach Luthers Lehre* [Theologische Bücherei, 15], München, 1961, 26-65.

Mueller, A. V.: *Luther und Tauler.* Bern, 1918.

Mueller, Hans-Mich.: "Der christliche Glaube und das 1. Gebot," (Ein Beitrag zum Verständnis von Luthers Rechtfertigungslehre, in Auseinandersetzung mit Karl Holl's Lutherdarstellung.) *Theologische Blätter,* 6, October, 1927.

Mueller, Hans-Mich.: "Der Glaube an Gott, den Schöpfer, als Glaube an Christus bei Luther," *Theologische Blätter,* 7, Feb. 1928, 37ff.

Mueller, Karl: *Kritische Beiträge zur "deutschen Theologie,"* II. Sitzungsberichte der preussischen Akademie der Wissenschaften, 1919, XXXVI, 631-658.

Nitzsch, Friedrich: "Über die Entstehung der scholastischen Lehre von der Synteresis: Ein historischer Beitrag zur Lehre vom Gewissen," *Jahrbücher für protestantische Theologie,* 5, 1879, 492ff.

Nitzsch, Friedrich: *Luther und Aristoteles.* Kiel, 1883.

Otto, Rudolf: *Die Anschauung vom heiligen Geist bei Luther.* Göttingen, 1898.

Otto, Rudolf: *West-östliche Mystik.* Gotha, 1926.

Plitt, G. L.: "Des heiligen Bernhard von Clairvaux Anschauungen vom christlichen Leben," *Zeitschrift für historische Theologie,* 1862, no. 2.

Plitt, G. L.: "Einige Bemerkungen über die deutsche Theologie," *Zeitschrift für die lutherische Theologie,* 26, 1865, no. 1, 49-62.

Pohlmann, Hans: *Die Grenze für die Bedeutung des religiösen Erlebnisses bei Luther.* Dissertation, Gütersloh, 1918.

Preger, Wilhelm: *Geschichte der deutschen Mystik im Mittelalter.* Vol. 3, Leipzig, 1893.

Preuss, Hans: *Die Entwicklung des Schriftprinzips bei Luther bis zur Leipziger Disputation.* Leipzig, 1901.

Preuss, Hans: "Was bedeutet die Formel: 'Convictus testimoniis scripturarum aut ratione evidente' in Luthers ungehörnter Antwort zu Worms," *Theologische Studien und Kritiken,* 81, 1908, 62ff.

Preuss, Hans: *Luthers Frömmigkeit—Gedanken über ihr Wesen und über ihre geschichtliche Stellung.* Leipzig, 1917.

Reichel: "Tauler," RGG ¹, V, 1112f.

Reifenrath, F.: *Die Deutsche Theologie des Frankfurter Gottesfreundes.* Halle, 1863.

Ritschl, Albrecht: "Geschichtliche Studien zur christlichen Lehre von Gott," 2. Art. *Gesammelte Aufsätze,* Neue Folge, No. 3, 65ff., 1896, Freiburg i.B. und Leipzig. Reprinted from *Jahrbücher für deutsche Theologie,* XIII, 1868, 67-133.

Ritschl, Albrecht: *Die christliche Lehre von der Rechtfertigung und Versöhnung,* 2. ed. I, Bonn, 1882.

Ritschl, Otto: *Dogmengeschichte des Protestantismus.* 2,I, Leipzig, 1912.

Scheel, Otto: "Die Entwicklung Luthers bis zum Abschluss der Vorlesung über den Römerbrief." *Schriften des Vereins für Reformationsgeschichte*, 27, no. 100, 61ff., Leipzig, 1910.

Scheel, Otto: "Ausschnitte aus dem Leben des jungen Luther," *Zeitschrift für Kirchengeschichte*, 32, 1911. No. III, 386ff.; No. IV, 531ff.

Scheel, Otto: *Dokumente zu Luthers Entwicklung (bis 1519).* Sammlung Krueger. 2. Reihe. No. 9, Tübingen, 1911.

Scheel, Otto: *Martin Luther*, 2 Vols. Tübingen, 1916/17.

Scheel, Otto: *Taulers Mystik und Luthers reformatorische Entdeckung. Festgabe für Julius Kaftan*, 298ff. Tübingen, 1920.

Schlatter, Adolf: *Luthers Deutung des Römerbriefs.* Beiträge zur Förderung christlicher Theologie, Vol. 21, No. 7, 1917.

Schmidt, Fried. Wilh.: *Der Gottesgedanke in Luthers Römerbriefvorlesung*, 3. Lutherheft der theol. Stud. u. Krit. 3/4, Heft 1920/21.

v. Schubert, Hans: *Luthers Frühentwicklung bis 1517/19. Schriften des Vereins für Reformationsgeschichte.* 34, 1916, No. 124.

Schulze, L.: "Brüder vom gemeinsamen Leben," RE [3], Vol. 3, 472-507.

Schulze, L.: "Thomas a Kempis," RE [3], Vol. 19, 719-733.

Seeberg, Reinhold: *Lehrbuch der Dogmengeschichte.* III and IV. 1., 2., and 3. ed., Leipzig, 1913 and 1917 ET.

Siedel, Gottlob: *Die Mystik Taulers.* Leipzig, 1911.

Stange, Carl: *Die ältesten ethischen Disputationen Luthers. Quellenschriften zur Geschichte des Protestantismus*, no. 1. Leipzig, 1904.

Stange, Carl: *Theologische Aufsätze* (5,8,9). Leipzig, 1905.

Stange, Carl: "Der Todesgedanke in Luthers Tauflehre," *Zeitschrift für systematische Theologie*, 5, 1928, no. 4, 758-844.

Staupitz, Joh.: *Tübinger Predigten*, ed. G. Buchwald und E. Wolf, mit Vorwort von O. Scheel. *Quellen und Forschungen zur Reformationsgeschichte*, VIII. Leipzig, 1927.

Steinlein, Herman: "Wandlungen in Luthers Auslegung der 3. Bitte," *Vierteljahrschrift der Luthergesellschaft*, 1927. No. 1/2, 13ff.

Tauler, Joh.: *Predigten.* Ed. Ferd. Vetter, Berlin, 1910.

Thieme, Karl: *Die christliche Demut.* 1. Hälfte: *Wortgeschichte und die Demut bei Jesus.* Giessen, 1906.

Thomas von Aquin: *Summa Theologica.* Ed. Parma, 1852.

Thomas a Kempis: *De Imitatione Christi.* Libri IV. ed. Karl Hirsche. Berlin, 1891.

Ullmann, Karl: *Reformatoren vor der Reformation*, II, 2. ed. Gotha, 1866.

v. Walter, Joh.: "Vom jungen Luther," *Neue kirchliche Zeitschrift*, 1914, 55ff.

Walther, Wilhelm: *Das Erbe der Reformation in Kampf der Gegenwart.* No. 1-4, Leipzig, 1903, 1904, 1909, 1917.

Winkler, Robert: *Das Geistproblem in seiner Bedeutung für die Prinzipienfrage der systematischen Theologie der Gegenwart.* Göttingen, 1926.

Wolf, Ernst: *Staupitz und Luther. Quellen und Forschungen zur Reformationsgeschichte.* IX, Leipzig, 1927.

Zickendraht, Karl: *Der Streit zwischen Erasmus und Luther über die Willensfreiheit.* Dargestellt und beurteilt. Leipzig, 1909.

Addendum to the Fourth Edition

My book, *Luther's Theology of the Cross,* first appeared in 1929 and was reprinted unchanged as the second and third editions in 1933 and 1939. Also this third edition was soon sold out. After the war the publisher and I seriously considered a new edition, but I could not bring myself to do it. I did not want to issue it again without revision; but other plans beckoned whose realization seemed more urgent to me. But in recent years requests came so often and so urgently from the most diverse circles to make the book available again that I felt I should no longer resist this pressure. This, of course, again raised the question about the shape of a new edition. If I were to write the book today, it would turn out differently both in content and style.[1] To make minor improvements, modify the content, and tone down the language would have produced a mere patch-work job whose seams would be disturbingly visible. After all, the book made its way as it is, with all its formulations that now seem a bit too pointed, and with its youthfully unconcerned figures of speech. The insertion of too many "ifs" and "buts" could only have blurred and weakened the purpose of this investigation (to which I still hold without qualification) namely, to work energetically for the acceptance of a specific point of view in comprehending Luther's theological thought. Therefore it seemed advisable to permit the original text to stand as is and, instead of a major revision, to include in an addendum what I wish to say from my present position by way of supplement or correction.

A new critical edition of the *Dictata super Psalterium* (W. III and

IV) is in process. Only after its appearance will a comprehensive scholarly use of this important material from the early Luther be possible. For the present, the reader is directed to Erich Vogelsang, *Die Anfänge von Luthers Christologie nach der ersten Psalmen-vorlesung (Arbeiten zur Kirchengeschichte,* published by E. Hirsch and Hans Lietzmann, Vol. 15, 1929, especially pp. 4-11), and to Gerhard Ebeling, "Luthers Psalterdruck vom Jahre 1513," *Zeitschrift für Theologie und Kirche,* Vol. 50, 1953, No. 1, pp. 43 to 99) and the literature cited there. Here the reader will be introduced to the problems of a critical study of the sources.

With regard to the use of the great lectures on Genesis, already the first edition (n. 4, 2) indicated critically that the printed version does not come from Luther himself and must therefore be cited with caution. Meanwhile Erich Seeberg has presented his *Studien zu Luthers Genesis-Vorlesung* (1932), and Peter Meinhold pub-lished a comprehensive, thorough investigation, *Die Genesis-Vor-lesung Luthers und ihre Herausgeber (Forschungen zur Kirchen— und Geistesgeschichte,* edited by E. Seeberg, E. Caspar, W. Weber, Vol. 8, Stuttgart, 1936). It will not be necessary to comment on them in detail. My a priori assumption that the ideas of the theol-ogy of the cross appearing in the Genesis lectures must not be charged to the publishers but belong to the "genuine" Luther, is corroborated by the exact analysis of Meinhold (cf. above all pp. 99ff., p. 157, p. 399). For the reference of the Genesis lectures to *The Bondage of the Will* with its warning against speculation about the hidden God and predestination (W. XLIII, 457, 32ff.; 458, 35ff.; LW 5, 42ff.), cf. Meinhold, pp. 293ff. Concerning the genuineness of the passage from W. XLIII, 463, 3ff.; LW 5, 50, I could get no information from Meinhold. I believe I have shown that the pas-sage, even assuming its genuineness, does not support the idea that the old Luther gave up the thought of the hidden God. Therefore the passages from the Genesis lectures cited in my book probably belong to the "genuine" Luther. At most, one might ask whether the fact that in the Genesis lectures the simultaneous relationship of hiddenness and revelation has become predominantly a succes-sive one, is to be traced back to the "old" Luther or the publishers. In any case the idea is perfectly conceivable also for Luther him-self.

We cannot here go into the numerous new publications on Lu-ther's theology since 1929. I call attention to Ernst Wolf's biblio-graphical report and my research report, "Zehn Jahre Lutherforschung." [3] The basic thesis of my book is that in the theology of the cross we are not dealing with a pre-Reformation preliminary stage, but with a persistent, abiding principle in Luther's theology. This thesis has, to my knowledge, nowhere been seriously challenged in the literature to date; it may therefore be regarded as a general view today.

This claim from the year 1954 can no longer be maintained today without further ado since the appearance of Ernst Bizer's book, *Fides ex auditu. Eine Untersuchung über die Entdeckung der Gerechtigkeit Gottes durch Martin Luther* (Neukirchen, 1958; 2nd ed., 1961; 3rd ed., 1966). Bizer, like others before him, placed Luther's Reformation turning point in the year 1518, and thus at the same time designated the theology of the cross, as Otto Ritschl had done earlier (1912), as a pre-Reformation, monkish stage of Luther's real theology. We cannot here go into a detailed review of Bizer's thesis, which had created quite a stir.

A summary of the almost limitless discussion since then is excellently reported by Otto H. Pesch in a thorough essay, "Zur Frage nach Luthers reformatorischer Wende" in the periodical *Catholica,* Vol. 20, Münster, 1966, No. 3, 216-246, and No. 4, 264-280. This essay deals exhaustively with all pertinent literature as well as the discussion at the Luther Congress in Järvenpää, 1966, and finally offers the author's own position. A uniform scholarly judgment on Bizer's conception has not been arrived at. Personally, I agree with H. Bornkamm in regarding Bizer's thesis as overdrawn. For the rest, I do not believe that taking a position for or against Bizer's thesis is decisive for what I tried to clarify in my book. The goal of my investigation was to show that the theology of the cross was a theological principle of knowledge for Luther. As such it can be traced in the theology of the Word, which Bizer has acknowledged as being exclusively "reformatory." The documentation for this in my book is not at all limited to the period before 1518. In conjunction with Bizer, Kurt Aland ("Der Weg zur Reformation. Zeitpunkt und Charakter des reformatorischen Erlebnisses Martin Luthers," *Theologische Existenz heute,* N.F., No. 123, München, 1965) dated the "breakthrough" around February/March, 1518, a date accepted by Bizer (3rd ed., p. 190).

Luther presented the "program of the theology of the cross" in the Heidelberg Disputation, April, 1518. Hence it can hardly stand in diametrical opposition to the reformatory theology of the Word, even if one follows Bizer and regards Luther's theology from 1513 to 1518 as pre-Reformation, and if one follows Aland (pp. 106ff.) and assumes a certain "undecidedness" (p. 108) with regard to the Heidelberg Disputation. What confronts us in the Heidelberg Disputation as the program of the theology of the cross confronts us also in Luther's later writings, for example, in *The Bondage of The Will* and even in the great lectures on Genesis, and hence cannot be confined in time to a preliminary stage of Luther's "real" theology. For the rest, I should like here also to warn against an all too pointed systematization of Luther's statements. This applies even to Luther's doctrine of justification. On this point see my work, "Duplex Justitia. Luthers Stellung zu einer Unionsformel des 16. Jahrhunderts" *(Veröffentlichungen des Instituts für europäische Geschichte,* Vol. 68, Wiesbaden, 1972).

Also the great works of Elert, E. Seeberg, and Joh. v. Walter deal with the basic thoughts of Luther's theology of the cross. In Vol. 2, 3rd and 4th editions of his biography of Luther, Otto Scheel has a section on it (pp. 594ff.). Still greater detail is presented by E. Vogelsang.[4] Lilje points up the significance of the theology of the cross for Luther's view of history."[5] On the relationship of theology and philosophy in Luther's thought, Wilhelm Link's superb but one-sided study has come out,[6] which touches a number of points I have also developed. In *Theologie und Liturgie,* pp. 145f., *Von Augustin zu Luther,* pp. 343ff., I have critically demonstrated my attitude toward Erich Seeberg's picture of Luther. On the question of the authorship of the *Imitation of Christ* of Thomas a Kempis, I point to the survey of Karl Bihlmeyer, pp. 432f.[7]

Because of the changed theological situation since 1929 and my own intellectual progress, portions of my book would be formulated differently today. This applies especially to the opening pages of the introduction. The Bibliography must be supplemented in the sense indicated above. Today I would no longer discuss Hunzinger's thesis on Luther's alleged Neoplatonism so extensively. In view of the measureless exaggerations of our time, Luther's battle against reason appears to me today essentially more problematical. Today I would formulate the judgment on Schleiermacher much more carefully. The same applies to the occasional remarks concerning the significance of metaphysics and "natural theology." But surely no one will deny that after the dreadful events of the past ten years the basic ideas of Luther's theology of the cross have become even more relevant than I expressed in the opening pages.

On two points I find myself compelled to revise, or at least modify, my earlier views. The one concerns the question about the significance of the hidden God in *The Bondage of the Will*. It had already been clear to me earlier that Luther's exegesis of the passage from Ezekiel (W. XVIII, 685) cannot simply be inserted in the "revelation-concealment" model. But the two views of the hidden God were still harmonized too much by me. Doerne has convinced me of this.[8]

I have thought through the whole complex of questions once more and have presented the fruits of my efforts in the essay, "Gott und Mensch in humanistischer und reformatorischer Schau. Eine Einführung in Luthers Schrift De servo arbitrio."[9] It must be conceded that the hidden God in the interpretation of the Ezekiel passage is not a form of manifestation of the revealed God; he is not the crucified God, but appears to be an absolute God, a God in himself, with whom we have nothing to do. He remains above us and has not included himself in his revelation. God's condescendence is in polar tension with his unlimited freedom and incomprehensibility. But this passage is thoroughly misunderstood if one suspects in it an intrusion of philosophy into theology or the need for a general metaphysical framework for the Christian idea of the love of God.

On the contrary, the view of the hidden God in the interpretation of the Ezekiel passage is the expression of a deep religious experience on the part of Luther. It is the experience of the stark aliveness and unsearchableness of God, of which Luther was profoundly conscious in spite of God's revelation in Jesus Christ. The reality of God shatters all our thinking about God, and Luther himself was ready to surrender unsparingly the dogmatic conclusion and systematic completeness. In that very fact lies his religious superiority over Erasmus. My earlier treatment should be supplemented in this direction. In addition to my essay, mentioned above, I call attention to my statement of the problems in *Theologie und Liturgie*, pp. 161ff., and my article on "Pharaoh's obduration" in the Meiser Festschrift.[10]

The other point concerns Luther's attitude toward mysticism. I continue to maintain that Luther's theology of the cross and the German mysticism of the Middle Ages are basic conceptions that diverge. But I have made this difference too pointed in a systematic way, and turned it into an absolute antithesis for the sake of the conclusion. With that I paid my tribute to the dominant theological view of the time, as given its pregnant expression, for example, in Emil Brunner's *Mysticism and the Word.* Today I would no longer dare to assert that in mysticism "strictly speaking, the idea of guilt has no place". I would no longer infer, in connection with Heinzelmann, that faith and mysticism are related "like fire and water". The judgment that "in its central point the mysticism of Tauler is theology of glory follows from the desire for the birth of God in the soul only for an abstract systematic way of thinking, but not for an unbiased consideration of the history of piety, which is more suitable here than a purely dogmatic approach. The ethics of the cross in the *Imitation of Christ* did not undertake a general attack on the high theological speculation with its metaphysical presuppositions, and did not break out of the spell of works piety, and to that extent it is "not at all conceivable without the church's theology of glory", but with regard to piety it is much closer to Luther's theology of the cross than any speculative theology of glory.

The Neoplatonic presuppositions of thought are surely unmistakable in German mysticism and they should not be overlooked in examining Luther's attitude toward mysticism. In fact, here is an antithesis between Luther's theology of the cross and mysticism that cannot be given up. But piety has a different logic than abstract dogmatic thought, and Luther was deeply touched by the piety of a Tauler. This feeling of kinship cannot simply be presented as a case of being deceived about the antithetical nature of the basic positions, as was done on page 156. Taking more pains with the historical question, only indicated on pp. 147f. might have warned against all too harsh antitheses at this point. Also Luther's Christ mysticism (pp. 105f.) is not really so far removed from that of a Tauler. Without prejudice to the longed-for mystical experience, the mystic also lives by faith and by grace. Christian mysticism is one of the most venerable phenomena of Christian piety, and should certainly not "be rejected in substance" (p. 83). Since then, my efforts to understand mysticism have found expression in my essays on Master Eckehart [11] and Bernard of Clairvaux.[12] Also the Apostle Paul was no stranger to a mystical experience together with ecstasy (2 Cor. 12), something that is occasionally ignored.[13] In summary: The drawing of systematic boundaries has its value but it does not comprehend the ultimate. The reader of Part Three, "The Theology of the Cross and Mysticism" will kindly bear this in mind.

At the close of my book I mentioned two further tasks which go

beyond the limits of this study. The one would be to demonstrate
the significance of the principle of thought set forth in the theology
of the cross for the separate doctrines in detail, hence to offer a
presentation of Luther's entire theology from the perspective of the
theology of the cross. This has not yet been done. In my writing,
Vom Abendmahl Christi,[14] I dealt with Luther's teaching on the
Lord's Supper. Here, too, we meet with his theology of the cross
(cf. especially pp. 87f.), no matter how much needs to be said in
criticism of it. In my booklet, *Luthers evangelische Botschaft,* (2nd
ed., München, 1948) I investigated the relationship between cross
and justification, and between cross and history.

I have concerned myself more extensively with the second task.
Was Luther able, by means of his theology of the cross, to present
the full riches of the biblical views, or was he a very one-sided
hearer of Holy Scripture after all? These problems are dealt with
in my two books, *Luther und das Johanneische Christentum*
(München, 1935), and *Luther als Ausleger der Synoptiker* (München-
en, 1954). But my little book on *Humanitas-Christianitas* (Gütersloh, 1948) came into being because of my concern lest the age-old
question regarding the relationship of these two entities might be
answered prematurely and one-sidedly in favor of a falsely-under-
stood theology of the cross.

Walther v. Loewenich
Erlangen, Spring, 1954

Notes

1. The interval of a quarter century—and what a span of 25 years it was!—surely had to be noticed.

2. *Christentum und Wissenschaft*, Vol. 10, 1934, pp. 6ff., 203ff., 259ff., 437ff.

3. *Theologie und Liturgie*, 1952, pp. 119-170 (Stauda Verlag, Kassel). Now also in the volume, *Von Augustin zu Luther*, Witten, 1959, pp. 307-378.

4. Cf. *Die Anfänge von Luthers Christologie*, pp. 15, 24, 88-129, 144ff. *Der angefochtene Christus bei Luther*, (*Arbeiten zur Kirchengeschichte 21*, 1932), pp. 21f.

5. *Furchestudien*, Vol. 2, 1932.

6. *Das Ringen Luthers um die Freiheit der Theologie von der Philosophie.* (*Forschuung zur Geschichte und Lehre des Protestantismus*, published by Ernst Wolf, 9th Series, Vol. III, Munich, 1940). Also see *Von Augustin zu Luther*, pp. 348ff. Link is to be consulted especially for the discussions in my book, pp. 103ff.

7. Karl Bihlmeyer, *Kirchengeschichte*, Part 2: "Das Mittelalter," 12th ed., 1948.

8. "Gottes Ehre am gebundenen Willen. Evangelische Grundlagen und theologische Spitzensätze in De servo arbitrio." *Lutherjahrbüch*, 1938, 45-92.

9. Printed in my booklet, *Humanitas-Christianitas*, Gütersloh, 1948, 65-102; cf. especially pp. 89ff. The user of my *Theology of the Cross* will kindly read my discussions there.

10. *Viva Vox Evangelii*. Munich, 1951, 196-213. Now also in *Von Augustin zu Luther*, Witten, 1959, 161-179.

11. *Jahrbüch des Martin Luther-Bundes*, 1947, 60ff. *Von Augustin zu Luther*, 136ff. See also the chapter on German mysticism in my *Geschichte der Kirche*, 4th ed., 1954, 172ff.

12. *Zeitwende*, 1953, No. 1, 325ff. *Von Augustin zu Luther*, 122ff.

13. Cf. my book *Paulus*, 2nd ed., Witten, 1949, p. 158.

14. Furcheverlag, Berlin, 1938, pp. 49ff.